The Sea Is a Continual Miracle

Seafaring America

RICHARD J. KING, Williams College-Mystic Seaport, Editor

Seafaring America is a series of original and classic works of fiction, nonfiction, poetry, and drama bearing on the history of America's engagement with our oceans and coastlines. Spanning diverse eras, populations, and geographical settings, the series strives to introduce, revive, and aggregate a wide range of exemplary and seminal stories about our American maritime heritage, including the accounts of First Peoples, explorers, voluntary and forced immigrants, fishermen, whalers, captains, common sailors, members of the navy and coast guard, marine biologists, and the crews of vessels ranging from lifeboats, riverboats, and tugboats to recreational yachts. As a sailor's library, Seafaring America introduces new stories of maritime interest and reprints books that have fallen out of circulation and deserve reappraisal, and publishes selections from well-known works that reward reconsideration because of the lessons they offer about our relationship with the ocean.

For a complete list of books available in this series, see www.upne.com

Photograph of Whitman by Matthew Brady
or Alexander Gardner, around 1862.

The Sea Is a Continual Miracle

Sea Poems and Other Writings by Walt Whitman

Edited by JEFFREY YANG

UNIVERSITY PRESS OF NEW ENGLAND   *Hanover and London*

University Press of New England
www.upne.com
© 2017 Jeffrey Yang
All rights reserved
Manufactured in the United States of America
Typeset in Utopia and Sentinel by Passumpsic Publishing

Seafaring America is supported and produced in part by the Maritime
Studies Program of Williams College and Mystic Seaport. Williams-Mystic
empowers global, creative citizens while inspiring an enduring relationship
with the ocean. We create an open-minded, interdisciplinary academic
community, with experiential learning at Mystic Seaport, along the coasts
of America, and at sea.

Library of Congress Cataloging-in-Publication Data
NAMES: Whitman, Walt, 1819–1892 author. | Yang, Jeffrey editor.
TITLE: The sea is a continual miracle: sea poems and other writings /
    by Walt Whitman; edited by Jeffrey Yang.
DESCRIPTION: Hanover: University Press of New England, 2017. | Series:
    Seafaring America | Includes bibliographical references and index.
IDENTIFIERS: LCCN 2016042857 (print) | LCCN 2017000895 (ebook) |
    ISBN 9781512600599 (cloth : alk. paper) | ISBN 9781611689228 (pbk.) |
    ISBN 9781512600605 (epub, mobi & pdf)
SUBJECTS: LCSH: Sea—Poetry. | Seafaring life—Poetry.
CLASSIFICATION: LCC PS3203 .Y36 2017 (print) | LCC PS3203 (ebook) |
    DDC 818/.308—dc23
LC record available at https://lccn.loc.gov/2016042857

5 4 3 2 1

To me the sea is a continual miracle,
The fishes that swim—the rocks—the motion
of the waves—the ships, with men in them
—what stranger miracles are there?

— Walt Whitman

Contents

Series Editor's Preface

SEAFARING AMERICA

The Inupiat of far northern Alaska have for centuries said that the bowhead whale lives two human lifetimes. In *Moby-Dick*, the primary entrepôt of all American literature of the sea, Ishmael yarns about a stone lance in an old whale: "It might have been darted by some Nor'-West Indian long before America was discovered." By studying amino acids in the eyes of legally killed bowhead whales and dating the old lances of stone, ivory, and steel found buried in the blubber, twenty-first century researchers have confirmed that some individuals of this species might indeed live over two hundred years. A bowhead swimming around the thinning ice of the Arctic in 2015, when the Cuban-American poet Richard Blanco wrote, "We all belong to the sea between us," likely also swam in 1859 when Emily Dickinson penciled the lines: "Exultation is the going / Of an inland soul to sea"—and then put them in her drawer.

Since the first human settlement of our coasts, the voices expressing the American relationship with the sea have been diverse in gender, race, ethnicity, geography, and experience. And the study of maritime literature and history continues to converge and circulate with marine science and contemporary policy.

Seafaring America seeks to inspire and explore ocean study in this twenty-first century. The Taino chief Hatuey, James Fenimore Cooper, Harriet Beecher Stowe, Frederick Douglass, Walt Whitman, Winslow Homer, Alexander Agassiz, Joshua Slocum, Kate Chopin, Samuel Eliot Morison, Langston Hughes, Rachel Carson, Ursula K. Le Guin, Jeffrey Yang, and generations of other American mariners, artists, writers, scientists, and historians have all known that the ocean is the dominant ecological, meteorological, political, and metaphorical force on Earth.

"The sea is History," wrote Derek Walcott in 1979, mourning the ꝑ horrors of the Middle Passage and the drowned African American cultural memory. By the 1970s the sea was history in a new way. Americans began to perceive the global ocean as vulnerable to our destructive reach. The realization rolled in with the discovery of the dead zone off the Mississippi River delta, industrial over-fishing off New England, and the massive oil spill that spoiled the same Santa Barbara sands on which Richard Henry Dana Jr. first landed his bare Boston Brahmin feet in 1835 after a passage of 150 days. Yet even today, the rising seas, floods, shipwrecks, and immutable tempests along the Great Lakes, the Gulf of Mexico, and America's Atlantic, Pacific, and Arctic coasts continue to re-mind us of an immortal and indifferent sea — a savage ocean that crashes and seeps over the transience of *Homo sapiens*.

Seafaring America is a series of new and classic works of fic-tion, nonfiction, history, poetry, and drama that engages with the country's enduring relationship with the oceans and coastlines. Seafaring America strives to introduce, revive, and aggregate a wide range of exemplary and seminal stories and verse about the American maritime heritage: to trace the footprints on the beach, the stone lances in the blubber, and the pearls in the drawer.

Richard J. King
Williams College-Mystic Seaport

Introduction: Apologia for the Sea

As idly drifting down the ebb,
Such ripples, half-caught voices, echo from the shore.
— Walt Whitman

Walt Whitman! The White Whale of American poetry. A vital amalgam of mythology and critical biography, invention and endless interpretation. His reflection of our nation as a "Centre of equal daughters, and equal sons . . . Perennial with the Earth, with Freedom, Law and Love," resounds across the land like a mourning song. His legendary names reach out to us across the formless waters: the Bard of Democracy, the Bard of America and of the Kosmos, the Bard of the Body (and of the Soul and Mortality), the Poet of Equality. He is our Pioneer, our Archetype, our Precedent, our prelapsarian Adam, our Dante, or along with Emily Dickinson, our Poet Progenitor, our Prototype, our Generative Figure, or simply, our Good Gray Poet. He is our Vast Albatross, as the poet Hilda Doolittle once wrote, "great, wide-winged, sea-soaked."

In Whitman's poetry, the Singer and the Song coincide with the birth of a literature that lives on and on, toward an unwavering, expectant future in our postexpectant present.

My first memory of him goes back to my sophomore year of high school. A friend had chosen to recite Whitman's elegy for President Lincoln, "O Captain! My Captain!" for a class assignment. She mounted a portrait of the president onto a cardboard altar, covered the image with thick drips of wax, and arranged the altar at the front of the classroom. She spread out some candles before the altar, lit them, turned out the lights, started the tape deck (I'm remembering the soundtrack to *Twin Peaks*), and proceeded to wail, "O Captain! my Captain! our fearful trip is done." I was hooked. I tracked down a used leather-bound copy of *Leaves of Grass*, illustrated with woodcuts. Many years later I would discover that edition was just one of many Whitman had published during his lifetime. That in fact, *Leaves of Grass*, as Roger

Asselineau's marvelous biography first showed, was a work in progress, part of a "constantly changing continuum" of revisions and editions, its design more open ended than not. A line by the poet Charles Reznikoff relates so aptly to this aspect of Whitman's lifework: "The ceaseless weaving of the uneven water"—a line I once saw collaged so small onto a gray, churning image of the sea painted by Mary Oppen.

Forty years ago in his encomium to the poet, Guy Davenport observed that "no one phrase is ever going to label Whitman's theme." The sea, though, can encompass it—puts it in place, gives it its pace. In line after line, the poet walks along it, breathes it, smells it, swims in it, sits by it, bathes in it, listens to it, sails and ferries and steamboats on it, talks to it. His young friend John Burroughs—a nature writer who became one of the most popular writers in America and the author of an early critical study of Whitman that Whitman himself contributed to and edited—observed late in the poet's life, "There is sea-salt in Whitman's poetry, strongly realistic epithets and phrases, that had their birth upon the shore, and that perpetually recur to one as he saunters on the beach. No phase of nature seems to have impressed him so deeply as the sea, or recurs so often in his poems." Burroughs even thought his friend had "a look about him of the gray, eternal sea that he so loved, near which he was born, and that had surely set its seal upon him."

This seal, set upon the poet as a child, was like an amulet that cast a spell upon him until his dying breath. In his twilight years, Whitman said of the sea in his prose sketches *Specimen Days*, "I remember well, I felt that I must one day write a book expressing this liquid, mystic theme. Afterward, I recollect, how it came to me that instead of any special lyrical or epical or literary attempt, the sea-shore should be an invisible *influence*, a pervading gauge and tally for me, in my composition." He goes on to describe

a dream, a picture, that for years at intervals, (sometimes quite long ones, but surely again, in time,) has come noiselessly up before me, and I really believe, fiction as it is, has enter'd largely into my practical life—certainly into my writings, and shaped and color'd them. It is nothing more or less than a stretch of interminable white-brown sand, hard and smooth and broad, with the ocean perpetually, grandly, rolling in upon it, with slow-measured sweep, with rustle and hiss and foam, and many a thump as of low bass drums. This scene, this picture, I say, has risen before me at times for years. Sometimes I wake at night and can hear and see it plainly.

Unlike many nineteenth-century authors whose experiences of long sea voyages fed directly into their writing, either through the navy or merchant marine or a whaling or scientific expedition, Whitman never shipped off to any lands beyond. Of traveling abroad, he once wrote, "Shall I journey four thousand miles to weigh the ashes of some corpses? Shall I not vivify myself with life here, rushing, tumultuous, scornful, masterful, oceanic—greater than ever before known?"

In 1848, six years after Baudelaire rounded the Cape of Good Hope, Whitman got as far south as the Gulf of Mexico, sailing down the Mississippi with his brother Jeff to work at a newspaper in New Orleans, returning to Brooklyn a few months later by way of the same river, up to the Great Lakes, and down the Hudson. Though Whitman once described his Mississippi journey as "monotonous and dull" and wrote only one early poem directly about it cloaked in the "murky darkness" of a Poe-inspired Gothic, the impact this trip had on the writing of *Leaves* was as profound as the impact Baudelaire's failed voyage to India had on the writing of *Fleurs du Mal*. Both books arose out of two wildly different experiences with boredom.

He got as far east as Boston, first visiting the capital in 1860 to oversee the printing of the third edition of *Leaves of Grass*. A couple years later, Whitman ferried and trained down to Washington, D.C., to look for his brother George, who had been wounded in battle. He continued his search down the Rappahannock River to

Falmouth, Virginia, spending most of the Civil War there and back in Washington helping the wounded in military hospitals, working part-time as a clerk in the Indian Bureau and later in the Attorney General's Office. He visited Emerson in Concord, as well other friends up the Hudson to West Point and Esopus, New York; he rode the ferry on the Delaware River up to Philadelphia to give a lecture; he sailed the bay at Cape May, where he wrote "With Husky-Haughty Lips, O Sea!"

In 1879, fifteen years after the slaughter of Cheyenne and Arapaho People in Colorado Territory, Whitman got as far west as Denver and Pueblo, riding the railroads, traveling through Kansas where he was expected to give a talk in Topeka for the celebration of the twenty-fifth anniversary of the state. Due to fatigue and poor health, however, he never delivered the speech. A year later in 1880, he got as far north as Canada (or "Kanada," as he liked to call it), his only trip outside the United States, stopping at Niagara Falls before spending four months touring around London, Ontario, to Sarnia, steam-yachting down the Saint Lawrence River to the Thousand Islands and over to Montreal, Quebec, up the Saguenay to Chicoutimi and Ha! Ha! Bay. "Such *amplitude*," Whitman writes in his Canada diary, "a river and necklace of vast lakes, pure, sweet, eligible, supplied by the chemistry of millions of square miles of gushing springs and melted snows." Whitman had gone to Canada on the invitation of an admirer, Dr. Richard Bucke, who accompanied him on his travels. Bucke, a prominent psychiatrist and superintendent of the London Insane Asylum, treated masturbation by inserting a metal wire into the patient's penis — a burning sign of the times.

In the "early candle-light of his old age," Whitman loafed by the waters of Timber Creek, near his friend Harry Stafford's family farm in Camden, New Jersey. After suffering a paralytic stroke in 1873, the same year his mother passed away, he moved to Camden, first with his brother George and after a decade to his own "little old shanty" near the Delaware River. There he "domicil'd . . . with a housekeeper and man nurse," his upstairs study "a low ceiling'd room something like a big old ship's cabin." It was filled with paper detritus, photographs, china vessels, cologne-water, twine, and a "hundred indescribable things besides," along with stacks of his own books he sold upon request. He lived there until his death on March 26, 1892. The pyramidal tomb he had designed himself cost almost twice as much as his house—a "plain and massive stone temple" with an iron gate and bronze lock inspired by Blake's engraving, "Death's Door." Thomas Eakins created a death mask and took a plaster cast of his hand. Thousands lined the Camden streets to watch his funeral procession.

Walter Whitman was born in 1819 in West Hills, New York, the second of eight children (another died as a nameless infant). When he was four, his father (English, Puritan stock) sold the family farm (his grandfather and great-grandfather owned numerous slaves) and moved to Brooklyn to take up carpentering and real estate speculation, without success. At age eleven he stopped his official schooling and worked as an office boy to help the family's financial situation. At age twelve Whitman apprenticed as a typesetter at a newspaper in Brooklyn; by age fourteen he was living on his own, as his family moved back to Long Island. The art of printing would become a lifelong passion for the poet, as well as solitude, comradery, and leisure—leisure as the neo-Thomist philosopher Josef Piefer defined it in the mid-twentieth century, as a "receptive attitude of mind, a condition of the soul" that manifests itself as "celebration." Like Dickinson and Poe, he belonged to no church, though he felt a kinship with his maternal Quaker (Low Dutch) roots, as well with Brahma, Bacchus, Buddha, Manito, Allah. He read actively throughout his life, with pen and scissors in hand, marking and cutting passages from newspapers, magazines, and books, binding them into bundles or reassembling them in scrapbooks and notebooks.

Of his Long Island birthplace (or "Paumanok," as he liked to call it), he wrote in *Specimen Days*, "The shores of this bay, winter and summer, and my doings there in early life, are woven all through L. of G." He took long walks on the coast there, by the "ceaseless roll of the Atlantic." As a boy he speared eels through the ice (see "Poem of Joys"); he sailed around Peconic Bay, circling Shelter Island down to Montauk, where he chatted with the fishermen on the rocks below the lighthouse; he enjoyed ferrying between Manhattan and Brooklyn, when the borough was a growing suburban town of 30,000 inhabitants, the East River still bridgeless. He told Horace Traubel, author of a nine-volume biography of the poet's last four years of life, "My own favorite loafing places have always been the rivers, the wharves, the boats—I like sailors, stevedores. I have never lived away from a big river."

Whitman wrote in a notebook,

Sea Winrows
Ocean Winrows
Beach
Beach Winrows
Winrows with sand and sea-hay, —Winrows Sand and scales
    and beach-hay
        Sands and Drifts
Winrows and Beach-hay Under-foot /
Walking the Beach /
Drift underfoot underfoot Drift /
Wash
Drift at your feet

After moving back in with his parents in 1836, Whitman spent a few depressing years working as a schoolteacher in various Long Island towns—one he described in a letter as "a sink of despair." He started a weekly newspaper and would continue to work as a journalist, compositor, editor, and publisher at various papers for some thirty years, punctuated by a stretch as a New York *flâneur* during the forties, strolling forth into the Battery, cane in hand. During this time, he began one article: "How I love a loafer!"; he wrote some short fiction and a temperance novel, *Franklin Evans; or The Inebriate*, which he'd later tell Traubel was "damned rot—rot of the worst sort." He regularly saw plays and operas, frequented music concerts, took long walks on the empty beach at Coney Island. He looked after his family when his father's arthritis became too debilitating. For a stint in the early fifties, he made money by building and selling houses in Brooklyn, as his father had attempted years before. In the late fifties and early sixties, he often caroused with the Fred Gray Association of gay men and other bohemians at Pfaff's Cellar on Broadway. After the Civil War, he formed a deep, adhesive bond with a streetcar conductor, Peter Doyle.

In 1855, a few days before his father's death, Whitman published his first edition of *Leaves of Grass*. Ralph Waldo Emerson memorably declared in his 1844 essay "The Poet" that Dante "dared to write his autobiography into colossal cipher, into universality," as no American poet, himself included, had yet to do. If Whitman can be seen to have answered this dare, as some commentators have suggested, he seemed to have accomplished it by parachuting in from out of nowhere. His book had no precedent in English: the bold prose manifesto that prefaced the book; the twelve untitled poems on quarto-size pages scattered with varied-length ellipses; the long lines expanding and contracting between the margins like the steady crash of waves, selves shifting and multiplying onward with the speed of a steam engine. Or rather, with the speed of a ship at full sail, for as the scholar Ed Folsom has pointed out, Whitman had originally wanted to include an image of "a large ship under full power of steady forward motion" somewhere in his book, perhaps even using it as a cover illustration —an emblematic vessel of passage for readers. The philosopher William James described its prosody as "the systematic expulsion of all contractile elements." The opening gambit of Whitman's exultant, metaphysical proposition has come to mark the most iconic beginning in the history American literature:

I CELEBRATE myself,
And what I assume you shall assume,
For every atom belonging to me as good belongs to you.

"America is a poem in our eyes; its ample geography dazzles the imagination, and it will not wait long for metres" was not written by Whitman but by Emerson in his essay, "The Poet." "Nothing actually new," Whitman wrote in a review of *Leaves* published under a different name, "only an accumulation or fruitage or carrying out of the old or its adaption to the modern." He said his book had been composed by "merging oneself in all the living flood and practicality and fervency of that period," and that "he felt in regard to his own agency in it like a somnambulist who is shown during his waking hours the giddy heights and impossible situations over which he has passed safely in his sleep."

One of the first things that strikes readers new to the 1855 *Leaves*, besides the absence of poem titles, is the many ellipses scattered throughout—a variation of two, three, and mostly four dots Whitman used to indicate breath pauses or voice interruptions—the visual play of utterance translated onto the printed page, heightening the "immediateness" and "ecstasy of statement." These dots disappeared with the publication of the second edition the following year, accompanied by many other changes that continued on for the rest of his life, the poet-bookmaker expanding, reorganizing, revising, cutting, and revising again edition after edition through eight U.S. incarnations, along with multiple issues and variant printings, to the last iteration in 1892, also known as "the deathbed edition." No poet since William Blake had been as intimately involved in the actual making of his books as Whitman was—from paper choice to interior and cover design, to typesetting and the working of the printing machine, to binding and proof sheets—what Whitman described as "the slow and laborious formation, type by type." A glance at his working proofs reveals a mass of handwritten markings and rewritings that brim over margins, squeeze between lines, and saturate blank spaces, scraps of rewritten text or whole poems pasted onto other scraps or into blank spaces—a chaotic mess that rivals Proust's surviving drafts. The gladness, the buoyancy, the sweet innocence, "the hopeful green stuff woven" even when he grieves, "looking in vain for light," pulses through the pages, thus echoing Whitman's own dictum of poetry embodying the ideal (as Alexis de Tocqueville also echoed in 1840: "the search after, and the delineation of the Ideal") and prose the real. Even as he began to group certain poems into sequences, or "clusters" as he called them, he described the theory of doing so as an idealized metonymy: "the Passion of Woman-Love" and "adhesiveness, manly love" ("adhesiveness" is one term, among other terms, that Whitman borrowed and adapted from the then fashionable phrenologists, who originally used it to signify the affection between women). It is as if he a priori imagined French poet Mallarmé's ideal of the book as "a hymn, all harmony and joy; an immaculate grouping of universal relationships come together for some miraculous and glittering occasion." When Whitman said that he sought "to break down the barriers of form between prose and poetry," he was also referring to a marrying of the real and ideal.

It is worth reminding ourselves the degree to which the first appearance of Whitman's verse must have felt like ultralight lunar beams reflected from elsewhere. Poets from England read in America at the time included Robert Browning and Elizabeth Barrett Browning, Christina Rossetti and Dante Gabriel Rossetti, and Alfred Lord Tennyson, as well as the devoutly popular Jean Ingelow, some thirty editions of her *Poems* published within four years in the mid-1860s. Gerard Manley Hopkins suffered in solitude, though he had read Whitman, writing to a friend, "I always knew in my heart Walt Whitman's mind to be more like my own than any other man's living." New England poets admired at the time included the so-called Fireside Poets—Henry Wadsworth Longfellow, John Greenleaf Whittier, James Russell Lowell, William Cullen Bryant—as well as Emerson and Edmund Stedman, among others. Dickinson, like Hopkins, needed the goodwill of a friend to publish her first book after her death. Outside of Amerindian indigenous songs and black slave songs, contemporary American verse still sounded more or less like this:

Yet whenever I cross the river
  On its bridge with wooden piers,
Like the odor of brine from the ocean
  Comes the thought of other years.

Until this:

Out of the cradle endlessly rocking,
Out of the mocking-bird's throat, the musical shuttle,
Out of the Ninth-month midnight,
Over the sterile sands and the fields beyond, where the child
  leaving his bed wander'd alone, bareheaded, barefoot,
Down from the shower'd halo

The Northumbrian poet Basil Bunting once observed that Whitman's melding of words and music broke "the general Spenserian model of English poetry." We have come to call it "free verse," though that conceals more than it reveals about the intricate interleaving of form and content, sound and meaning. The lines above sway back and forth with onomatopoetic birdsong; their measured lengths are patterned after the movement of waves and musically unfold through anaphoric lilt, spondaic shift, subtle assonance, and alliteration. As the cradle rocks on, switching between "the sinking aria" and stretches of recitative, the motion of the lines echoes the birth taking place at the center of the poem—out of the memories of the boy on the beach rises an awareness of love and death, his wakening into a poetic vocation. Whitman described his poetry to Traubel as analogous to "*the Ocean*. Its verses are the liquid, billowy waves, ever rising and falling, perhaps sunny and smooth, perhaps wild with storm, always moving, always alike in their nature as rolling waves, but hardly any two exactly alike in size or measure (metre), never having the sense of something finished and fixed, always suggesting something beyond."

  Whitman wrote in a notebook,

To the liquid
To the
   As I sat
To the music of ebb-tide ripples softly
Alone
To the ripples ~~flo~~
~~Floa~~ ~~Idly floating~~
Idly I float

Many literary scholars (Basil De Sélincourt, F. O. Matthiessen, Angus Fletcher, Betsy Erkkila) and poets (Robert Duncan, Muriel Rukeyser, William Bronk), to name a few, have touched on the centrality of the ocean in Whitman's work. In a chapter titled "Walt Whitman's Marine Democracy" in *The Brother in Elysium*, Bronk recognized that both poet and sea "shared a cosmic and elemental passion," and that "he was that same substance as the sea, which united all substances and all diversity within its similitude." In his book *Language and Style in Leaves of Grass*, C. Carroll Hollis explored the influence of oratory, the "great art of the nineteenth century," on Whitman's verse. Whitman had grown up attending the sermons of preachers such as Elias Hicks and the former sailor Father Taylor, and as a young man he had even harbored hopes to make his way in the lucrative speaking circuit. Hollis called the early, pre-1860 poetry a "speech act . . . the imagined utterance of an imagined prophetic speaker transposed to the printed page . . . lines printed in a way to draw attention to the oral patterns of his message." At the heart of this pattern that Whitman adapts, Hollis discerned, is a medieval Latin rhetorical device called the *cursus*, which marks the accents at the end of a phrase and lends language its "beautiful flow," the *cursus* "shaped and limited by breathing and utterance" so that "equal thoughts have equal words and equal emphasis and equal time-span of expression." *Cursus* means course, way, voyage, passage. The word also has a geographic dimension, as adopted by archaeologists to name those early Roman ritual barrows found on the British Isles

—running earthworks that look like waveforms rolling across the grass—the deathless grass a sea of grass.

Whitman wrote in a notebook,

Sea-cabbage; salt hay; sea-rushes; ooze—sea-ooze; gluten— sea-gluten; sea-scum; spawn; surf; beach salt-perfume; mud; sound of walking barefoot ankle deep in the edge of the water by the sea.

The manifold cipher of the sea frames the shores of Whitman's poetry. The Earth is "the divine ship sailing the divine sea." The ocean is the "brine of life . . . the always-ready grave." It is, like the poet himself, "of one phase, and of all phases." From the first edition of *Leaves*, he merges with it (or a brook) and with nature itself ("I effuse my flesh in eddies and drift it in lacy jags"). It is his "lover" and his sexual libido ("Seas of bright juice suffuse heaven"). It carries the Ship of Democracy. Of music's elusive, beautiful mystery, "I can only tell you of it, as one might tell who reaches his neck at night and looks far over sea after the headland of the morning." It is a metaphor for Manhattan and Brooklyn ("The splendor, pic- turesqueness, and oceanic amplitude and rush of these great cit- ies") and for birds ("Such oceans, such successions of them") and for compost ("it's transparent green-wash . . . so amorous after me . . . clean forever and forever"). It is a fountain of type and a font: "These ocean waves arousable to fury and to death / Or sooth'd to ease and sheeny sun and sleep." A soldier in the field "sinks like a wave." In "Passage to India," one of his most wave-patterned poems—"a voyage of the soul . . . on the trackless seas"—he cele- brates the opening of the Suez Canal, the railroads, and the "gen- tle wires" laid across the Atlantic. It is the ultimate mystery ("All, all, toward the mystic Ocean tending"), a "prophetic spirit," "ex- tasy," the "wondrous interplay between the seen and unseen." It is a "savage old mother," a site of violence and shipwreck.

Whitman wrote in a notebook,

The soul or spirit transmutes itself into all matter—into rocks, and can [*illeg.*] live the life of a rock—into the sea, and can feel itself the sea.

In the concluding essay of the deathbed edition, Whitman confessed that "from a worldly and business point of view *Leaves of Grass* has been worse than a failure." Little could he know the oceanic influence he would become for poets around the world, his book setting off a series of seismic waves through the twentieth century, his spirit translated with tidalectic ebullience. Franz Kafka felt Whitman "gave his whole heart to every leaf of grass"; Fernando Pessoa annotated *Leaves of Grass* and thought Whitman "had all modern times in him"; César Vallejo wrote in 1929, "Walt Whitman is indisputably the most authentic precursor of new poetry worldwide"; Aimé Césaire praised his "physiological need for space and his *great heart*"; Van Gogh, who assembled a number of personal poetry albums, found Whitman's "Prayer of Columbus" *fort belle*. Of a well-known naval battle depicted in "Song of Myself," Jorge Luis Borges considered "Whitman as having at last discovered how poetry should be written."

Poets Velimir Khlebnikov and Vladimir Mayakovsky both swan-dived from Whitman into Russian futurism.

Federico García Lorca's black child in his "Ode" announces Whitman's spirit as "the coming reign of wheat." American poet Alfredo Ortiz Vargas fused Whitmanian "Democracity" with Huidobro's *Altazor* in his *Las torres de Manhattan* before being shot to death in Kansas City in 1951 at age fifty-four.

Italian poet and novelist Cesar Pavese described Whitman's poetry in his college thesis as the "discovery of a world new in history and of the singing of it." Dino Campana, who spent the last fourteen years of his life alone in an insane asylum near Florence, begins and ends the only book of poems he published, *Orphic Songs* (titled after an Italian critic's description of Whitman's poetry as "real, unprecedented Orphic songs"), with an unattributed misquotation of Whitman: "They were all torn and cover'd with the boy's blood."

There was *Whitmanisme* in France and *Whitmanismo* in Brazil. Henri Michaux's line could be Whitman's: "Streams move onward, but not the sea." Whitman was a living stream for Blaise Cendrars, who followed it to "Panama," for Guillaume Apollinaire, who followed it to "Zone," for John Dos Passos, Frank O'Hara, and Hart Crane, as well as for Rabindranath Tagore, José Martí, Rubén Darío, Pablo Neruda, Kenneth Rexroth, Jean Toomer. Muriel Rukeyser, like D. H. Lawrence, thought him impossible to imitate. She said, "He remembered his body as other poets of his time remembered English verse. Out of his body, and its relation to itself and the sea, he drew his basic rhythms. They are not the rhythms, as has been asserted, of work and love-making; but rather of the relation of our breathing to our heartbeat." Allen Ginsberg famously howled in creative imitation. In a one-act play by Amiri Baraka, Tonto says to the Lone Ranger, "Your Manifest Destiny! Even Walt Whitman went for it."

Langston Hughes edited three separate anthologies of his work. Ezra Pound made a public pact with him and assimilated his rhythms through the musical patterns of nineteenth-century composers such as Liszt and Berlioz. William Carlos Williams wrestled with Whitman his whole life, trading barbs with bits of praise, and yet he learned so much from him. Hilda Doolittle— our Helen in America who furthered the "gem-school" (as she grouped Emerson, Poe, Frost, Moore)—called Whitman a "lazy loafer [who] created a continent [with his] immortal 'leaves,' not shining laurel, it is true, but fragrant, simply 'of grass.'" She pointed to Whitman as a direct precursor of the Imagists.

American poet and art critic Sadakichi Hartmann (who appears in Pound's "Canto 80") communed with Whitman's "soul atoms," translated German correspondence for him, and published his Boswellian pamphlet *Conversations with Whitman* in 1895. The first thing the nineteen-year-old Hartmann saw when the Camden transplant opened his front door was his naked breast. He said Whitman's "favorite ejaculation" was "Oy! Oy?," or "Oy?!" which he'd often repeat in reply to strangers' questions. Unlike his hero, Sadakichi spent time in jail for something he wrote—a verse play about Jesus. Sadakichi said his conversations with Whitman were "calm, invigorating, softly flowing on like a summer day in the open fields or on the ocean."

It's almost incredible that Whitman hasn't appeared on our currency, like the Japanese novelist Natsume Sōseki on the 1,000 yen note. Sōseki drank from the Bard of Democracy's wellspring, too, describing him as "a giant descended from the heavens, exhaling great flames on behalf of the United States, creating wildly extravagant poems, with the power of the buffalo that roams the prairies. His voice skimmed the waves to the other side of the Atlantic . . . becoming what one must declare as truly the happiest event of recent years."

The wildly inventive Chinese poet Gu Cheng, who wore a cutoff pant leg on his head to keep people from stealing his thoughts, described his encounter with Whitman as a religious experience:

I first read Whitman's poems at an early age but got reawakened much later. I was a reserved person. It was not until one morning in 1983 that the electricity of my anguish dissolved my skin, which had been as stiff as lead, and as a result I came to perceive the great ontological being—Whitman. His sound came down vertically from the air, blowing on me and shaking my every hour and minute. The century between us no longer exists; nor does the Pacific Ocean, leaving Whitman himself —the visible but untouchable "I" and himself only—the eternity that was getting nearer and clearer. I was stunned, almost desirous to throw myself away and give up my work grinding flowers on the glass of images. I was shaken again and again, lying there and feeling like a wooden piece in a piano. From morning until night, I just listened to the sound of the falling raindrops. On that day I ate nothing.*

American poet Robert Creeley once spoke about not reading Whitman until his thirties. He said it was considered "bad taste" to have an active interest in Whitman when he was in college during the 1940s due to the "naively affirmative" effusions that were out of step with the cynical times. Simon Ortiz memorably wrote in his 1981 book *From Sand Creek*, "When I was younger — and America was young too in the 19th century — Whitman was a poet I loved, and I grew older. And Whitman was dead." Ortiz's contemporary, Lucille Clifton, prefaced each chapter of her auto-biography with lines from "Song of Myself." San Francisco Renaissance poet Robert Duncan once said, "Yet it is Whitman's Sea that remains primary for me."

The impulse to embrace multitudes grew into multitudes embracing him. Sometimes the embrace became a fruitful resistance. Whitman wrote in a notebook,

The flukes of a whale   they are as quick as light.

When I spoke to a friend about editing this book, he replied enthusiastically, "That's easy! Just include everything." In practice, the task of making the selection proved more difficult than this. Whitman, of course, wrote many poems that had little or nothing to do with the ocean. But given the deeply personal and powerful influence nature's great ontological being had on the poet his whole life, it's easy to feel that its primordial waters permeated his whole unconsciousness, its briny air smelt everywhere in his work, breaking the surface of all content. Afoot as he was

*Slightly adapted from Liu Shusen's essay, "Gu Cheng and Walt Whitman: In Search of a New Poetics," in *Whitman East and West: New Contexts for Reading Walt Whitman*, ed. by Ed Folsom (Iowa City: University of Iowa Press, 2002), 208–220.

with his vision of infusing as many facets of America into his book as his powers could muster, the all-absorbing ocean seemed to meld with the mystical essence of his soul. Whitman would hint as much in his poems: "To glide with thee, O Soul, o'er all, in all, as a ship o'er the waters!"

After much consideration, eventually three main aims were determined to guide the selection and structure of this anthology. The first aim was to include poems where the sea or its connected bodies of water (a creek or lake or river as outlet to the sea, subject to tides) figured prominently, or pivotally. Second was to include a handful of poems where the form itself seemed directly related or emulative of the sea's character and cadence: the gradual accretion of linked things into a song list, for example, as if a swelling wave that never breaks or a widening whirlpool that swallows more and more around it. Or take "Respondez!" — Whitman's "greatest poem" for the poet Louis Zukofsky, and in many ways his queerest, with its anaphoric combers crashing on and on against diverse tyrannies through satire and dithyrambic irony. The ocean, though largely unseen in such poems, appears to play an essential role in their composition (along with countless other natural influences, intertwined). Third was to arrange the book so that readers might get some sense of the trajectory of Whitman's evolving, expanding *Leaves*, however fragmented this sense might be in the context and constraint of the sea. As Whitman himself once said, "Yet the last edition is as necessary to my scheme as the first edition: no one could be superior to another because all are of equal importance in the fulfillment of the design."

With these words in mind, the selection proceeds chronologically by date of publication, each section culled from the various editions of *Leaves* from the first 1855 edition to the last in 1892 (in Whitman's words, "seven or eight stages and struggles"). Poems new to each original edition, or newly arranged in a cluster, make up each respective section. Other sections consist of poems taken from collections Whitman initially published as individual volumes, such as *Drum Taps*—arising directly out of the Civil War—and *Two Rivulets*—Whitman's most overtly experimental interweaving of prose and poetry, the two "streams" (Real and Ideal) running one above the other across the page divided by a wavy line, the three strands of time (Present, Future, Past) twining with the ebb and flow of Day and Night. All these volumes eventually made their way, in some form, into his *Leaves of Grass*—his life-spanning book of books he called his *"carte visite"* for future generations. These volumes were often even hand-stitched into the back of the latest printing of *Leaves*. Additionally, an ample selection of Whitman's sea-shimmering prose from *Specimen Days*, written late in his life when he was a "half-Paralytic" (he had originally thought of titling the book "Notes of a Half-Paralytic"), along with a few other prose pieces plus one pre-*Leaves* poem, have been integrated into the chronological whole.

One last thing to note about this book's assemblage: for a couple of poems, two versions from different editions of *Leaves* have been included in the spirit of our oceanic theme, like variations on a recurring wave, half-caught echoes on the shore, lines rippling back and forth. Moreover, readers can get a keyhole glimpse for themselves into Whitman's restless process of revision, from word choice down to his changing thoughts about punctuation and rhythm. Compare, for example, the opening of Whitman's "Out of the Cradle Endlessly Rocking" excerpted above with its first appearance in the 1860–61 edition as "A Word Out of the Sea":

OUT of the rocked cradle,
Out of the mocking-bird's throat, the musical shuttle,
Out of the boy's mother's womb, and from the nipples of her
    breasts,
Out of the Ninth Month midnight,
Over the sterile sands, and the fields beyond, where the child,
    leaving his bed, wandered alone, bareheaded, barefoot,
Down from the showered halo

Marked changes can be noted between the two even in this short passage: at the start, the switch from past tense to the eternal present progressive, the line physically extending with time; the excised third line that alters the rhythmic pattern completely, quickening the birth into birdsong while leaving the direct treatment of the womb and the mother's nipples from which the boy flows out to be inferred from the succinct fullness of the fourth line; the added apostrophes that slightly contract the final two lines while suggesting a slanglike looseness (slang, Whitman thought, aspiring to poetry in its "attempt of common humanity to escape from bald literalism, and express itself illimitably"). His 1867 version of this poem adds semicolons that were later taken out. Or follow the tributary back to a much different draft when it was first published in the New York *Saturday Press* in 1859 as "A Child's Reminiscence."

Whitman viewed the sea as both cradle and grave. He had embarked into the public sphere as a poet at age forty-six, "My ties and ballasts leave me. . . . I travel. . . . I sail. . . . my elbows rest in the sea-gaps," seeing the immortality in every living thing. During the dark years of the Civil War, he could still write buoyantly of "a Ship, spreading all her sails . . . as she speeds, she speeds so stately —below, emulous waves press forward . . . with shining curving motions, and foam." As he ebb'd closer to death this image transformed into the body of "a gray and batter'd ship . . . rusting, mouldering" in "some nameless bay." Looking east across the watery expanse from Montauk Point, he felt "the wild unrest . . . that inbound urge and urge of waves, / Seeking the shores forever." The sea called him back ("By that long scan of waves, myself call'd back, resumed upon myself"), as he wended the beach like he had as a child three-score plus years ago, listening to "The first and last confession of the globe . . . / The tale of cosmic elemental passion." The sea's mysterious undertow pulled him further into its open depths, "to the deepest, freest waters." The "truest" voyage awaited him, "the endless cruise" of "the unseen soul of me." Like Hermes, whom he summoned in an early poem, Whitman would leave "solid earth" on the "eidélon yacht of me" — "eidolon," a Greek word referring to an idol, a reflection in water or a mirror, an apparition or phantom, that Whitman invoked as the "image of the ideal": "The infinite oceans where the rivers empty! . . . The true realities . . . the real I myself."

Whitman's favorite line of Tennyson's: "For the mighty wind arises roaring seaward and I go."

After his final eidélonic departure, there could be no return — only untried seas, ports, gravitation, unvisited of shores, leaving behind his ceaselessly weaving continuum of *Leaves*. Who was to know what should come home to us? What he could in no way foresee in one aspect of the sea: its ecological fragility. The temporality of the continual miracle in the face of humanity. The poet's dream of the sea, of the white-brown strip of shore the child walks along, listening to the constant bass drum of waves rolling upon it, source of infinite renewal, dependent on flesh and bone and a spirit of home to uphold.

Jeffrey Yang

Beacon, NY

A Note on the Text

Most of the poems and prose in this volume were compiled from the original editions of Whitman's books published during his lifetime, available online at the amazing Walt Whitman Archive directed by Kenneth M. Price and Ed Folsom at whitmanarchive.org. Individually scanned page images of each original publication of *Leaves of Grass* accompany the digital text. All issues of typesetting attempted to follow Whitman's original setting in the context of this new design. An 1876 edition of *Two Rivulets* (volume 2 of the Centennial Edition of *Leaves*) in the Special Collections Library at Vassar College was used for poems not yet available on the Whitman Archive.

Other texts were taken directly from *Walt Whitman of the New York Aurora*, edited by Joseph Jay Rubin and Charles H. Brown (Bald Eagle Press, 1950), *Notebooks and Unpublished Prose Manuscripts*, edited by Edward Grier (NYU Press, 1961–1984, six vols.), and *The Collected Writings of Walt Whitman: The Early Poems and the Fiction*, edited by Thomas L. Brasher (New York University Press, 1963). Additional primary sources consulted include the following: *Leaves of Grass: A Textual Variorum of the Printed Poem*, edited by Sculley Bradley, Harold W. Blodgett, Arthur Golden, and William White (NYU Press, 2008; 3 vols.); *Walt Whitman: Poetry and Prose*, edited by Justin Kaplan (Library of America, 1996); *Specimen Days & Collect* (Wilson & McCormick, 1883; Dover republication, 1995); *Complete Prose Works* (Small, Maynard & Company, 1898); and *The Uncollected Poetry and Prose of Walt Whitman*, edited by Emory Halloway (Doubleday, 1921, two vols.).

In the poems from the 1855 edition and in a handful of others of longer length, a three-dot ellipsis in brackets signifies deleted text. Though there is precedent for editing Whitman's work by cutting sections out for specific reasons (one extreme example being Elizabeth Porter Gould's *Gems of Walt Whitman* [1889]), one would naturally want to avoid any needless meddling. However, for our purposes here, given the structure and constraints of this book, the elisions serve a necessary function, like riding a new curl of a breaking wave. These poems in their entirety can be found easily outside this anthology.

For more detailed information about the various editions of *Leaves of Grass* and the karmic history of specific poems, readers are directed to the notes section in the back of this volume.

Here I would like to thank Richard King at Williams College–Mystic Seaport for the invitation to edit this volume. His enthusiasm, encouragement, and advice through the publication process kept this ship afloat. Thanks also to his two research assistants, Rani Onyango and Jae Hyun Jeong, for their help in assembling a very different, earlier version of this book. Thanks to Vassar College Libraries for the generous use of their stacks and to Mark Seidl in the Archives and Special Collections Library for his assistance. A deep thanks, too, to Stephen Hull, Lauren Seidman, Andrew Lohse, and the rest of the University Press of New England for their support, guidance, and attentiveness, and to Lee Motteler for his expert copyediting. Lastly, I would like to thank an anonymous reviewer of another earlier version of this book for making it a better book.

[The sound of the anchor heaved . . .]

The Sea Is a Continual Miracle

The Ocean

[First published in the *New York Aurora*, April 21, 1842.]

It is not easy for a person who has resided only upon the seaboard, to conceive of the feelings which fill the bosom of one, when for the first time he comes in sight of the ocean. How many thousands pass their lives without one glimpse of that glorious "creature," which, next to the canopy above, is the most magnificent object of material creation.

Here is one who has spent the years of childhood, youth, and early manhood in the far off inland districts. The green hills, briar studded crags, and mossy battlements of rock, have echoed with the bellowing of the thunder and the mountain blast, but with the deep, rolling murmur of the ocean, never. He has seen the flowers of the glen nod, and the treetops of the forest wave in the wind, and when the fury of the tempest came, the air filled with mangled branches and stripped off verdure; but never has he seen the ocean "wrought up to madness by the storm," the angry billows leaping up, and in battle array invading the province of the very clouds, or dashing in spent fury upon the trembling rocks. Calmly has he seen the moon throw down her light upon the rural bound, and all things reveling in quiet beauty; but never the moonlight rocked upon the rolling deep, nor the reflected stars rising and falling there, gems upon a mighty bosom swelling with darkness and mystery. Over wide spread fields of green, dotted with copse and mansion, has his eye wandered; but never over a boundless field of brightest blue, variegated only by the sunny sail and sable hull. What, then, can we imagine to be his feelings, as he stands now for the first time upon some lofty sea shore crag, with the boundless expanse before him? His soul must be stirred by its magnificence, and his thoughts take a new and loftier flight into regions of beauty and grandeur.

A few days ago we were quietly treading our way among the bales, boxes and crates upon one of the East River quays, when our progress was arrested by a very aged man, who wished to have pointed out to him the different kinds of vessels. He said he had never before seen vessels of any kind, this being the first time he had ever been near the ocean. He had read of the various classes, but had no definite conception on the subject. At first, we thought him quizzing, but after being satisfied of his perfect sincerity, endeavored to point out the peculiarities. He soon had no difficulty in recognizing the various denominations—ships, barks, brigs, schooners, sloops, &c.'; and as well as our limited nautical attainments would admit of, we endeavored to show the peculiar advantages of the different modes of rigging. The old man seemed much gratified, and doubtless will with pleasure, should it ever be our lot to peregrinate in the region of his home, point out to us the peculiarities, virtues, beauties and uses of the various productions of his soil. And that practical knowledge of his is of far greater value than all the fanciful smattering that is usually caught up in the city rounds. A man cannot acquire all knowledge, and therefore it becomes him to direct his attention to the acquisition of that which is of the greatest worth. Teaching a bean to wind up its pole, is a more useful, though perhaps not so *manly* or elegant an employment, as teaching a lap dog to jump.

But we were speaking of the ocean—that eternal fountain of the sublime and mysterious. We love to listen to the deep and ceaseless tones of its music, when the repose of midnight has fallen upon it. There is a sublimity in its angry tossing, when wrought to madness by the assaults and goadings of the storm king. We love to think of the riches, and the lost, that lie beneath its waves, and to carry the thoughts forward to that eventful hour when it must give up its treasures and its dead—when the sands which now form its bound will melt away with "the fervent heat," and its waves be lost in the ocean of eternity.

The Mississippi at Midnight

[First published in the *New Orleans Daily Crescent*, March 6, 1848.]

How solemn! sweeping this dense black tide!
   No friendly lights i' the heaven o'er us;
A murky darkness on either side,
   And kindred darkness all before us!

Now, drawn nearer, the shelving rim,
   Weird-like shadows suddenly rise;
Shapes of mist and phantoms dim
   Baffle the gazer's straining eyes.

River fiends, with malignant faces!
   Wild and wide their arms are thrown,
As if to clutch in fatal embraces
   Him who sails their realms upon.

Then, by the trick of our swift motion,
   Straight, tall giants, an army vast,
Rank by rank, like the waves of ocean,
   On the shore march stiffly past,

How solemn! the river a trailing pall,
   Which takes, but never again gives back;
And moonless and starless the heaven's arch'd wall,
   Responding an equal black!

Oh, tireless waters! like Life's quick dream,
   Onward and onward ever hurrying—
Like Death in this midnight hour you seem,
   Life in your chill drops greedily burying!

from *Leaves of Grass* (1855)

The American poets are to enclose old and new for America is the race of races. Of them a bard is to be commensurate with a people. To him the other continents arrive as contributions . . . he gives them reception for their sake and his own sake. His spirit responds to his country's spirit . . . . he incarnates its geography and natural life and rivers and lakes. Mississippi with annual freshets and changing chutes, Missouri and Columbia and Ohio and Saint Lawrence with the falls and beautiful masculine Hudson, do not embouchure where they spend themselves more than they embouchure into him. The blue breadth over the inland sea of Virginia and Maryland and the sea off Massachusetts and Maine and over Manhattan bay and over Champlain and Erie and over Ontario and Huron and Michigan and Superior, and over the Texan and Mexican and Floridian and Cuban seas and over the seas off California and Oregon, is not tallied by the blue breadth of the waters below more than the breadth of above and below is tallied by him. When the long Atlantic coast stretches longer and the Pacific coast stretches longer he easily stretches with them north or south. He spans between them also from east to west and reflects what is between them.

—1855 Preface

I CELEBRATE myself,
And what I assume you shall assume,
For every atom belonging to me as good belongs to you.

I loafe and invite my soul,
I lean and loafe at my ease . . . . observing a spear of summer grass.

Houses and rooms are full of perfumes . . . . the shelves are
    crowded with perfumes,
I breathe the fragrance myself, and know it and like it,
The distillation would intoxicate me also, but I shall not let it.

The atmosphere is not a perfume . . . . it has no taste of the
    distillation . . . . it is odorless,
It is for my mouth forever . . . . I am in love with it,
I will go to the bank by the wood and become undisguised and naked,
I am mad for it to be in contact with me.

The smoke of my own breath,
Echoes, ripples, and buzzed whispers . . . . loveroot, silkthread,
    crotch and vine,
My respiration and inspiration . . . . the beating of my heart . . . .
    the passing of blood and air through my lungs,
The sniff of green leaves and dry leaves, and of the shore and
    darkcolored sea-rocks, and of hay in the barn,
The sound of the belched words of my voice . . . . words loosed to
    the eddies of the wind,
A few light kisses . . . . a few embraces . . . . a reaching around of arms,
The play of shine and shade on the trees as the supple boughs wag,
The delight alone or in the rush of the streets, or along the fields
    and hillsides,
The feeling of health . . . . the full-noon trill . . . . the song of me
    rising from bed and meeting the sun.

from *Leaves of Grass* (1855)   7

[...]

A child said, What is the grass? fetching it to me with full hands;
How could I answer the child? .... I do not know what it is any
   more than he.

I guess it must be the flag of my disposition, out of hopeful green
   stuff woven.

Or I guess it is the handkerchief of the Lord,
A scented gift and remembrancer designedly dropped,
Bearing the owner's name someway in the corners, that we may
   see and remark, and say Whose?

Or I guess the grass is itself a child .... the produced babe of the
   vegetation.
Or I guess it is a uniform hieroglyphic,
And it means, Sprouting alike in broad zones and narrow zones,
Growing among black folks as among white,
Kanuck, Tuckahoe, Congressman, Cuff, I give them the same,
   I receive them the same.

And now it seems to me the beautiful uncut hair of graves.

[...]

Alone far in the wilds and mountains I hunt,
Wandering amazed at my own lightness and glee,
In the late afternoon choosing a safe spot to pass the night,
Kindling a fire and broiling the freshkilled game,
Soundly falling asleep on the gathered leaves, my dog and gun
   by my side.
The Yankee clipper is under her three skysails .... she cuts the
   sparkle and scud,
My eyes settle the land .... I bend at her prow or shout joyously
   from the deck.

The boatmen and clamdiggers arose early and stopped for me,
I tucked my trowser-ends in my boots and went and had a good time,
You should have been with us that day round the chowder-kettle.

[. . .]

Twenty-eight young men bathe by the shore,
Twenty-eight young men, and all so friendly,
Twenty-eight years of womanly life, and all so lonesome.

She owns the fine house by the rise of the bank,
She hides handsome and richly drest aft the blinds of the window.

Which of the young men does she like the best?
Ah the homeliest of them is beautiful to her.

Where are you off to, lady? for I see you,
You splash in the water there, yet stay stock still in your room.

Dancing and laughing along the beach came the twenty-ninth
    bather,
The rest did not see her, but she saw them and loved them.

The beards of the young men glistened with wet, it ran from their
    long hair,
Little streams passed all over their bodies.

An unseen hand also passed over their bodies,
It descended tremblingly from their temples and ribs.

The young men float on their backs, their white bellies swell to
    the sun . . . . they do not ask who seizes fast to them,
They do not know who puffs and declines with pendant and
    bending arch,
They do not think whom they souse with spray.

[. . .]

I am enamored of growing outdoors,
Of men that live among cattle or taste of the ocean or woods,
Of the builders and steerers of ships, of the wielders of axes and
    mauls, of the drivers of horses,
I can eat and sleep with them week in and week out.

[. . .]

This is the grass that grows wherever the land is and the water is,
This is the common air that bathes the globe.

[. . .]

You sea! I resign myself to you also . . . . I guess what you mean,
I behold from the beach your crooked inviting fingers,
I believe you refuse to go back without feeling of me;
We must have a turn together . . . . I undress . . . . hurry me out of
    sight of the land,
Cushion me soft . . . . rock me in billowy drowse,
Dash me with amorous wet . . . . I can repay you.

Sea of stretched ground-swells!
Sea breathing broad and convulsive breaths!
Sea of the brine of life! Sea of unshovelled and always-ready graves!
Howler and scooper of storms! Capricious and dainty sea!
I am integral with you . . . . I too am of one phase and of all phases.

Partaker of influx and efflux . . . . extoler of hate and conciliation,
Extoler of amies and those that sleep in each others' arms.

[. . .]

To behold the daybreak!
The little light fades the immense and diaphanous shadows,
The air tastes good to my palate.

Hefts of the moving world at innocent gambols, silently rising,
    freshly exuding,
Scooting obliquely high and low.

Something I cannot see puts upward libidinous prongs,
Seas of bright juice suffuse heaven.

The earth by the sky staid with . . . . the daily close of their junction,
The heaved challenge from the east that moment over my head,
The mocking taunt, See then whether you shall be master!

Dazzling and tremendous how quick the sunrise would kill me,
If I could not now and always send sunrise out of me.

We also ascend dazzling and tremendous as the sun,
We found our own my soul in the calm and cool of the daybreak.

My voice goes after what my eyes cannot reach,
With the twirl of my tongue I encompass worlds and volumes of
    worlds.
Speech is the twin of my vision . . . . it is unequal to measure itself.

It provokes me forever,
It says sarcastically, Walt, you understand enough . . . . why don't
    you let it out then?

Come now I will not be tantalized . . . . you conceive too much of
    articulation.

[. . .]

I hear the trained soprano . . . . she convulses me like the climax
    of my love-grip;
The orchestra whirls me wider than Uranus flies,
It wrenches unnamable ardors from my breast,
It throbs me to gulps of the farthest down horror,
It sails me . . . . I dab with bare feet . . . . they are licked by the
    indolent waves,
I am exposed . . . . cut by bitter and poisoned hail,
Steeped amid honeyed morphine . . . . my windpipe squeezed in
    the fakes of death,
Let up again to feel the puzzle of puzzles,
And that we call Being.

To be in any form, what is that?
If nothing lay more developed the quahaug and its callous shell
    were enough.

Mine is no callous shell,
I have instant conductors all over me whether I pass or stop,
They seize every object and lead it harmlessly through me.

I merely stir, press, feel with my fingers, and am happy,
To touch my person to some one else's is about as much as I
    can stand.

[. . .]

Swift wind! Space! My Soul! Now I know it is true what I guessed at;
What I guessed when I loafed on the grass,
What I guessed while I lay alone in my bed . . . . and again as I
    walked the beach under the paling stars of the morning.

My ties and ballasts leave me . . . . I travel . . . . I sail . . . . my elbows
    rest in the sea-gaps,
I skirt the sierras . . . . my palms cover continents,
I am afoot with my vision.

By the city's quadrangular houses . . . . in log-huts, or camping
with lumbermen,
Along the ruts of the turnpike . . . . along the dry gulch and rivulet bed,
Hoeing my onion-patch, and rows of carrots and parsnips . . . .
crossing savannas . . . trailing in forests,
Prospecting . . . . gold-digging . . . . girdling the trees of a new purchase,
Scorched ankle-deep by the hot sand . . . . hauling my boat down the
shallow river;
Where the panther walks to and fro on a limb overhead . . . . where the
buck turns furiously at the hunter,
Where the rattlesnake suns his flabby length on a rock . . . . where the
otter is feeding on fish,
Where the alligator in his tough pimples sleeps by the bayou,
Where the black bear is searching for roots or honey . . . . where the
beaver pats the mud with his paddle-tail;
Over the growing sugar . . . . over the cottonplant . . . . over the rice
in its low moist field;
Over the sharp-peaked farmhouse with its scalloped scum and
slender shoots from the gutters;
Over the western persimmon . . . . over the longleaved corn and
the delicate blue-flowered flax;
Over the white and brown buckwheat, a hummer and a buzzer there
with the rest,
Over the dusky green of the rye as it ripples and shades in the breeze;
Scaling mountains . . . . pulling myself cautiously up . . . . holding on
by low scragged limbs,
Walking the path worn in the grass and beat through the leaves of
the brush;
Where the quail is whistling betwixt the woods and the wheatlot,
Where the bat flies in the July eve . . . . where the great goldbug
drops through the dark;
Where the flails keep time on the barn floor,
Where the brook puts out of the roots of the old tree and flows to
the meadow,

Where cattle stand and shake away flies with the tremulous
  shuddering of their hides,
Where the cheese-cloth hangs in the kitchen, and andirons straddle
  the hearth-slab, and cobwebs fall in festoons from the rafters;
Where triphammers crash . . . . where the press is whirling its
  cylinders;
Wherever the human heart beats with terrible throes out of its ribs;
Where the pear-shaped balloon is floating aloft . . . . floating in it
  myself and looking composedly down;
Where the life-car is drawn on the slipnoose . . . . where the heat
  hatches pale-green eggs in the dented sand,
Where the she-whale swims with her calves and never forsakes them,
Where the steamship trails hindways its long pennant of smoke,
Where the ground-shark's fin cuts like a black chip out of the water,
Where the half-burned brig is riding on unknown currents,
Where shells grow to her slimy deck, and the dead are corrupting
  below;
Where the striped and starred flag is borne at the head of the
  regiments;
Approaching Manhattan, up by the long-stretching island,
Under Niagara, the cataract falling like a veil over my countenance;
Upon a door-step . . . .

[. . .]

I fly the flight of the fluid and swallowing soul,
My course runs below the soundings of plummets.

I help myself to material and immaterial,
No guard can shut me off, no law can prevent me.

I anchor my ship for a little while only,
My messengers continually cruise away or bring their returns to me.

I go hunting polar furs and the seal . . . . leaping chasms with a
  pike-pointed staff . . . . clinging to topples of brittle and blue.

I ascend to the foretruck . . . . I take my place late at night in the crow's
   nest . . . . we sail through the arctic sea . . . . it is plenty light enough,
Through the clear atmosphere I stretch around on the wonderful
   beauty,
The enormous masses of ice pass me and I pass them . . . . the scenery
   is plain in all directions,
The white-topped mountains point up in the distance . . . . I fling out
   my fancies toward them;
We are about approaching some great battlefield in which we are soon
   to be engaged,
We pass the colossal outposts of the encampments . . . . we pass with
   still feet and caution;
Or we are entering by the suburbs some vast and ruined city . . . .
   the blocks and fallen architecture more than all the living cities
   of the globe.

I am a free companion . . . . I bivouac by invading watchfires.

I turn the bridegroom out of bed and stay with the bride myself,
And tighten her all night to my thighs and lips.

My voice is the wife's voice, the screech by the rail of the stairs,
They fetch my man's body up dripping and drowned.

I understand the large hearts of heroes,
The courage of present times and all times;
How the skipper saw the crowded and rudderless wreck of the
   steamship, and death chasing it up and down the storm,
How he knuckled tight and gave not back one inch, and was faithful
   of days and faithful of nights,
And chalked in large letters on a board, Be of good cheer, We will not
   desert you;
How he saved the drifting company at last,
How the lank loose-gowned women looked when boated from the side
   of their prepared graves,
How the silent old-faced infants, and the lifted sick, and the
   sharp-lipped unshaved men;

All this I swallow and it tastes good . . . . I like it well, and it
   becomes mine,
I am the man . . . . I suffered . . . . I was there.

[. . .]

Did you read in the seabooks of the oldfashioned frigate-fight?
Did you learn who won by the light of the moon and stars?

Our foe was no skulk in his ship, I tell you,
His was the English pluck, and there is no tougher or truer, and
   never was, and never will be;
Along the lowered eve he came, horribly raking us.
We closed with him . . . . the yards entangled . . . . the cannon touched,
My captain lashed fast with his own hands.

We had received some eighteen-pound shots under the water,
On our lower-gun-deck two large pieces had burst at the first fire,
   killing all around and blowing up overhead.

Ten o'clock at night, and the full moon shining and the leaks on
   the gain, and five feet of water reported,
The master-at-arms loosing the prisoners confined in the after-hold
   to give them a chance for themselves.

The transit to and from the magazine was now stopped by the
   sentinels,
They saw so many strange faces they did not know whom to trust.

Our frigate was afire . . . . the other asked if we demanded quarters?
   if our colors were struck and the fighting done?

I laughed content when I heard the voice of my little captain,
We have not struck, he composedly cried, We have just begun
   our part of the fighting.

Only three guns were in use,
One was directed by the captain himself against the enemy's mainmast,
Two well-served with grape and canister silenced his musketry and
   cleared his decks.

The tops alone seconded the fire of this little battery, especially the
   maintop,
They all held out bravely during the whole of the action.

Not a moment's cease,
The leaks gained fast on the pumps . . . . the fire eat toward the
   powder-magazine,
One of the pumps was shot away . . . . it was generally thought we
   were sinking.
Serene stood the little captain,
He was not hurried . . . . his voice was neither high nor low,
His eyes gave more light to us than our battle-lanterns.

Toward twelve at night, there in the beams of the moon they
   surrendered to us.

Stretched and still lay the midnight,
Two great hulls motionless on the breast of the darkness,
Our vessel riddled and slowly sinking . . . . preparations to pass to
   the one we had conquered,
The captain on the quarter deck coldly giving his orders through
   a countenance white as a sheet,
Near by the corpse of the child that served in the cabin,
The dead face of an old salt with long white hair and carefully
   curled whiskers,
The flames spite of all that could be done flickering aloft and below,
The husky voices of the two or three officers yet fit for duty,
Formless stacks of bodies and bodies by themselves . . . . dabs of
   flesh upon the masts and spars,
The cut of cordage and dangle of rigging . . . . the slight shock of the
   soothe of waves,

Black and impassive guns, and litter of powder-parcels, and the
strong scent,
Delicate sniffs of the seabreeze . . . . smells of sedgy grass and fields
by the shore . . . death-messages given in charge to survivors,
The hiss of the surgeon's knife and the gnawing teeth of his saw,
The wheeze, the cluck, the swash of falling blood . . . . the short
wild scream, the long dull tapering groan,
These so . . . . these irretrievable.

[. . .]

I rise extatic through all, and sweep with the true gravitation,
The whirling and whirling is elemental within me.

[. . .]

My words are words of a questioning, and to indicate reality;
This printed and bound book . . . . but the printer and the printing-
office boy?
The marriage estate and settlement . . . . but the body and mind of
the bridegroom? also those of the bride?
The panorama of the sea . . . . but the sea itself?
The well-taken photographs . . . . but your wife or friend close and
solid in your arms?
The fleet of ships of the line and all the modern improvements . . . .
but the craft and pluck of the admiral?
The dishes and fare and furniture . . . . but the host and hostess,
and the look out of their eyes?
The sky up there . . . . yet here or next door or across the way?
The saints and sages in history . . . . but you yourself?
Sermons and creeds and theology . . . . but the human brain, and
what is called reason, and what is called love, and what is
called life?

[. . .]

Rise after rise bow the phantoms behind me,
Afar down I see the huge first Nothing, the vapor from the nostrils
    of death,
I know I was even there . . . . I waited unseen and always,
And slept while God carried me through the lethargic mist,
And took my time . . . . and took no hurt from the foetid carbon.

Long I was hugged close . . . . long and long.

Immense have been the preparations for me,
Faithful and friendly the arms that have helped me.

Cycles ferried my cradle, rowing and rowing like cheerful boatmen;
For room to me stars kept aside in their own rings,
They sent influences to look after what was to hold me.

Before I was born out of my mother generations guided me,
My embryo has never been torpid . . . . nothing could overlay it;
For it the nebula cohered to an orb . . . . the long slow strata piled
    to rest it on . . . . vast vegetables gave it sustenance,
Monstrous sauroids transported it in their mouths and deposited it
    with care.

All forces have been steadily employed to complete and delight me,
Now I stand on this spot with my soul.

Span of youth! Ever-pushed elasticity! Manhood balanced and
    florid and full!

[. . .]

Long enough have you dreamed contemptible dreams,
Now I wash the gum from your eyes,
You must habit yourself to the dazzle of the light and of every moment
    of your life

Long have you timidly waded, holding a plank by the shore,
Now I will you to be a bold swimmer,
To jump off in the midst of the sea, and rise again and nod to me
and shout, and laughingly dash with your hair.

I am the teacher of athletes,
He that by me spreads a wider breast than my own proves the
width of my own,
He most honors my style who learns under it to destroy the teacher.

The boy I love, the same becomes a man not through derived power
but in his own right,
Wicked, rather than virtuous out of conformity or fear,
Fond of his sweetheart, relishing well his steak,
Unrequited love or a slight cutting him worse than a wound cuts,
First rate to ride, to fight, to hit the bull's eye, to sail a skiff, to sing
a song or play on the banjo,
Preferring scars and faces pitted with smallpox over all latherers
and those that keep out of the sun.

[. . .]

If you would understand me go to the heights or water-shore,
The nearest gnat is an explanation and a drop or the motion of waves
a key,
The maul the oar and the handsaw second my words.

[. . .]

Do I contradict myself?
Very well then . . . . I contradict myself;
I am large . . . . I contain multitudes.

I concentrate toward them that are nigh . . . . I wait on the door-slab.

Who has done his day's work and will soonest be through with
   his supper?
Who wishes to walk with me?

Will you speak before I am gone? Will you prove already too late?

The spotted hawk swoops by and accuses me . . . . he complains of
   my gab and my loitering.

I too am not a bit tamed . . . . I too am untranslatable,
I sound my barbaric yawp over the roofs of the world.

The last scud of day holds back for me,
It flings my likeness after the rest and true as any on the shadowed
   wilds,
It coaxes me to the vapor and the dusk.

I depart as air . . . . I shake my white locks at the runaway sun,
I effuse my flesh in eddies and drift it in lacy jags.

I bequeath myself to the dirt to grow from the grass I love,
If you want me again look for me under your bootsoles.

You will hardly know who I am or what I mean,
But I shall be good health to you nevertheless,
And filter and fibre your blood.

Failing to fetch me me at first keep encouraged,
Missing me one place search another,
I stop some where waiting for you

❖

[. . .]

The sun and stars that float in the open air . . . . the appleshaped
    earth and we upon it . . . . surely the drift of them is something
    grand;
I do not know what it is except that it is grand, and that it is happiness,
And that the enclosing purport of us here is not a speculation, or
    bon-mot or reconnoissance,
And that it is not something which by luck may turn out well for us,
    and without luck must be a failure for us,
And not something which may yet be retracted in a certain
    contingency.

The light and shade — the curious sense of body and identity —
    the greed that with perfect complaisance devours all things —
    the endless pride and out-stretching of man — unspeakable
    joys and sorrows,
The wonder every one sees in every one else he sees . . . . and the
    wonders that fill each minute of time forever and each acre of
    surface and space forever,
Have you reckoned them as mainly for a trade or farmwork? or for
    the profits of a store? or to achieve yourself a position? or to fill
    a gentleman's leisure or a lady's leisure?

Have you reckoned the landscape took substance and form that it
    might be painted in a picture?
Or men and women that they might be written of, and songs sung?
Or the attraction of gravity and the great laws and harmonious
combinations and the fluids of the air as subjects for the savans?
Or the brown land and the blue sea for maps and charts?
Or the stars to be put in constellations and named fancy names?
Or that the growth of seeds is for agricultural tables or agriculture
    itself?

[. . .]

The ship's compass . . the sailor's tarpaulin . . the stays and lanyards,
    and the ground-tackle for anchoring or mooring,
The sloop's tiller . . the pilot's wheel and bell . . the yacht or
    fish-smack . . the great gay-pennanted three-hundred-foot
    steamboat under full headway, with her proud fat breasts and
    her delicate swift-flashing paddles;
The trail and line and hooks and sinkers . . the seine, and hauling
    the seine;
Smallarms and rifles . . . . the powder and shot and caps and
    wadding . . . . the ordnance for war . . . . the carriages:
Everyday objects . . . .

[. . .]

❖

TO think of time . . . . to think through the retrospection,
To think of today . . and the ages continued henceforward.

[. . .]

To think that the rivers will come to flow, and the snow fall, and
    fruits ripen . . and act upon others as upon us now . . . . yet not
    act upon us;
To think of all these wonders of city and country . . and others taking
    great interest in them . . and we taking small interest in them.

[. . .]

Slowmoving and black lines creep over the whole earth . . . . they
    never cease . . . .
they are the burial lines,

He that was President was buried, and he that is now President
    shall surely be buried.

Cold dash of waves at the ferrywharf,
Posh and ice in the river . . . . half-frozen mud in the streets,
A gray discouraged sky overhead . . . . the short last daylight of
    December,
A hearse and stages . . . . other vehicles give place,
The funeral of an old stagedriver . . . . the cortege mostly drivers.

Rapid the trot to the cemetery,
Duly rattles the deathbell . . . . the gate is passed . . . . the grave is
    halted at . . . . the living alight . . . . the hearse uncloses,
The coffin is lowered and settled . . . . the whip is laid on the coffin,
The earth is swiftly shovelled in . . . . a minute . . no one moves or
    speaks . . . . it is done,
He is decently put away . . . . is there anything more?

[...]

The law of the past cannot be eluded.
The law of the present and future cannot be eluded,
The law of the living cannot be eluded . . . . it is eternal,
The law of promotion and transformation cannot be eluded,
The law of heroes and good-doers cannot be eluded,
The law of drunkards and informers and mean persons cannot
    be eluded.

Slowmoving and black lines go ceaselessly over the earth,
Northerner goes carried and southerner goes carried . . . . and they
    on the Atlantic side and they on the Pacific, and they between, and
    all through the Mississippi country . . . . and all over the earth.

[...]

How beautiful and perfect are the animals! How perfect is my soul!
How perfect the earth, and the minutest thing upon it!
What is called good is perfect, and what is called sin is just as perfect;
The vegetables and minerals are all perfect . . and the imponderable
    fluids are perfect;
Slowly and surely they have passed on to this, and slowly and surely
    they will yet pass on.

O my soul! if I realize you I have satisfaction,
Animals and vegetables! if I realize you I have satisfaction,
Laws of the earth and air! if I realize you I have satisfaction.

I cannot define my satisfaction . . yet it is so,
I cannot define my life . . yet it is so.

I swear I see now that every thing has an eternal soul!
The trees have, rooted in the ground . . . . the weeds of the sea have . . . .
    the animals.

from *Leaves of Grass* (1855) **25**

I swear I think there is nothing but immortality!
That the exquisite scheme is for it, and the nebulous float is for it,
and the cohering is for it,
And all preparation is for it . . and identity is for it . . and life and
death are for it.

[. . .]

Pier that I saw dimly last night when I looked from the windows,
Pier out from the main, let me catch myself with you and stay . . . .
    I will not chafe you;
I feel ashamed to go naked about the world,
And am curious to know where my feet stand . . . . and what is this
    flooding me, childhood or manhood . . . . and the hunger that
    crosses the bridge between.

The cloth laps a first sweet eating and drinking,
Laps life-swelling yolks . . . . laps ear of rose-corn, milky and just
    ripened:
The white teeth stay, and the boss-tooth advances in darkness,
And liquor is spilled on lips and bosoms by touching glasses, and
    the best liquor afterward.

I descend my western course . . . . my sinews are flaccid,
Perfume and youth course through me, and I am their wake.

[. . .]

I see a beautiful gigantic swimmer swimming naked through the
    eddies of the sea,
His brown hair lies close and even to his head . . . . he strikes out
    with courageous arms . . . . he urges himself with his legs.
I see his white body . . . . I see his undaunted eyes;
I hate the swift-running eddies that would dash him headforemost
    on the rocks.

What are you doing you ruffianly red-trickled waves?
Will you kill the courageous giant? Will you kill him in the prime
    of his middle age?

Steady and long he struggles;

He is baffled and banged and bruised . . . . he holds out while his
strength holds out,

The slapping eddies are spotted with his blood . . . . they bear him
away . . . . they roll him and swing him and turn him:

His beautiful body is borne in the circling eddies . . . . it is continually
bruised on rocks,

Swiftly and out of sight is borne the brave corpse.

I turn but do not extricate myself;

Confused . . . . a pastreading . . . . another, but with darkness yet.

The beach is cut by the razory ice-wind . . . . the wreck-guns sound,

The tempest lulls and the moon comes floundering through the drifts.

I look where the ship helplessly heads end on . . . . I hear the burst
as she strikes . . I hear the howls of dismay . . . . they grow fainter
and fainter.

I cannot aid with my wringing fingers;

I can but rush to the surf and let it drench me and freeze upon me.

I search with the crowd . . . . not one of the company is washed to
us alive;

In the morning I help pick up the dead and lay them in rows in a barn.

[. . .]

Elements merge in the night . . . . ships make tacks in the dreams
. . . . the sailor sails . . . . the exile returns home,

The fugitive returns unharmed . . . . the immigrant is back beyond
months and years;

The poor Irishman lives in the simple house of his childhood, with
the wellknown neighbors and faces,

They warmly welcome him . . . . he is barefoot again . . . . he forgets
he is welloff;

The Dutchman voyages home, and the Scotchman and Welchman
voyage home . . and the native of the Mediterranean voyages
home;
To every port of England and France and Spain enter wellfilled ships;
The Swiss foots it toward his hills . . . . the Prussian goes his way,
and the Hungarian his way, and the Pole goes his way,
The Swede returns, and the Dane and Norwegian return.

[. . .]

The soul is always beautiful,
The universe is duly in order . . . . every thing is in its place,
What is arrived is in its place, and what waits is in its place;
The twisted skull waits . . . . the watery or rotten blood waits,
The child of the glutton or venerealee waits long, and the child of the
drunkard waits long, and the drunkard himself waits long,
The sleepers that lived and died wait . . . . the far advanced are to go on
in their turns, and the far behind are to go on in their turns,
The diverse shall be no less diverse, but they shall flow and unite
. . . . they unite now.

❖

[...]

The sprawl and fulness of babes . . . . the bosoms and heads of
   women . . . . the folds of their dress . . . . their style as we pass in
   the street . . . . the contour of their shape downwards;
The swimmer naked in the swimmingbath . . seen as he swims
   through the salt transparent greenshine, or lies on his back and
   rolls silently with the heave of the water;
Framers bare-armed framing a house . . hoisting the beams in their
   places . . or using the mallet and mortising-chisel,
The bending forward and backward of rowers in rowboats . . . .

[...]

I knew a man . . . . he was a common farmer . . . . he was the father
   of five sons . . . and in them were the fathers of sons . . . and in
   them were the fathers of sons.

This man was of wonderful vigor and calmness and beauty of person;
The shape of his head, the richness and breadth of his manners, the
   pale yellow and white of his hair and beard, the immeasurable
   meaning of his black eyes,
These I used to go and visit him to see . . . . He was wise also,
He was six feet tall . . . . he was over eighty years old . . . . his sons
   were massive clean bearded tanfaced and handsome,
They and his daughters loved him . . . all who saw him loved him . . .
   they did not love him by allowance . . . they loved him with
   personal love;
He drank water only . . . . the blood showed like scarlet through
   the clear brown skin of his face;
He was a frequent gunner and fisher . . . he sailed his boat himself . . .
   he had a fine one presented to him by a shipjoiner . . . . he had
   fowling-pieces, presented to him by men that loved him;

When he went with his five sons and many grandsons to hunt or fish
  you would pick him out as the most beautiful and vigorous of
  the gang,
You would wish long and long to be with him . . . . you would wish to
  sit by him in the boat that you and he might touch each other.

I have perceived that to be with those I like is enough,
To stop in company with the rest at evening is enough,
To be surrounded by beautiful curious breathing laughing flesh is
  enough,
To pass among them . . to touch any one . . . . to rest my arm ever so
  lightly round his or her neck for a moment . . . . what is this then?
I do not ask any more delight . . . . I swim in it as in a sea.

There is something in staying close to men and women and looking
  on them and in the contact and odor of them that pleases the
  soul well,
All things please the soul, but these please the soul well.

This is the female form,
A divine nimbus exhales from it from head to foot,
It attracts with fierce undeniable attraction,
I am drawn by its breath as if I were no more than a helpless vapor . . . .
  all falls aside but myself and it,
Books, art, religion, time . . the visible and solid earth . . the atmosphere
  and the fringed clouds . . what was expected of heaven or feared of
  hell are now consumed,
Mad filaments, ungovernable shoots play out of it . . the response
  likewise ungovernable,
Hair, bosom, hips, bend of legs, negligent falling hands — all diffused
  . . . . mine too diffused,
Ebb stung by the flow, and flow stung by the ebb . . . . loveflesh swelling
  and deliciously aching,
Limitless limpid jets of love hot and enormous . . . . quivering jelly
  of love . . . white-blow and delirious juice,

from *Leaves of Grass* (1855)   31

Bridegroom-night of love working surely and softly into the
    prostrate dawn,
Undulating into the willing and yielding day,
Lost in the cleave of the clasping and sweetfleshed day.

This is the nucleus . . . after the child is born of woman the man is
    born of woman,
This is the bath of birth . . . this is the merge of small and large and
    the outlet again.

[. . .]

Each belongs here or anywhere just as much as the welloff . . . .
    just as much as you,
Each has his or her place in the procession.

All is a procession,
The universe is a procession with measured and beautiful motion.

[. . .]

[...]

.... The sense of what is real .... the thought if after all it should
  prove unreal,
The doubts of daytime and the doubts of nighttime ... the curious
  whether and how,
Whether that which appears so is so .... Or is it all flashes and specks?
Men and women crowding fast in the streets .. if they are not flashes
  and specks what are they?
The streets themselves, and the facades of houses .... the goods in
  the windows,
Vehicles .. teams .. the tiered wharves, and the huge crossing at
  the ferries;
The village on the highland seen from afar at sunset .... the river
  between,
Shadows .. aureola and mist .. light falling on roofs and gables of
  white or brown, three miles off,
The schooner near by sleepily dropping down the tide .. the little
  boat slacktowed astern,
The hurrying tumbling waves and quickbroken crests and slapping;
The strata of colored clouds .... the long bar of maroontint away
  solitary by itself .... the spread of purity it lies motionless in,
The horizon's edge, the flying seacrow, the fragrance of saltmarsh
  and shoremud;
These became part of that child who went forth every day, and who
  now goes and will always go forth every day,
And these become of him or her that peruses them now.

GREAT are the myths . . . . I too delight in them,
Great are Adam and Eve . . . . I too look back and accept them;
Great the risen and fallen nations, and their poets, women, sages,
    inventors, rulers, warriors and priests.

Great is liberty! Great is equality! I am their follower,
Helmsmen of nations, choose your craft . . . . where you sail I sail,
Yours is the muscle of life or death . . . . yours is the perfect science
    . . . . in you I have absolute faith.

Great is today, and beautiful,
It is good to live in this age . . . . there never was any better.

Great are the plunges and throes and triumphs and falls of
    democracy,
Great the reformers with their lapses and screams,
Great the daring and venture of sailors on new explorations.

Great are yourself and myself,
We are just as good and bad as the oldest and youngest or any,
What the best and worst did we could do,
What they felt . . do not we feel it in ourselves?
What they wished . . do we not wish the same?

Great is youth, and equally great is old age . . . . great are the day
    and night;
Great is wealth and great is poverty . . . . great is expression and
    great is silence.

[. . .]

Great is the greatest nation . . the nation of clusters of equal nations.

Great is the earth, and the way it became what it is,
Do you imagine it is stopped at this? . . . . and the increase abandoned?
Understand then that it goes as far onward from this as this is from
    the times when it lay in covering waters and gases.

Great is the quality of truth in man,
The quality of truth in man supports itself through all changes,
It is inevitably in the man . . . . He and it are in love, and never leave
    each other.
The truth in man is no dictum . . . . it is vital as eyesight,
If there be any soul there is truth . . . . if there be man or woman
    there is truth . . . . If there be physical or moral there is truth,
If there be equilibrium or volition there is truth . . . . if there be
    things at all upon the earth there is truth.

O truth of the earth! O truth of things! I am determined to press
    the whole way toward you,
Sound your voice! I scale mountains or dive in the sea after you.

Great is language . . . . it is the mightiest of the sciences,
It is the fulness and color and form and diversity of the earth . . . .
    and of men and women . . . . and of all qualities and processes;
It is greater than wealth . . . . it is greater than buildings or ships or
    religions or paintings or music.

[. . .]

Great is life . . and real and mystical . . wherever and whoever,
Great is death . . . . Sure as life holds all parts together, death holds
    all parts together;
Sure as the stars return again after they merge in the light, death is
    great as life.

from *Leaves of Grass* (1856)

With Ohio, Illinois, Missouri, Oregon—with the states around the Mexican sea—with cheerfully welcomed immigrants from Europe, Asia, Africa—with Connecticut, Vermont, New Hampshire, Rhode Island—with all varied interests, facts, beliefs, parties, genesis—there is being fused a determined character, fit for the broadest use for the freewomen and freemen of The States, accomplished and to be accomplished, without any exception whatever—each indeed free, each idiomatic, as becomes live states and men, but each adhering to one enclosing general form of politics, manners, talk, personal style, as the plenteous varieties of the race adhere to one physical form. Such character is the brain and spine to all, including literature, including poems. Such character, strong, limber, just, open-mouthed, American-blooded, full of pride, full of ease, of passionate friendliness, is to stand compact upon that vast basis of the supremacy of Individuality—that new moral American continent without which, I see, the physical continent remained incomplete, may-be a carcass, a bloat—that newer America, answering face to face with The States, with ever-satisfying and ever-unsurveyable seas and shores.

> —letter to Ralph Waldo Emerson
> included in an appendix titled "Leaves-Droppings"

3. *from* Poem of Salutation

O TAKE my hand, Walt Whitman!
Such gliding wonders! Such sights and sounds!
Such joined unended links, each hooked to the next!
Each answering all, each sharing the earth with all.

What widens within you, Walt Whitman?
What waves and soils exuding?
What climes? what persons and lands are here?
Who are the infants? some playing, some slumbering?
Who are the girls? Who are the married women?
Who are the three old men going slowly with their arms about
    each others' necks?
What rivers are these? What forests and fruits are these?
What are the mountains called that rise so high in the mists?
What myriads of dwellings are they, filled with dwellers?

Within me latitude widens, longitude lengthens,
Asia, Africa, Europe, are to the east—America is provided for in
    the west,
Banding the bulge of the earth winds the hot equator,
Curiously north and south turn the axis-ends;
Within me is the longest day, the sun wheels in slanting rings, it
    does not set for months,
Stretched in due time within me the midnight sun just rises above
    the horizon, and sinks again;
Within me zones, seas, cataracts, plains, volcanoes, groups,
Oceanica, Australasia, Polynesia, and the great West Indian islands.

[. . .]

What do you see, Walt Whitman?
Who are they you salute, and that one after another salute you?

I see a great round wonder rolling through the air,
I see diminute farms, hamlets, ruins, graveyards, jails, factories,
    palaces, hovels, huts of barbarians, tents of nomads, upon the
    surface,
I see the shaded part on one side where the sleepers are sleeping,
    and the sun-lit part on the other side,
I see the curious silent change of the light and shade,
I see distant lands, as real and near to the inhabitants of them as
    my land is to me.

I see plenteous waters,
I see mountain peaks — I see the sierras of Andes and Alleghanies,
    I see where they range,

I see plainly the Himmalehs, Chian Shahs, Altays, Gauts,
I see the Rocky Mountains, and the Peak of Winds,
I see the Styrian Alps and the Karnac Alps,
I see the Pyrenees, Balks, Carpathians, and to the north the Dofrafields,
    and off at sea Mount Hecla,
I see Vesuvius and Etna — I see the Anahuacs,
I see the Mountains of the Moon, and the Snow Mountains, and
    the Red Mountains of Madagascar,
I see the Vermont hills, and the long string of Cordilleras;
I see the vast deserts of Western America,
I see the Libyan, Arabian, and Asiatic deserts;
I see huge dreadful Arctic and Antarctic icebergs,
I see the superior oceans and the inferior ones — the Atlantic and
    Pacific, the sea of Mexico, the Brazilian sea, and the sea of Peru,
The Japan waters, those of Hindostan, the China Sea, and the Gulf
    of Guinea,
The spread of the Baltic, Caspian, Bothnia, the British shores, and
    the Bay of Biscay,
The clear-sunned Mediterranean, and from one to another of its
    islands,
The inland fresh-tasted seas of North America,
The White Sea, and the sea around Greenland.

I behold the mariners of the world,
Some are in storms, some in the night, with the watch on the look-out,
some drifting helplessly, some with contagious diseases.

I behold the steam-ships of the world,
Some double the Cape of Storms, some Cape Verde, others Cape
Guardafui, Bon, or Bajadore,
Others Dondra Head, others pass the Straits of Sunda, others Cape
Lopatka, others Behring's Straits,
Others Cape Horn, others the Gulf of Mexico, or along Cuba or Hayti,
others Hudson's Bay or Baffin's Bay,
Others pass the Straits of Dover, others enter the Wash, others the
Firth of Solway, others round Cape Clear, others the Land's End,
Others traverse the Zuyder Zee or the Scheld,
Others add to the exits and entrances at Sandy Hook,
Others to the comers and goers at Gibraltar or the Dardanelles,
Others sternly push their way through the northern winter-packs,
Others descend or ascend the Obi or the Lena,
Others the Niger or the Congo, others the Hoang-ho and Amoor,
others the Indus, the Burampooter and Cambodia,
Others wait at the wharves of Manahatta, steamed up, ready to start,
Wait swift and swarthy in the ports of Australia,
Wait at Liverpool, Glasgow, Dublin, Marseilles, Lisbon, Naples,
Hamburgh, Bremen, Bordeaux, the Hague, Copenhagen,
Wait at Valparaiso, Rio Janeiro, Panama,
Wait at their moorings at Boston, Philadelphia, Baltimore, Charleston,
New Orleans, Galveston, San Francisco.

I see the tracks of the rail-roads of the earth,
I see them welding state to state, county to county, city to city, through
North America,
I see them in Great Britain, I see them in Europe,
I see them in Asia and in Africa.

I see the electric telegraphs of the earth,
I see the filaments of the news of the wars, deaths, losses, gains,
　　passions, of my race.

I see the long thick river-stripes of the earth,
I see where the Mississippi flows, I see where the Columbia flows,
I see the St. Lawrence and the falls of Niagara,
I see the Amazon and the Paraguay,
I see where the Seine flows, and where the Loire, the Rhone, and
　　the Guadalquivir flow,
I see the windings of the Volga, the Dnieper, the Oder,
I see the Tuscan going down the Arno, and the Venetian along
　　the Po,
I see the Greek seaman sailing out of Egina bay.

I see the site of the great old empire of Assyria, and that of Persia,
　　and that of India,
I see the falling of the Ganges over the high rim of Saukara.

I see the place of the idea of the Deity incarnated by avatars in
　　human forms,
I see the spots of the successions of priests on the earth, oracles,
　　sacrificers, brahmins, sabians, lamas, monks, muftis, exhorters,
I see where druids walked the groves of Mona, I see the misletoe
　　and vervain,
I see the temples of the deaths of the bodies of gods, I see the old
　　signifiers,
I see Christ once more eating the bread of his last supper in the
　　midst of youths and old persons,
I see where the strong divine young man, the Hercules, toiled
　　faithfully and long, and then died,
I see the place of the innocent rich life and hapless fate of the
　　beautiful nocturnal son, the full-limbed Bacchus,
I see Kneph, blooming, dressed in blue, with the crown of feathers
　　on his head,

I see Hermes, unsuspected, dying, well-beloved, saying to the people,
  Do not weep for me, this is not my true country, I have lived banished
  from my true country, I now go back there, I return to the celestial
  sphere where every one goes in his turn.

[. . .]

I see the little and large sea-dots, some inhabited, some uninhabited;
I see two boats with nets, lying off the shore of Paumanok, quite still,
I see ten fishermen waiting—they discover now a thick school of
  mossbonkers, they drop the joined seine-ends in the water,
The boats separate, they diverge and row off, each on its rounding
  course to the beach, enclosing the mossbonkers,
The net is drawn in by a windlass by those who stop ashore,
Some of the fishermen lounge in the boats, others stand negligently
  ankle-deep in the water, poised on strong legs,
The boats are partly drawn up, the water slaps against them,
On the sand, in heaps and winrows, well out from the water, lie the
  green-backed spotted mossbonkers.

I see the despondent red man in the west, lingering about the banks of
  Moingo, and about Lake Pepin,
He has beheld the quail and honey-bee, and sadly prepared to depart.

I see the regions of snow and ice,
I see the sharp-eyed Samoiede and the Finn,
I see the seal-seeker in his boat, poising his lance,
I see the Siberian on his slight-built sledge, drawn by dogs,
I see the porpoise-hunters, I see the whale-crews of the South Pacific
  and the North Atlantic,
I see the cliffs, glaciers, torrents, valleys, of Switzerland—I mark the
  long winters and the isolation.

[. . .]

My spirit has passed in compassion and determination around
the whole earth,
I have looked for brothers, sisters, lovers, and found them ready
for me in all lands.

I think I have risen with you, you vapors, and moved away to
distant continents, and fallen down there, for reasons,
I think I have blown with you, you winds,
I think, you waters, I have fingered every shore with you,
I think I have run through what any river or strait of the globe has
run through,
I think I have taken my stand on the bases of peninsulas, and on
imbedded rocks.

What cities the light or warmth penetrates, I penetrate those cities
myself,
All islands to which birds wing their way, I wing my way myself,
I find my home wherever there are any homes of men.

11. Sun-Down Poem

FLOOD-TIDE of the river, flow on! I watch you, face to face,
Clouds of the west! sun half an hour high! I see you also face to face.

Crowds of men and women attired in the usual costumes, how curious
    you are to me!
On the ferry-boats the hundreds and hundreds that cross are more
    curious to me than you suppose,
And you that shall cross from shore to shore years hence, are more
    to me, and more in my meditations, than you might suppose.

The impalpable sustenance of me from all things at all hours of the day,
The simple, compact, well-joined scheme — myself disintegrated,
    every one disintegrated, yet part of the scheme,
The similitudes of the past and those of the future,
The glories strung like beads on my smallest sights and hearings —
    on the walk in the street, and the passage over the river,
The current rushing so swiftly, and swimming with me far away,
The others that are to follow me, the ties between me and them,
The certainty of others — the life, love, sight, hearing of others.

Others will enter the gates of the ferry, and cross from shore to shore,
Others will watch the run of the flood-tide,
Others will see the shipping of Manhattan north and west, and the
    heights of Brooklyn to the south and east,
Others will see the islands large and small,
Fifty years hence others will see them as they cross, the sun half an hour
    high,
A hundred years hence, or ever so many hundred years hence, others
    will see them,
Will enjoy the sun-set, the pouring in of the flood-tide, the falling back
    to the sea of the ebb-tide.

It avails not, neither time or place—distance avails not,
I am with you, you men and women of a generation, or ever so
    many generations hence,
I project myself, also I return—I am with you, and know how it is.

Just as you feel when you look on the river and sky, so I felt,
Just as any of you is one of a living crowd, I was one of a crowd,
Just as you are refreshed by the gladness of the river, and the
    bright flow, I was refreshed,
Just as you stand and lean on the rail, yet hurry with the swift current,
    I stood, yet was hurried,
Just as you look on the numberless masts of ships, and the thick-
    stemmed pipes of steamboats, I looked.

I too many and many a time crossed the river, the sun half an hour
    high,
I watched the December sea-gulls, I saw them high in the air floating
    with motionless wings oscillating their bodies,
I saw how the glistening yellow lit up parts of their bodies, and left
    the rest in strong shadow,
I saw the slow-wheeling circles and the gradual edging toward the
    south.

I too saw the reflection of the summer-sky in the water.
Had my eyes dazzled by the shimmering track of beams,
Looked at the fine centrifugal spokes of light round the shape of
    my head in the sun-lit water,
Looked on the haze on the hills southward and southwestward,
Looked on the vapor as it flew in fleeces tinged with violet,
Looked toward the lower bay to notice the arriving ships,
Saw their approach, saw aboard those that were near me,
Saw the white sails of schooners and sloops, saw the ships at anchor,
The sailors at work in the rigging or out astride the spars,
The round masts, the swinging motion of the hulls, the slender
    serpentine pennants,

The large and small steamers in motion, the pilots in their pilot-houses,
The white wake left by the passage, the quick tremulous whirl of the
     wheels,
The flags of all nations, the falling of them at sun-set,
The scallop-edged waves in the twilight, the ladled cups, the frolicsome
     crests and glistening,
The stretch afar growing dimmer and dimmer, the gray walls of the
     granite store-houses by the docks,
On the river the shadowy group, the big steam-tug closely flanked
     on each side by the barges — the hay-boat, the belated lighter,
On the neighboring shore the fires from the foundry chimneys burning
     high and glaringly into the night,
Casting their flicker of black, contrasted with wild red and yellow light,
     over the tops of houses, and down into the clefts of streets.

These and all else were to me the same as they are to you,
I project myself a moment to tell you — also I return.

I loved well those cities,
I loved well the stately and rapid river,
The men and women I saw were all near to me,
Others the same — others who look back on me, because I looked
     forward to them,
The time will come, though I stop here today and tonight.

What is it, then, between us? What is the count of the scores or hundreds
     of years between us?
Whatever it is, it avails not — distance avails not, and place avails not.

I too lived,
I too walked the streets of Manhattan Island, and bathed in the waters
     around it;
I too felt the curious abrupt questionings stir within me,
In the day, among crowds of people, sometimes they came upon me,
In my walks home late at night, or as I lay in my bed, they came upon me.

I too had been struck from the float forever held in solution,
I too had received identity by my body,
That I was, I knew was of my body, and what I should be, I knew
    I should be of my body.

It is not upon you alone the dark patches fall,
The dark threw patches down upon me also,
The best I had done seemed to me blank and suspicious,
My great thoughts, as I supposed them, were they not in reality
    meagre? Would not people laugh at me?

It is not you alone who know what it is to be evil,
I am he who knew what it was to be evil,
I too knitted the old knot of contrariety,
Blabbed, blushed, resented, lied, stole, grudged,
Had guile, anger, lust, hot wishes I dared not speak,
Was wayward, vain, greedy, shallow, sly, a solitary committer,
    a coward, a malignant person,
The wolf, the snake, the hog, not wanting in me,
The cheating look, the frivolous word, the adulterous wish, not wanting,
Refusals, hates, postponements, meanness, laziness, none of these
    wanting.

But I was a Manhattanese, free, friendly, and proud!
I was called by my nighest name by clear loud voices of young men
    as they saw me approaching or passing,
Felt their arms on my neck as I stood, or the negligent leaning of
    their flesh against me as I sat,
Saw many I loved in the street, or ferry-boat, or public assembly,
    yet never told them a word,
Lived the same life with the rest, the same old laughing, gnawing,
    sleeping,
Played the part that still looks back on the actor or actress,
The same old role, the role that is what we make it, as great as
    we like, or as small as we like, or both great and small.

Closer yet I approach you,

What thought you have of me, I had as much of you—I laid in my stores in advance,

I considered long and seriously of you before you were born.

Who was to know what should come home to me?

Who knows but I am enjoying this?

Who knows but I am as good as looking at you now, for all you cannot see me?

It is not you alone, nor I alone,

Not a few races, not a few generations, not a few centuries,

It is that each came, or comes, or shall come, from its due emission, without fail, either now, or then, or henceforth.

Every thing indicates—the smallest does, and the largest does,

A necessary film envelops all, and envelops the soul for a proper time.

Now I am curious what sight can ever be more stately and admirable to me than my mast-hemm'd Manahatta, my river and sun-set, and my scallop-edged waves of flood-tide, the sea-gulls oscillating their bodies, the hay-boat in the twilight, and the belated lighter,

Curious what gods can exceed these that clasp me by the hand, and with voices I love call me promptly and loudly by my nighest name as I approach,

Curious what is more subtle than this which ties me to the woman or man that looks in my face,

Which fuses me into you now, and pours my meaning into you.

We understand, then, do we not?

What I promised without mentioning it, have you not accepted?

What the study could not teach—what the preaching could not accomplish is accomplished, is it not?

What the push of reading could not start is started by me personally, is it not?

Flow on, river! Flow with the flood-tide, and ebb with the ebb-tide!
Frolic on, crested and scallop-edged waves!
Gorgeous clouds of the sun-set, drench with your splendor me, or
the men and women generations after me!
Cross from shore to shore, countless crowds of passengers!
Stand up, tall masts of Manahatta!—stand up, beautiful hills of
Brooklyn!
Bully for you! you proud, friendly, free Manhattanese!
Throb, baffled and curious brain! throw out questions and answers!
Suspend here and everywhere, eternal float of solution!
Blab, blush, lie, steal, you or I or any one after us!
Gaze, loving and thirsting eyes, in the house or street or public
assembly!
Sound out, voices of young men! loudly and musically call me by
my nighest name!
Live, old life! play the part that looks back on the actor or actress!
Play the old role, the role that is great or small, according as one
makes it!
Consider, you who peruse me, whether I may not in unknown ways
be looking upon you!
Be firm, rail over the river, to support those who lean idly, yet haste
with the hasting current!
Fly on, sea-birds! fly sideways, or wheel in large circles high in
the air!
Receive the summer-sky, you water! faithfully hold it till all
downcast eyes have time to take it from you!
Diverge, fine spokes of light, from the shape of my head, or any one's
head, in the sun-lit water!
Come on, ships, from the lower bay! pass up or down, white-sailed
schooners, sloops, lighters!
Flaunt away, flags of all nations! be duly lowered at sun-set!
Burn high your fires, foundry chimneys! cast black shadows at
night-fall! cast red and yellow light over the tops of the houses!
Appearances, now or henceforth, indicate what you are!
You necessary film, continue to envelop the soul!

About my body for me, and your body for you, be hung our divinest
  aromas!
Thrive, cities! Bring your freight, bring your shows, ample and sufficient
  rivers!
Expand, being than which none else is perhaps more spiritual!
Keep your places, objects than which none else is more lasting!

We descend upon you and all things, we arrest you all,
We realize the soul only by you, you faithful solids and fluids,
Through you color, form, location, sublimity, ideality,
Through you every proof, comparison, and all the suggestions and
  determinations of ourselves.
You have waited, you always wait, you dumb beautiful ministers!
  you novices!
We receive you with free sense at last, and are insatiate henceforward,
Not you any more shall be able to foil us, or with-hold yourselves
  from us,
We use you, and do not cast you aside — we plant you permanently
  within us,
We fathom you not — we love you — there is perfection in you also,
You furnish your parts toward eternity,
Great or small, you furnish your parts toward the soul.

24. Poem of Perfect Miracles

REALISM is mine, my miracles,
Take all of the rest—take freely—I keep but my own—I give only
  of them,
I offer them without end—I offer them to you wherever your feet
  can carry you, or your eyes reach.

Why! who makes much of a miracle?
As to me, I know of nothing else but miracles,
Whether I walk the streets of Manhattan,
Or dart my sight over the roofs of houses toward the sky,
Or wade with naked feet along the beach, just in the edge of the water,
Or stand under trees in the woods,
Or talk by day with any one I love—or sleep in the bed at night with
  any one I love,
Or sit at the table at dinner with my mother,
Or look at strangers opposite me riding in the car,
Or watch honey-bees busy around the hive, of an August forenoon,
Or animals feeding in the fields,
Or birds—or the wonderfulness of insects in the air,
Or the wonderfulness of the sun-down—or of stars shining so quiet
  and bright,
Or the exquisite, delicate, thin curve of the new-moon in May,
Or whether I go among those I like best, and that like me best—
  mechanics, boatmen, farmers,
Or among the savans—or to the soiree—or to the opera,
Or stand a long while looking at the movements of machinery,
Or behold children at their sports,
Or the admirable sight of the perfect old man, or the perfect old
  woman,
Or the sick in hospitals, or the dead carried to burial,
Or my own eyes and figure in the glass,
These, with the rest, one and all, are to me miracles,
The whole referring—yet each distinct and in its place.

To me, every hour of the light and dark is a miracle,
Every inch of space is a miracle,
Every square yard of the surface of the earth is spread with the same,
Every cubic foot of the interior swarms with the same;
Every spear of grass — the frames, limbs, organs, of men and women,
    and all that concerns them,
All these to me are unspeakably perfect miracles.

To me the sea is a continual miracle,
The fishes that swim — the rocks — the motion of the waves — the ships,
    with men in them — what stranger miracles are there?

28. Bunch Poem

THE friend I am happy with,
The arm of my friend hanging idly over my shoulder,
The hill-side whitened with blossoms of the mountain ash,
The same, late in autumn—the gorgeous hues of red, yellow, drab,
   purple, and light and dark green,
The rich coverlid of the grass—animals and birds—the private
   untrimmed bank—the primitive apples—the pebble-stones,
Beautiful dripping fragments—the negligent list of one after another,
   as I happen to call them to me, or think of them,
The real poems, (what we call poems being merely pictures,)
The poems of the privacy of the night, and of men like me,
This poem, drooping shy and unseen, that I always carry, and that
   all men carry,
(Know, once for all, avowed on purpose, wherever are men like me,
   are our lusty, lurking, masculine poems,)
Love-thoughts, love-juice, love-odor, love-yielding, love-climbers,
   and the climbing sap,
Arms and hands of love—lips of love—phallic thumb of love—
   breasts of love—bellies, pressed and glued together with love,
Earth of chaste love—life that is only life after love,
The body of my love—the body of the woman I love—the body of
   the man—the body of the earth,
Soft forenoon airs that blow from the south-west,
The hairy wild-bee that murmurs and hankers up and down—that
   gripes the full-grown lady-flower, curves upon her with amorous
   firm legs, takes his will of her, and holds himself tremulous and
   tight upon her till he is satisfied,
The wet of woods through the early hours,
Two sleepers at night lying close together as they sleep, one with
   an arm slanting down across and below the waist of the other,
The smell of apples, aromas from crushed sage-plant, mint, birch-bark,
The boy's longings, the glow and pressure as he confides to me what
   he was dreaming,

The dead leaf whirling its spiral whirl, and falling still and content to
    the ground,
The no-formed stings that sights, people, objects, sting me with,
The hubbed sting of myself, stinging me as much as it ever can any one,
The sensitive, orbic, underlapped brothers, that only privileged feelers
    may be intimate where they are,
The curious roamer, the hand, roaming all over the body—the bashful
    withdrawing of flesh where the fingers soothingly pause and edge
    themselves,
The limpid liquid within the young man,
The vexed corrosion, so pensive and so painful,
The torment—the irritable tide that will not be at rest,
The like of the same I feel—the like of the same in others,
The young woman that flushes and flushes, and the young man that
    flushes and flushes,
The young man that wakes, deep at night, the hot hand seeking to
    repress what would master him—the strange half-welcome pangs,
    visions, sweats—the pulse pounding through palms and trembling
    encircling fingers—the young man all colored, red, ashamed, angry;
The souse upon me of my lover the sea, as I lie willing and naked,
The merriment of the twin-babes that crawl over the grass in the sun,
    the mother never turning her vigilant eyes from them,
The walnut-trunk, the walnut-husks, and the ripening or ripened
    long-round walnuts,
The continence of vegetables, birds, animals,
The consequent meanness of me should I skulk or find myself indecent,
    while birds and animals never once skulk or find themselves
    indecent,
The great chastity of paternity, to match the great chastity of maternity,
The oath of procreation I have sworn,
The greed that eats in me day and night with hungry gnaw, till I
    saturate what shall produce boys to fill my place when I am through,
The wholesome relief, repose, content,
And this bunch plucked at random from myself,
It has done its work—I toss it carelessly to fall where it may.

31. Poem of The Sayers of The Words of The Earth

EARTH, round, rolling, compact—suns, moons, animals—all these
    are words,
Watery, vegetable, sauroid advances—beings, premonitions,
    lispings of the future—these are vast words.

Were you thinking that those were the words—those upright lines?
    those curves, angles, dots?
No, those are not the words—the substantial words are in the
    ground and sea,
They are in the air—they are in you.

Were you thinking that those were the words—those delicious
    sounds out of your friends' mouths?
No, the real words are more delicious than they.

Human bodies are words, myriads of words,
In the best poems re-appears the body, man's or woman's,
    well-shaped, natural, gay,
Every part able, active, receptive, without shame or the need of
    shame.

Air, soil, water, fire, these are words,
I myself am a word with them—my qualities interpenetrate with
    theirs—my name is nothing to them,
Though it were told in the three thousand languages, what would
    air, soil, water, fire, know of my name?

A healthy presence, a friendly or commanding gesture, are words,
    sayings, meanings,
The charms that go with the mere looks of some men and women
    are sayings and meanings also.

The workmanship of souls is by the inaudible words of the earth,
The great masters, the sayers, know the earth's words, and use them
more than the audible words.

Syllables are not the earth's words,
Beauty, reality, manhood, time, life — the realities of such as these are
the earth's words.

Amelioration is one of the earth's words,
The earth neither lags nor hastens,
It has all attributes, growths, effects, latent in itself from the jump,
It is not half beautiful only — defects and excrescences show just as
much as perfections show.

The earth does not withhold, it is generous enough,
The truths of the earth continually wait, they are not so concealed either,
They are calm, subtle, untransmissible by print,
They are imbued through all things, conveying themselves willingly,
Conveying a sentiment and invitation of the earth — I utter and utter,
I speak not, yet if you hear me not, of what avail am I to you?
To bear — to better — lacking these, of what avail am I?

Accouche! Accouchez!
Will you rot your own fruit in yourself there?
Will you squat and stifle there?

The earth does not argue,
Is not pathetic, has no arrangements,
Does not scream, haste, persuade, threaten, promise,
Makes no discriminations, has no conceivable failures,
Closes nothing, refuses nothing, shuts none out,
Of all the powers, objects, states, it notifies, shuts none out.

The earth does not exhibit itself nor refuse to exhibit itself—
    possesses still underneath,
Underneath the ostensible sounds, the august chorus of heroes,
    the wail of slaves,
Persuasions of lovers, curses, gasps of the dying, laughter of young
    people, accents of bargainers,
Underneath these possessing the words that never fail.

To her children the words of the eloquent dumb great mother
    never fail,
The true words do not fail, for motion does not fail, and reflection
    does not fail,
Also the day and night do not fail, and the voyage we pursue does
    not fail.

Of the interminable sisters,
Of the ceaseless cotillions of sisters,
Of the centripetal and centrifugal sisters, the elder and younger sisters,
The beautiful sister we know dances on with the rest.

With her ample back toward every beholder,
With the fascinations of youth and the equal fascinations of age,
Sits she whom I too love like the rest, sits undisturbed,
Holding up in her hand what has the character of a mirror,
    her eyes glancing back from it,
Glancing thence as she sits, inviting none, denying none,
Holding a mirror day and night tirelessly before her own face.

Seen at hand, or seen at a distance,
Duly the twenty-four appear in public every day,
Duly approach and pass with their companions, or a companion,
Looking from no countenances of their own, but from the
    countenances of those who are with them,
From the countenances of children or women, or the manly
    countenance,

From the open countenances of animals, from inanimate things,
From the landscape or waters, or from the exquisite apparition of
    the sky,
From our own countenances, mine and yours, faithfully returning them,
Every day in public appearing without fail, but never twice with the
    same companions.
Embracing man, embracing all, proceed the three hundred and
    sixty-five resistlessly round the sun,
Embracing all, soothing, supporting, follow close three hundred and
    sixty-five offsets of the first, sure and necessary as they.

Tumbling on steadily, nothing dreading,
Sunshine, storm, cold, heat, forever withstanding, passing, carrying,
The soul's realization and determination still inheriting,
The liquid vacuum around and ahead still entering and dividing,
No balk retarding, no anchor anchoring, on no rock striking,
Swift, glad, content, unbereaved, nothing losing,
Of all able and ready at any time to give strict account,
The divine ship sails the divine sea.

Whoever you are! motion and reflection are especially for you,
The divine ship sails the divine sea for you.

Whoever you are! you are he or she for whom the earth is solid and
    liquid,
You are he or she for whom the sun and moon hang in the sky,
For none more than you are the present and the past,
For none more than you is immortality.

Each man to himself, and each woman to herself, is the word of the past
    and present, and the word of immortality,
Not one can acquire for another—not one!
Not one can grow for another—not one!

The song is to the singer, and comes back most to him,
The teaching is to the teacher, and comes back most to him,
The murder is to the murderer, and comes back most to him,
The theft is to the thief, and comes back most to him,
The love is to the lover, and comes back most to him,
The gift is to the giver, and comes back most to him — it cannot fail,
The oration is to the orator, and the acting is to the actor and actress,
    not to the audience,
And no man understands any greatness or goodness but his own,
    or the indication of his own.

I swear the earth shall surely be complete to him or her who shall
    be complete!
I swear the earth remains broken and jagged only to him or her
    who remains broken and jagged!

I swear there is no greatness or power that does not emulate those
    of the earth!
I swear there can be no theory of any account, unless it corroborate
    the theory of the earth!
No politics, art, religion, behaviour, or what not, is of account,
    unless it compare with the amplitude of the earth,
Unless it face the exactness, vitality, impartiality, rectitude of
    the earth.

I swear I begin to see love with sweeter spasms than that which
    responds love!
It is that which contains itself, which never invites and never refuses.

I swear I begin to see little or nothing in audible words!
I swear I think all merges toward the presentation of the unspoken
    meanings of the earth!
Toward him who sings the songs of the body, and of the truths of
    the earth,
Toward him who makes the dictionaries of the words that print
    cannot touch.

I swear I see what is better than to tell the best,
It is always to leave the best untold.
When I undertake to tell the best, I find I cannot,
My tongue is ineffectual on its pivots,
My breath will not be obedient to its organs,
I become a dumb man.

The best of the earth cannot be told anyhow—all or any is best,
It is not what you anticipated, it is cheaper, easier, nearer,
Things are not dismissed from the places they held before,
The earth is just as positive and direct as it was before,
Facts, religions, improvements, politics, trades, are as real as before,
But the soul is also real, it too is positive and direct,
No reasoning, no proof has established it,
Undeniable growth has established it.

This is a poem for the sayers of the earth—these are hints of meanings,
These are they that echo the tones of souls, and the phrases of souls;
If they did not echo the phrases of souls, what were they then?
If they had not reference to you in especial, what were they then?
I swear I will never henceforth have to do with the faith that tells the best!
I will have to do with that faith only that leaves the best untold.

Say on, sayers of the earth!
Delve! mould! pile the substantial words of the earth!
Work on, age after age! nothing is to be lost,
It may have to wait long, but it will certainly come in use,
When the materials are all prepared, the architects shall appear,
I swear to you the architects shall appear without fail! I announce them
    and lead them!
I swear to you they will understand you and justify you!
I swear to you the greatest among them shall be he who best knows you,
    and encloses all, and is faithful to all!
I swear to you, he and the rest shall not forget you! they shall perceive
    that you are not an iota less than they!
I swear to you, you shall be glorified in them!

from *Leaves of Grass* (1860–61)

Mysterious ocean where the streams empty,
Prophetic spirit of materials shifting and flickering around me,
Wondrous interplay between the seen and unseen . . .

— "Proto-Leaf"

Passions there — wars, pursuits, tribes — sight in those ocean-
    depths — breathing that thick-breathing air, as so many do,
The change thence to the sight here, and to the subtle air
    breathed by beings like us, who walk this sphere;
The change onward from ours to that of beings who walk other
    spheres.

— "Leaves of Grass," No. 16
[later titled "The World Below The Brine"]

from Proto-Leaf

FREE, fresh, savage,
Fluent, luxuriant, self-content, fond of persons and places,
Fond of fish-shape Paumanok, where I was born,
Fond of the sea—lusty-begotten and various,
Boy of the Mannahatta, the city of ships, my city,
Or raised inland, or of the south savannas,
Or full-breath'd on Californian air, or Texan or Cuban air,
Tallying, vocalizing all—resounding Niagara—resounding Missouri,
Or rude in my home in Kanuck woods,
Or wandering and hunting, my drink water, my diet meat,
Or withdrawn to muse and meditate in some deep recess,
Far from the clank of crowds, an interval passing, rapt and happy,
Stars, vapor, snow, the hills, rocks, the Fifth Month flowers, my amaze,
    my love,
Aware of the buffalo, the peace-herds, the bull, strong-breasted
    and hairy,
Aware of the mocking-bird of the wilds at daybreak,
Solitary, singing in the west, I strike up for a new world.

[. . .]

O I see the following poems are indeed to drop in the earth the germs
    of a greater Religion.

My comrade!
For you, to share with me, two greatnesses—And a third one, rising
    inclusive and more resplendent,
The greatness of Love and Democracy—and the greatness of Religion.

Melange mine!
Mysterious ocean where the streams empty,
Prophetic spirit of materials shifting and flickering around me,
Wondrous interplay between the seen and unseen,

Living beings, identities, now doubtless near us, in the air, that we
  know not of,
Extasy everywhere touching and thrilling me,
Contact daily and hourly that will not release me,
These selecting—These, in hints, demanded of me.

Not he, adhesive, kissing me so long with his daily kiss,
Has winded and twisted around me that which holds me to him,
Any more than I am held to the heavens, to the spiritual world,
And to the identities of the Gods, my unknown lovers,
After what they have done to me, suggesting such themes.

O such themes! Equalities!
O amazement of things! O divine average!
O warblings under the sun—ushered, as now, or at noon, or setting!
O strain, musical, flowing through ages—now reaching hither,
I take to your reckless and composite chords—I add to them, and
  cheerfully pass them forward.

As I have walked in Alabama my morning walk, I have seen where
  the she-bird, the mocking-bird, sat on her nest in the briers,
  hatching her brood.

I have seen the he-bird also,
I have paused to hear him, near at hand, inflating his throat, and
  joyfully singing.

And while I paused, it came to me that what he really sang for was
  not there only,
Nor for his mate nor himself only, nor all sent back by the echoes,
But subtle, clandestine, away beyond,
A charge transmitted, and gift occult, for those being born.

Democracy!
Near at hand to you a throat is now inflating itself and joyfully
  singing.

[. . .]

On my way a moment I pause,
Here for you! And here for America!
Still the Present I raise aloft—Still the Future of The States I harbinge,
  glad and sublime,
And for the Past I pronounce what the air holds of the red aborigines.

The red aborigines!
Leaving natural breaths, sounds of rain and winds, calls as of birds and
  animals in the woods, syllabled to us for names, Okonee, Koosa,
  Ottawa, Monongahela, Sauk, Natchez, Chattahoochee, Kaqueta,
  Oronoco.
Wabash, Miami, Saginaw, Chippewa, Oshkosh, WallaWalla,
Leaving such to The States, they melt, they depart, charging the water
  and the land with names.

O expanding and swift! O henceforth,
Elements, breeds, adjustments, turbulent, quick, and audacious,
A world primal again—Vistas of glory, incessant and branching,
A new race, dominating previous ones, and grander far,
New politics—New literatures and religions—New inventions and arts.
These! These, my voice announcing—I will sleep no more, but arise;
You oceans that have been calm within me! how I feel you, fathomless,
  stirring, preparing unprecedented waves and storms.

See! steamers steaming through my poems!
See, in my poems immigrants continually coming and landing;
See, in arriere, the wigwam, the trail, the hunter's hut, the flat-boat,
  the maize-leaf, the claim, the rude fence, and the backwoods village;
See, on the one side the Western Sea, and on the other side the Eastern
  Sea, how they advance and retreat upon my poems, as upon their
  own shores;
See, pastures and forests in my poems—See, animals, wild and tame—
  See, beyond the Kanzas, countless herds of buffalo, feeding on
  short curly grass;

See, in my poems, old and new cities, solid, vast, inland, with
   paved streets, with iron and stone edifices, and ceaseless vehicles,
   and commerce;
See the populace, millions upon millions, handsome, tall, muscular,
   both sexes, clothed in easy and dignified clothes—teaching,
   commanding, marrying, generating, equally electing and elective;
See, the many-cylinder'd steam printing-press—See, the electric
   telegraph—See, the strong and quick locomotive, as it departs,
   panting, blowing the steam-whistle;
See, ploughmen, ploughing farms—See, miners, digging mines—
   See, the numberless factories;
See, mechanics, busy at their benches, with tools—See from
   among them, superior judges, philosophs, Presidents, emerge,
   dressed in working dresses;
See, lounging through the shops and fields of The States, me,
   well-beloved, close-held by day and night,
Hear the loud echo of my songs there! Read the hints come at last.

O my comrade!
O you and me at last—and us two only;
O power, liberty, eternity at last!
O to be relieved of distinctions! to make as much of vices as virtues!
O to level occupations and the sexes! O to bring all to common
   ground! O adhesiveness!
O the pensive aching to be together—you know not why, and I
   know not why.

O a word to clear one's path ahead endlessly!
O something extatic and undemonstrable! O music wild!
O now I triumph—and you shall also;
O hand in hand—O wholesome pleasure—O one more desirer
   and lover,
O haste, firm holding—haste, haste on, with me.

from Chants Democratic
and Native American

Apostroph

O mater! O fils!
O brood continental!
O flowers of the prairies!
O space boundless! O hum of mighty products!
O you teeming cities! O so invincible, turbulent, proud!
O race of the future! O women!
O fathers! O you men of passion and the storm!
O native power only! O beauty!
O yourself! O God! O divine average!
O you bearded roughs! O bards! O all those slumberers!
O arouse! the dawn-bird's throat sounds shrill! Do you not hear the
    cock crowing?
O, as I walk'd the beach, I heard the mournful notes foreboding
    a tempest—the low, oft-repeated shriek of the diver, the
    long-lived loon;
O I heard, and yet hear, angry thunder; — O you sailors! O ships!
    make quick preparation!
O from his masterful sweep, the warning cry of the eagle!
(Give way there, all! It is useless! Give up your spoils;)
O sarcasms! Propositions! (O if the whole world should prove indeed
    a sham, a sell!)
O I believe there is nothing real but America and freedom!
O to sternly reject all except Democracy!
O imperator! O who dare confront you and me?
O to promulgate our own! O to build for that which builds for mankind!
O feuillage! O North! O the slope drained by the Mexican sea!
O all, all inseparable—ages, ages, ages!
O a curse on him that would dissever this Union for any reason
    whatever!
O climates, labors! O good and evil! O death!

O you strong with iron and wood! O Personality!
O the village or place which has the greatest man or woman! even
    if it be only a few ragged huts;
O the city where women walk in public processions in the streets,
    the same as the men;
O a wan and terrible emblem, by me adopted!
O shapes arising! shapes of the future centuries!
O muscle and pluck forever for me!
O workmen and workwomen forever for me!
O farmers and sailors! O drivers of horses forever for me!
O I will make the new bardic list of trades and tools!
O you coarse and wilful! I love you!
O South! O longings for my dear home! O soft and sunny airs!
O pensive! O I must return where the palm grows and the mocking-
    bird sings, or else I die!
O equality! O organic compacts! I am come to be your born poet!
O whirl, contest, sounding and resounding! I am your poet, because
    I am part of you;
O days by-gone! Enthusiasts! Antecedents!
O vast preparations for These States! O years!
O what is now being sent forward thousands of years to come!
O mediums! O to teach! to convey the invisible faith!
To promulge real things! to journey through all The States!
O creation! O to-day! O laws! O unmitigated adoration!
O for mightier broods of orators, artists, and singers!
O for native songs! carpenter's, boatman's, ploughman's songs!
    shoemaker's songs!
O haughtiest growth of time! O free and extatic!
O what I, here, preparing, warble for!
O you hastening light! O the sun of the world will ascend, dazzling,
    and take his height — and you too will ascend;
O so amazing and so broad! up there resplendent, darting and
    burning;
O prophetic! O vision staggered with weight of light! with pouring
    glories!

O copious! O hitherto unequalled!
O Libertad! O compact! O union impossible to dissever!
O my Soul! O lips becoming tremulous, powerless!
O centuries, centuries yet ahead!
O voices of greater orators! I pause—I listen for you!
O you States! Cities! defiant of all outside authority!
I spring at once into your arms! you I most love!
O you grand Presidentiads! I wait for you!
New history! New heroes! I project you!
Visions of poets! only you really last! O sweep on! sweep on!
O Death! O you striding there! O I cannot yet!
O heights! O infinitely too swift and dizzy yet!
O purged lumine! you threaten me more than I can stand!
O present! I return while yet I may to you!
O poets to come, I depend upon you!

from Leaves of Grass

4.

SOMETHING startles me where I thought I was safest,
I withdraw from the still woods I loved,
I will not go now on the pastures to walk,
I will not strip the clothes from my body to meet my lover the sea,
I will not touch my flesh to the earth, as to other flesh, to renew me.

O Earth!
O how can the ground of you not sicken?
How can you be alive, you growths of spring?
How can you furnish health, you blood of herbs, roots, orchards,
    grain?
Are they not continually putting distempered corpses in you?
Is not every continent worked over and over with sour dead?

Where have you disposed of those carcasses of the drunkards and
    gluttons of so many generations?
Where have you drawn off all the foul liquid and meat?
I do not see any of it upon you to-day — or perhaps I am deceived,
I will run a furrow with my plough — I will press my spade through
    the sod, and turn it up underneath,
I am sure I shall expose some of the foul meat.

Behold!
This is the compost of billions of premature corpses,
Perhaps every mite has once formed part of a sick person —
    Yet behold!
The grass covers the prairies,
The bean bursts noiselessly through the mould in the garden,
The delicate spear of the onion pierces upward,
The apple-buds cluster together on the apple-branches,
The resurrection of the wheat appears with pale visage out of its graves,

The tinge awakes over the willow-tree and the mulberry-tree,
The he-birds carol mornings and evenings, while the she-birds sit
    on their nests,
The young of poultry break through the hatched eggs,
The new-born of animals appear—the calf is dropt from the cow,
    the colt from the mare,
Out of its little hill faithfully rise the potato's dark green leaves,
Out of its hill rises the yellow maize-stalk;
The summer growth is innocent and disdainful above all those strata
    of sour dead.

What chemistry!
That the winds are really not infectious,
That this is no cheat, this transparent green-wash of the sea, which is
    so amorous after me,
That it is safe to allow it to lick my naked body all over with its tongues,
That it will not endanger me with the fevers that have deposited
    themselves in it,
That all is clean, forever and forever,
That the cool drink from the well tastes so good,
That blackberries are so flavorous and juicy,
That the fruits of the apple-orchard, and of the orange-orchard—that
    melons, grapes, peaches, plums, will none of them poison me,
That when I recline on the grass I do not catch any disease,
Though probably every spear of grass rises out of what was once a
    catching disease.

Now I am terrified at the Earth! it is that calm and patient,
It grows such sweet things out of such corruptions,
It turns harmless and stainless on its axis, with such endless successions
    of diseased corpses,
It distils such exquisite winds out of such infused fetor,
It renews, with such unwitting looks, its prodigal, annual, sumptuous
    crops,
It gives such divine materials to men, and accepts such leavings
    from them at last.

❖

Poem of Joys

O TO make a most jubilant poem!
O full of music! Full of manhood, womanhood, infancy!
O full of common employments! Full of grain and trees.

O for the voices of animals! O for the swiftness and balance of fishes!
O for the dropping of rain-drops in a poem!
O for the sunshine and motion of waves in a poem.

O to be on the sea! the wind, the wide waters around;
O to sail in a ship under full sail at sea.

O the joy of my spirit! It is uncaged! It darts like lightning!
It is not enough to have this globe, or a certain time—I will have
      thousands of globes, and all time.

O the engineer's joys!
To go with a locomotive!
To hear the hiss of steam—the merry shriek—the steam-whistle—
      the laughing locomotive!
To push with resistless way, and speed off in the distance.
O the horseman's and horsewoman's joys!
The saddle—the gallop—the pressure upon the seat—the cool
      gurgling by the ears and hair.

O the fireman's joys!
I hear the alarm at dead of night,
I hear bells—shouts!—I pass the crowd—I run!
The sight of the flames maddens me with pleasure.

O the joy of the strong-brawned fighter, towering in the arena,
      in perfect condition, conscious of power, thirsting to meet
      his opponent.

O the joy of that vast elemental sympathy which only the human Soul
    is capable of generating and emitting in steady and limitless floods.

O the mother's joys!
The watching—the endurance—the precious love—the anguish—
    the patiently yielded life.

O the joy of increase, growth, recuperation,
The joy of soothing and pacifying—the joy of concord and harmony.

O to go back to the place where I was born!
O to hear the birds sing once more!
To ramble about the house and barn, and over the fields, once more,
And through the orchard and along the old lanes once more.

O male and female!
O the presence of women! (I swear, nothing is more exquisite to me than
    the presence of women;)
O for the girl, my mate! O for happiness with my mate!
O the young man as I pass! O I am sick after the friendship of him who,
    I fear, is indifferent to me.

O the streets of cities!
The flitting faces—the expressions, eyes, feet, costumes! O I cannot tell
    how welcome they are to me;
O of men—of women toward me as I pass—The memory of only one
    look—the boy lingering and waiting.

O to have been brought up on bays, lagoons, creeks, or along the coast!
O to continue and be employed there all my life!
O the briny and damp smell—the shore—the salt weeds exposed at
    low water,
The work of fishermen—the work of the eel-fisher and clam-fisher.

O it is I!
I come with my clam-rake and spade! I come with my eel-spear;
Is the tide out? I join the group of clam-diggers on the flats,
I laugh and work with them — I joke at my work, like a mettlesome
young man.

In winter I take my eel-basket and eel-spear and travel out on foot
on the ice — I have a small axe to cut holes in the ice;
Behold me, well-clothed, going gayly, or returning in the afternoon —
my brood of tough boys accompanying me,
My brood of grown and part-grown boys, who love to be with
none else so well as they love to be with me,
By day to work with me, and by night to sleep with me.

Or, another time, in warm weather, out in a boat, to lift the lobster-
pots, where they are sunk with heavy stones, (I know the buoys;)
O the sweetness of the Fifth Month morning upon the water, as I row,
just before sunrise, toward the buoys;
I pull the wicker pots up slantingly — the dark green lobsters are
desperate with their claws, as I take them out — I insert
wooden pegs in the joints of their pincers,
I go to all the places, one after another, and then row back to the shore,
There, in a huge kettle of boiling water, the lobsters shall be boiled
till their color becomes scarlet.

Or, another time, mackerel-taking,
Voracious, mad for the hook, near the surface, they seem to fill the
water for miles;
Or, another time, fishing for rock-fish in Chesapeake Bay — I one
of the brown-faced crew;
Or, another time, trailing for blue-fish off Paumanok, I stand with
braced body,
My left foot is on the gunwale — my right arm throws the coils of
slender rope,
In sight around me the quick veering and darting of fifty skiffs,
my companions.

O boating on the rivers!
The voyage down the Niagara, (the St. Lawrence,) — the superb scenery
— the steamers,
The ships sailing — the Thousand Islands — the occasional timber-raft,
and the raftsmen with long-reaching sweep-oars,
The little huts on the rafts, and the stream of smoke when they cook
supper at evening.

O something pernicious and dread!
Something far away from a puny and pious life!
Something unproved! Something in a trance!
Something escaped from the anchorage, and driving free.

O to work in mines, or forging iron!
Foundry casting — the foundry itself — the rude high roof — the ample
and shadowed space,
The furnace — the hot liquid poured out and running.

O the joys of the soldier!
To feel the presence of a brave general! to feel his sympathy!
To behold his calmness! to be warmed in the rays of his smile!
To go to battle! to hear the bugles play, and the drums beat!
To hear the artillery! to see the glittering of the bayonets and
musket-barrels in the sun!
To see men fall and die and not complain!
To taste the savage taste of blood! to be so devilish!
To gloat so over the wounds and deaths of the enemy.

O the whaleman's joys! O I cruise my old cruise again!
I feel the ship's motion under me — I feel the Atlantic breezes
fanning me,
I hear the cry again sent down from the mast-head, *There she blows*,
Again I spring up the rigging, to look with the rest — We see —
we descend, wild with excitement,
I leap in the lowered boat — We row toward our prey, where he lies,

We approach, stealthy and silent — I see the mountainous mass,
    lethargic, basking,
I see the harpooner standing up — I see the weapon dart from his
    vigorous arm;
O swift, again, now, far out in the ocean, the wounded whale,
    settling, running to windward, tows me,
Again I see him rise to breathe — We row close again,
I see a lance driven through his side, pressed deep, turned in the
    wound,
Again we back off — I see him settle again — the life is leaving him fast,
As he rises, he spouts blood — I see him swim in circles narrower
    and narrower, swiftly cutting the water — I see him die,
He gives one convulsive leap in the centre of the circle, and then
    falls flat and still in the bloody foam.

O the old manhood of me, my joy!
My children and grand-children — my white hair and beard,
My largeness, calmness, majesty, out of the long stretch of my life.

O the ripened joy of womanhood!
O perfect happiness at last!
I am more than eighty years of age — my hair, too, is pure white —
    I am the most venerable mother;
How clear is my mind! how all people draw nigh to me!
What attractions are these, beyond any before? what bloom, more
    than the bloom of youth?
What beauty is this that descends upon me, and rises out of me?

O the joy of my Soul leaning poised on itself — receiving identity
    through materials, and loving them — observing characters,
    and absorbing them;
O my Soul, vibrated back to me, from them — from facts, sight,
    hearing, touch, my phrenology, reason, articulation, comparison,
    memory, and the like;

O the real life of my senses and flesh, transcending my senses and flesh;
O my body, done with materials—my sight, done with my material eyes;
O what is proved to me this day, beyond cavil, that it is not my material
    eyes which finally see,
Nor my material body which finally loves, walks, laughs, shouts,
    embraces, procreates.

O the farmer's joys!
Ohioan's, Illinoisian's, Wisconsinese', Kanadian's, Iowan's, Kansian's,
    Missourian's, Oregonese' joys,
To rise at peep of day, and pass forth nimbly to work,
To plough land in the fall for winter-sown crops,
To plough land in the spring for maize,
To train orchards—to graft the trees—to gather apples in the fall.

O the pleasure with trees!
The orchard—the forest—the oak, cedar, pine, pekan-tree,
The honey-locust, black-walnut, cottonwood, and magnolia.

O Death!
O the beautiful touch of Death, soothing and benumbing a few
    moments, for reasons;
O that of myself, discharging my excrementitious body, to be burned,
    or rendered to powder, or buried,
My real body doubtless left to me for other spheres,
My voided body, nothing more to me, returning to the purifications,
    further offices, eternal uses of the earth.

O to bathe in the swimming-bath, or in a good place along shore!
To splash the water! to walk ankle-deep; to race naked along the shore.
O to realize space!
The plenteousness of all—that there are no bounds;
To emerge, and be of the sky—of the sun and moon, and the flying
    clouds, as one with them.

O, while I live, to be the ruler of life — not a slave,
To meet life as a powerful conqueror,
No fumes — no ennui — no more complaints or scornful criticisms.

O me repellent and ugly!
O to these proud laws of the air, the water, and the ground, proving
    my interior Soul impregnable,
And nothing exterior shall ever take command of me.

O to attract by more than attraction!
How it is I know not — yet behold! the something which obeys
    none of the rest,
It is offensive, never defensive — yet how magnetic it draws.

O the joy of suffering!
To struggle against great odds! to meet enemies undaunted!
To be entirely alone with them! to find how much I can stand!
To look strife, torture, prison, popular odium, death, face to face!
To mount the scaffold! to advance to the muzzles of guns with
    perfect nonchalance!
To be indeed a God!
O the gleesome saunter over fields and hill-sides!
The leaves and flowers of the commonest weeds — the moist fresh
    stillness of the woods,
The exquisite smell of the earth at day-break, and all through the
    forenoon.

O love-branches! love-root! love-apples!
O chaste and electric torrents! O mad-sweet drops.

O the orator's joys!
To inflate the chest — to roll the thunder of the voice out from the
    ribs and throat,
To make the people rage, weep, hate, desire, with yourself,
To lead America — to quell America with a great tongue.

O the joy of a manly self-hood!
Personality — to be servile to none — to defer to none — not to any
 tyrant, known or unknown,
To walk with erect carriage, a step springy and elastic,
To look with calm gaze, or with a flashing eye,
To speak with a full and sonorous voice, out of a broad chest,
To confront with your personality all the other personalities of the earth.

O to have my life henceforth my poem of joys!
To dance, clap hands, exult, shout, skip, leap, roll on, float on,
An athlete — full of rich words — full of joys.

A Word Out of the Sea

OUT of the rocked cradle,
Out of the mocking-bird's throat, the musical shuttle,
Out of the boy's mother's womb, and from the nipples of her breasts,
Out of the Ninth Month midnight,
Over the sterile sands, and the fields beyond, where the child,
     leaving his bed, wandered alone, bareheaded, barefoot,
Down from the showered halo,
Up from the mystic play of shadows, twining and twisting as if
     they were alive,
Out from the patches of briers and blackberries,
From the memories of the bird that chanted to me,
From your memories, sad brother—from the fitful risings and
     fallings I heard,
From under that yellow half-moon, late-risen, and swollen as if
     with tears,
From those beginning notes of sickness and love, there in the
     transparent mist,
From the thousand responses of my heart, never to cease,
From the myriad thence-aroused words,
From the word stronger and more delicious than any,
From such, as now they start, the scene revisiting,
As a flock, twittering, rising, or overhead passing,
Borne hither—ere all eludes me, hurriedly,
A man—yet by these tears a little boy again,
Throwing myself on the sand, confronting the waves,
I, chanter of pains and joys, uniter of here and hereafter,
Taking all hints to use them—but swiftly leaping beyond them,
A reminiscence sing.

•

Reminiscence

ONCE, Paumanok,
When the snows had melted, and the Fifth Month grass was growing,
Up this sea-shore, in some briers,
Two guests from Alabama—two together,
And their nest, and four light-green eggs, spotted with brown,
And every day the he-bird, to and fro, near at hand,
And every day the she-bird, crouched on her nest, silent, with
    bright eyes,
And every day I, a curious boy, never too close, never disturbing them,
Cautiously peering, absorbing, translating.

Shine! Shine!
Pour down your warmth, great Sun!
While we bask—we two together.
Two together!
Winds blow South, or winds blow North,
Day come white, or night come black,
Home, or rivers and mountains from home,
Singing all time, minding no time,
If we two but keep together.

Till of a sudden,
May-be killed, unknown to her mate,
One forenoon the she-bird crouched not on the nest,
Nor returned that afternoon, nor the next,
Nor ever appeared again.

And thenceforward, all summer, in the sound of the sea,
And at night, under the full of the moon, in calmer weather,
Over the hoarse surging of the sea,

Or flitting from brier to brier by day,
I saw, I heard at intervals, the remaining one, the he-bird,
The solitary guest from Alabama.

Blow! Blow!
Blow up sea-winds along Paumanok's shore;
I wait and I wait, till you blow my mate to me.

Yes, when the stars glistened,
All night long, on the prong of a moss-scallop'd stake,
Down, almost amid the slapping waves,
Sat the lone singer, wonderful, causing tears.

He called on his mate,
He poured forth the meanings which I, of all men, know.
Yes, my brother, I know,
The rest might not — but I have treasured every note,
For once, and more than once, dimly, down to the beach gliding,
Silent, avoiding the moonbeams, blending myself with the shadows,
Recalling now the obscure shapes, the echoes, the sounds and
   sights after their sorts,
The white arms out in the breakers tirelessly tossing,
I, with bare feet, a child, the wind wafting my hair,
Listened long and long.

Listened, to keep, to sing — now translating the notes,
Following you, my brother.

Soothe! Soothe!
Close on its wave soothes the wave behind,
And again another behind, embracing and lapping, every one close,
But my love soothes not me.

Low hangs the moon — it rose late,
O it is lagging — O I think it is heavy with love.

O madly the sea pushes upon the land,
With love — with love.

O night!
O do I not see my love fluttering out there among the breakers?
What is that little black thing I see there in the white?
Loud! Loud!
Loud I call to you my love!
High and clear I shoot my voice over the waves,
Surely you must know who is here,
You must know who I am, my love.

Low-hanging moon!
What is that dusky spot in your brown yellow?
O it is the shape of my mate!
O moon, do not keep her from me any longer.

Land! O land!
Whichever way I turn, O I think you could give me my mate back again,
*   if you would,*
For I am almost sure I see her dimly whichever way I look.

O rising stars!
Perhaps the one I want so much will rise with some of you.

O throat!
Sound clearer through the atmosphere!
Pierce the woods, the earth,
Somewhere listening to catch you must be the one I want.

Shake out, carols!
Solitary here—the night's carols!
Carols of lonesome love! Death's carols!
Carols under that lagging, yellow, waning moon!
O, under that moon, where she droops almost down into the sea!

from *Leaves of Grass* (1860–61)   **85**

O reckless, despairing carols.
But soft!
Sink low—soft!
Soft! Let me just murmur,
And do you wait a moment, you husky-noised sea,
For somewhere I believe I heard my mate responding to me,
So faint—I must be still to listen,
But not altogether still, for then she might not come immediately
   to me.

Hither, my love!
Here I am! Here!
With this just-sustained note I announce myself to you,
This gentle call is for you, my love.

Do not be decoyed elsewhere!
That is the whistle of the wind—it is not my voice,
That is the fluttering of the spray,
Those are the shadows of leaves.

O darkness! O in vain!
O I am very sick and sorrowful.

O brown halo in the sky, near the moon, drooping upon the sea!
O troubled reflection in the sea!
O throat! O throbbing heart!
O all—and I singing uselessly all the night.

Murmur! Murmur on!
O murmurs—you yourselves make me continue to sing, I know not why.
O past! O joy!
In the air—in the woods—over fields,
Loved! Loved! Loved! Loved! Loved!
Loved—but no more with me,
We two together no more.

The aria sinking,
All else continuing—the stars shining,
The winds blowing—the notes of the wondrous bird echoing,
With angry moans the fierce old mother yet, as ever, incessantly
    moaning,
On the sands of Paumanok's shore gray and rustling,
The yellow half-moon, enlarged, sagging down, drooping, the face
    of the sea almost touching,
The boy extatic—with his bare feet the waves, with his hair the
    atmosphere dallying,
The love in the heart pent, now loose, now at last tumultuously bursting,
The aria's meaning, the ears, the Soul, swiftly depositing,
The strange tears down the cheeks coursing,
The colloquy there—the trio—each uttering,
The undertone—the savage old mother, incessantly crying,
To the boy's Soul's questions sullenly timing—some drowned secret
    hissing,
To the outsetting bard of love.

Bird! (then said the boy's Soul,)
Is it indeed toward your mate you sing? or is it mostly to me?
For I that was a child, my tongue's use sleeping,
Now that I have heard you,
Now in a moment I know what I am for—I awake,
And already a thousand singers—a thousand songs, clearer, louder,
    more sorrowful than yours,
A thousand warbling echoes have started to life within me,
Never to die.

O throes!
O you demon, singing by yourself—projecting me,
O solitary me, listening—never more shall I cease imitating,
    perpetuating you,
Never more shall I escape,
Never more shall the reverberations,

Never more the cries of unsatisfied love be absent from me,
Never again leave me to be the peaceful child I was before what
    there, in the night,
By the sea, under the yellow and sagging moon,
The dusky demon aroused—the fire, the sweet hell within,
The unknown want, the destiny of me.

O give me some clew!
O if I am to have so much, let me have more!
O a word! O what is my destination?
O I fear it is henceforth chaos!
O how joys, dreads, convolutions, human shapes, and all shapes,
    spring as from graves around me!
O phantoms! you cover all the land, and all the sea!
O I cannot see in the dimness whether you smile or frown upon me;
O vapor, a look, a word! O well-beloved!
O you dear women's and men's phantoms!
A word then, (for I will conquer it,)
The word final, superior to all,
Subtle, sent up—what is it?—I listen;
Are you whispering it, and have been all the time, you sea-waves?
Is that it from your liquid rims and wet sands?

Answering, the sea,
Delaying not, hurrying not,
Whispered me through the night, and very plainly before daybreak,
Lisped to me constantly the low and delicious word DEATH,
And again Death—ever Death, Death, Death,
Hissing melodious, neither like the bird, nor like my aroused
    child's heart,
But edging near, as privately for me, rustling at my feet,
And creeping thence steadily up to my ears,
Death, Death, Death, Death, Death.

Which I do not forget,
But fuse the song of two together,
That was sung to me in the moonlight on Paumanok's gray beach,
With the thousand responsive songs, at random,
My own songs, awaked from that hour,
And with them the key, the word up from the waves,
The word of the sweetest song, and all songs,
That strong and delicious word which, creeping to my feet,
The sea whispered me.

from Enfans d'Adam

7.

YOU and I—what the earth is, we are,
We two—how long we were fooled!
Now delicious, transmuted, swiftly we escape, as Nature escapes,
We are Nature—long have we been absent, but now we return,
We become plants, leaves, foliage, roots, bark,
We are bedded in the ground—we are rocks,
We are oaks—we grow in the openings side by side,
We browse—we are two among the wild herds, spontaneous as any,
We are two fishes swimming in the sea together,
We are what the locust blossoms are—we drop scent around the
     lanes, mornings and evenings,
We are also the coarse smut of beasts, vegetables, minerals,
We are what the flowing wet of the Tennessee is—we are two peaks
     of the Blue Mountains, rising up in Virginia,
We are two predatory hawks—we soar above and look down,
We are two resplendent suns—we it is who balance ourselves orbic
     and stellar—we are as two comets;
We prowl fanged and four-footed in the woods—we spring on prey;
We are two clouds, forenoons and afternoons, driving overhead,
We are seas mingling—we are two of those cheerful waves, rolling
     over each other, and interwetting each other,
We are what the atmosphere is, transparent, receptive, pervious,
     impervious,
We are snow, rain, cold, darkness—we are each product and
     influence of the globe,
We have circled and circled till we have arrived home again—
     we two have,
We have voided all but freedom, and all but our own joy.

10.

INQUIRING, tireless, seeking that yet unfound,
I, a child, very old, over waves, toward the house of maternity, the
    land of migrations, look afar,
Look off the shores of my Western Sea—having arrived at last where
    I am—the circle almost circled;
For coming westward from Hindustan, from the vales of Kashmere,
From Asia—from the north—from the God, the sage, and the hero,
From the south—from the flowery peninsulas, and the spice islands,
Now I face the old home again—looking over to it, joyous, as after
    long travel, growth, and sleep;
But where is what I started for, so long ago?
And why is it yet unfound?

from Calamus

3.

WHOEVER you are holding me now in hand,
Without one thing all will be useless,
I give you fair warning, before you attempt me further,
I am not what you supposed, but far different.

Who is he that would become my follower?
Who would sign himself a candidate for my affections? Are you he?

The way is suspicious — the result slow, uncertain, may-be
    destructive;
You would have to give up all else — I alone would expect to be your
    God, sole and exclusive,
Your novitiate would even then be long and exhausting,
The whole past theory of your life, and all conformity to the lives
    around you, would have to be abandoned;
Therefore release me now, before troubling yourself any further —
    Let go your hand from my shoulders,
Put me down, and depart on your way.

Or else, only by stealth, in some wood, for trial,
Or back of a rock, in the open air,
(For in any roofed room of a house I emerge not — nor in company,
And in libraries I lie as one dumb, a gawk, or unborn, or dead,)
But just possibly with you on a high hill — first watching lest any
    person, for miles around, approach unawares,
Or possibly with you sailing at sea, or on the beach of the sea,
    or some quiet island,
Here to put your lips upon mine I permit you,
With the comrade's long-dwelling kiss, or the new husband's kiss,
For I am the new husband, and I am the comrade.

Or, if you will, thrusting me beneath your clothing,
Where I may feel the throbs of your heart, or rest upon your hip,
Carry me when you go forth over land or sea;
For thus, merely touching you, is enough—is best,
And thus, touching you, would I silently sleep and be carried eternally.

But these leaves conning, you con at peril,
For these leaves, and me, you will not understand,
They will elude you at first, and still more afterward—I will certainly
    elude you,
Even while you should think you had unquestionably caught me,
    behold!
Already you see I have escaped from you.

For it is not for what I have put into it that I have written this book,
Nor is it by reading it you will acquire it,
Nor do those know me best who admire me, and vauntingly praise me,
Nor will the candidates for my love, (unless at most a very few,) prove
    victorious,
Nor will my poems do good only—they will do just as much evil,
    perhaps more,
For all is useless without that which you may guess at many times
    and not hit—that which I hinted at,
Therefore release me, and depart on your way.

4.

THESE I, singing in spring, collect for lovers,
(For who but I should understand lovers, and all their sorrow and joy?
And who but I should be the poet of comrades?)
Collecting, I traverse the garden, the world—but soon I pass the gates,
Now along the pond-side—now wading in a little, fearing not the wet,
Now by the post-and-rail fences, where the old stones thrown there,
    picked from the fields, have accumulated,

Wild-flowers and vines and weeds come up through the stones,
and partly cover them — Beyond these I pass,
Far, far in the forest, before I think where I get,
Solitary, smelling the earthy smell, stopping now and then in
the silence,
Alone I had thought — yet soon a silent troop gathers around me,
Some walk by my side, and some behind, and some embrace my
arms or neck,
They, the spirits of friends, dead or alive — thicker they come,
a great crowd, and I in the middle,
Collecting, dispensing, singing in spring, there I wander with them,
Plucking something for tokens — something for these, till I hit upon
a name — tossing toward whoever is near me,
Here! lilac, with a branch of pine,
Here, out of my pocket, some moss which I pulled off a live-oak
in Florida, as it hung trailing down,
Here, some pinks and laurel leaves, and a handful of sage,
And here what I now draw from the water, wading in the pond-side,
(O here I last saw him that tenderly loves me — and returns again,
never to separate from me,
And this, O this shall henceforth be the token of comrades — this
calamus-root shall,
Interchange it, youths, with each other! Let none render it back!)
And twigs of maple, and a bunch of wild orange, and chestnut,
And stems of currants, and plum-blows, and the aromatic cedar;
These I, compassed around by a thick cloud of spirits,
Wandering, point to, or touch as I pass, or throw them loosely
from me,
Indicating to each one what he shall have — giving something
to each,
But what I drew from the water by the pond-side, that I reserve,
I will give of it — but only to them that love, as I myself am capable
of loving.

11.

WHEN I heard at the close of the day how my name had been received
  with plaudits in the capitol, still it was not a happy night for me that
  followed;
And else, when I caroused, or when my plans were accomplished, still
  I was not happy;
But the day when I rose at dawn from the bed of perfect health,
  refreshed, singing, inhaling the ripe breath of autumn,
When I saw the full moon in the west grow pale and disappear in the
  morning light,
When I wandered alone over the beach, and, undressing, bathed,
  laughing with the cool waters, and saw the sun rise,
And when I thought how my dear friend, my lover, was on his way
  coming, O then I was happy;
O then each breath tasted sweeter—and all that day my food nourished
  me more—And the beautiful day passed well,
And the next came with equal joy—And with the next, at evening,
  came my friend;
And that night, while all was still, I heard the waters roll slowly
  continually up the shores,
I heard the hissing rustle of the liquid and sands, as directed to me,
  whispering, to congratulate me,
For the one I love most lay sleeping by me under the same cover in
  the cool night,
In the stillness, in the autumn moonbeams, his face was inclined
  toward me,
And his arm lay lightly around my breast—And that night I was happy.

13.

CALAMUS taste,
(For I must change the strain—these are not to be pensive leaves,
but leaves of joy,)
Roots and leaves unlike any but themselves,
Scents brought to men and women from the wild woods, and from
the pond-side,
Breast-sorrel and pinks of love—fingers that wind around tighter
than vines,
Gushes from the throats of birds, hid in the foliage of trees, as the
sun is risen,
Breezes of land and love—Breezes set from living shores out to you
on the living sea—to you, O sailors!
Frost-mellowed berries, and Third Month twigs, offered fresh to
young persons wandering out in the fields when the winter
breaks up,
Love-buds, put before you and within you, whoever you are,
Buds to be unfolded on the old terms,
If you bring the warmth of the sun to them, they will open, and
bring form, color, perfume, to you,
If you become the aliment and the wet, they will become flowers,
fruits, tall branches and trees,
They are comprised in you just as much as in themselves—
perhaps more than in themselves,
They are not comprised in one season or succession, but many
successions,
They have come slowly up out of the earth and me, and are to come
slowly up out of you.

14.

NOT heat flames up and consumes,
Not sea-waves hurry in and out,
Not the air, delicious and dry, the air of the ripe summer, bears lightly
along white down-balls of myriads of seeds, wafted, sailing
gracefully, to drop where they may,
Not these—O none of these, more than the flames of me, consuming,
burning for his love whom I love!
O none, more than I, hurrying in and out;
Does the tide hurry, seeking something, and never give up?
O I the same;
O nor down-balls, nor perfumes, nor the high rain-emitting clouds,
are borne through the open air,
Any more than my Soul is borne through the open air,
Wafted in all directions, O love, for friendship, for you.

19.

MIND you the timid models of the rest, the majority?
Long I minded them, but hence I will not—for I have adopted models
for myself, and now offer them to The Lands.

Behold this swarthy and unrefined face—these gray eyes,
This beard—the white wool, unclipt upon my neck,
My brown hands, and the silent manner of me, without charm;
Yet comes one, a Manhattanese, and ever at parting, kisses me lightly
on the lips with robust love,
And I, in the public room, or on the crossing of the street, or on
the ship's deck, kiss him in return;
We observe that salute of American comrades, land and sea,
We are those two natural and nonchalant persons.

26.

WE two boys together clinging,
One the other never leaving,
Up and down the roads going—North and South excursions making,
Power enjoying—elbows stretching—fingers clutching,
Armed and fearless—eating, drinking, sleeping, loving,
No law less than ourselves owning—sailing, soldiering, thieving,
    threatening,
Misers, menials, priests alarming—air breathing, water drinking,
    on the turf or the sea-beach dancing,
With birds singing—With fishes swimming—With trees branching
    and leafing,
Cities wrenching, ease scorning, statutes mocking, feebleness chasing,
Fulfilling our foray.

31.

WHAT ship, puzzled at sea, cons for the true reckoning?
Or, coming in, to avoid the bars, and follow the channel, a perfect
    pilot needs?
Here, sailor! Here, ship! take aboard the most perfect pilot,
Whom, in a little boat, putting off, and rowing, I, hailing you, offer.

What place is besieged, and vainly tries to raise the siege?
Lo! I send to that place a commander, swift, brave, immortal,
And with him horse and foot—and parks of artillery,
And artillerymen, the deadliest that ever fired gun.

32.

WHAT think you I take my pen in hand to record?
The battle-ship, perfect-model'd, majestic, that I saw pass the offing
    to-day under full sail?
The splendors of the past day? Or the splendor of the night that
    envelops me?
Or the vaunted glory and growth of the great city spread around me?
    —No;
But I record of two simple men I saw to-day, on the pier, in the midst
    of the crowd, parting the parting of dear friends,
The one to remain hung on the other's neck, and passionately
    kissed him,
While the one to depart, tightly prest the one to remain in his arms.

37.

A LEAF for hand in hand!
You natural persons old and young! You on the Eastern Sea, and you
    on the Western!
You on the Mississippi, and on all the branches and bayous of the
    Mississippi!
You friendly boatmen and mechanics! You roughs!
You twain! And all processions moving along the streets!
I wish to infuse myself among you till I see it common for you to walk
    hand in hand.

Longings for Home

O MAGNET-SOUTH! O glistening, perfumed South! My South!
O quick mettle, rich blood, impulse, and love! Good and evil! O all
    dear to me!
O dear to me my birth-things — All moving things, and the trees
    where I was born — the grains, plants, rivers;
Dear to me my own slow sluggish rivers where they flow, distant,
    over flats of silvery sands, or through swamps,
Dear to me the Roanoke, the Savannah, the Altamahaw, the Pedee,
    the Tombigbee, the Santee, the Coosa, and the Sabine;
O pensive, far away wandering, I return with my Soul to haunt their
    banks again,
Again in Florida I float on transparent lakes — I float on the
    Okeechobee — I cross the hummock land, or through pleasant
    openings, or dense forests,
I see the parrots in the woods — I see the papaw tree and the
    blossoming titi;
Again, sailing in my coaster, on deck, I coast off Georgia — I coast
    up the Carolinas,
I see where the live-oak is growing — I see where the yellow-pine,
    the scented bay-tree, the lemon and orange, the cypress, the
    graceful palmetto;
I pass rude sea-headlands and enter Pamlico Sound through an inlet,
    and dart my vision inland,
O the cotton plant! the growing fields of rice, sugar, hemp!
The cactus, guarded with thorns — the laurel-tree, with large white
    flowers,
The range afar — the richness and barrenness — the old woods
    charged with mistletoe and trailing moss,
The piney odor and the gloom — the awful natural stillness, (Here
    in these dense swamps the free-booter carries his gun, and the
    fugitive slave has his concealed hut;)

O the strange fascination of these half-known, half-impassable swamps,
   infested by reptiles, resounding with the bellow of the alligator,
   the sad noises of the night-owl and the wild-cat, and the whirr of
   the rattlesnake;
The mocking-bird, the American mimic, singing all the forenoon —
   singing through the moon-lit night,
The humming-bird, the wild-turkey, the raccoon, the opossum;
A Tennessee corn-field — the tall, graceful, long-leaved corn — slender,
   flapping, bright green, with tassels — with beautiful ears, each
   well-sheathed in its husk,
An Arkansas prairie — a sleeping lake, or still bayou;
O my heart! O tender and fierce pangs — I can stand them not —
   I will depart;
O to be a Virginian, where I grew up! O to be a Carolinian!
O longings irrepressible! O I will go back to old Tennessee, and
   never wander more!

from Messenger Leaves

To Old Age

I SEE in you the estuary that enlarges and spreads itself grandly
    as it pours in the great sea.

Mannahatta

I WAS asking for something specific and perfect for my city, and
    behold! here is the aboriginal name!
Now I see what there is in a name, a word, liquid, sane, unruly,
    musical, self-sufficient,
I see that the word of my city, is that word up there,
Because I see that word nested in nests of water-bays, superb,
    with tall and wonderful spires,
Rich, hemmed thick all around with sailships and steamships—
    an island sixteen miles long, solid-founded,
Numberless crowded streets—high growths of iron, slender, strong,
    light, splendidly uprising toward clear skies;
Tides swift and ample, well-loved by me, toward sun-down,
The flowing sea-currents, the little islands, the larger adjoining
    islands, the heights, the villas,
The countless masts, the white shore-steamers, the lighters, the
    ferry-boats, the black sea-steamers, well-model'd;
The down-town streets, the jobbers' houses of business—the
    houses of business of the ship-merchants, and money-brokers—
    the river-streets,
Immigrants arriving, fifteen or twenty thousand in a week,
The carts hauling goods—the manly race of drivers of horses—
    the brown-faced sailors,
The summer-air, the bright sun shining, and the sailing clouds aloft,
The winter snows, the sleigh-bells—the broken ice in the river,
    passing along, up or down, with the flood-tide or ebb-tide;

The mechanics of the city, the masters, well-formed, beautiful-faced,
   looking you straight in the eyes;
Trottoirs thronged — vehicles — Broadway — the women — the shops
   and shows,
The parades, processions, bugles playing, flags flying, drums beating;
A million people — manners free and superb — open voices —
   hospitality — the most courageous and friendly young men;
The free city! no slaves! no owners of slaves!
The beautiful city! the city of hurried and sparkling waters! the city
   of spires and masts!
The city nested in bays! my city!
The city of such women, I am mad to be with them! I will return
   after death to be with them!
The city of such young men, I swear I cannot live happy, without
   I often go talk, walk, eat, drink, sleep, with them!

from *Drum-Taps* (1865) and *Sequel to Drum-Taps: When Lilacs Last in the Door-yard Bloom'd and Other Poems* (1865–66)

But I am perhaps mainly satisfied with *Drum-Taps* because it delivers my ambition of the task that has haunted me, namely, to express in a poem (& in the way I like, which is not at all by directly stating it) the pending action of this *Time & Land we swim in*, with all their large conflicting fluctuations of despair & hope, the shiftings, masses, & the whirl & deafening din, (yet over all, as by invisible hand, a definite purport & idea) — with the unprecedented anguish of wounded & suffering, the beautiful young men, in wholesale death & agony, everything sometimes as if in blood color, & dripping blood.

—a letter to William D. O'Connor (January 6, 1865)

Rise O Days from Your Fathomless Deeps

1

RISE, O days, from your fathomless deeps, till you loftier and fiercer
sweep!
Long for my soul, hungering gymnastic, I devour'd what the earth
gave me;
Long I roam'd the woods of the north—long I watch'd Niagara pouring;
I travel'd the prairies over, and slept on their breast—I cross'd the
Nevadas, I cross'd the plateaus;
I ascended the towering rocks along the Pacific, I sail'd out to sea;
I sail'd through the storm, I was refresh'd by the storm;
I watch'd with joy the threatening maws of the waves;
I mark'd the white combs where they career'd so high, curling over;
I heard the wind piping, I saw the black clouds;
Saw from below what arose and mounted, (O superb! O wild as
my heart, and powerful!)
Heard the continuous thunder, as it bellow'd after the lightning;
Noted the slender and jagged threads of lightning, as sudden and fast
amid the din they chased each other across the sky;
— These, and such as these, I, elate, saw—saw with wonder, yet
pensive and masterful;
All the menacing might of the globe uprisen around me;
Yet there with my soul I fed—I fed content, supercilious.

2

'Twas well, O soul! 'twas a good preparation you gave me!
Now we advance our latent and ampler hunger to fill;
Now we go forth to receive what the earth and the sea never gave us;
Not through the mighty woods we go, but through the mightier cities;
Something for us is pouring now, more than Niagara pouring;
Torrents of men, (sources and rills of the Northwest, are you indeed
inexhaustible?)
What, to pavements and homesteads here—what were those storms
of the mountains and sea?

What, to passions I witness around me to-day? Was the sea risen?
Was the wind piping the pipe of death under the black clouds?
Lo! from deeps more unfathomable, something more deadly and
    savage;
Manhattan, rising, advancing with menacing front—Cincinnati,
    Chicago, unchain'd;
—What was that swell I saw on the ocean? behold what comes here!
How it climbs with daring feet and hands! how it dashes!
How the true thunder bellows after the lightning! how bright the
    flashes of lightning!
How DEMOCRACY, with desperate vengeful port strides on, shown
    through the dark by those flashes of lightning!
(Yet a mournful wail and low sob I fancied I heard through the dark,
In a lull of the deafening confusion.)

3
Thunder on! stride on Democracy! strike with vengeful stroke!
And do you rise higher than ever yet, O days, O cities!
Crash heavier, heavier yet, O storms! you have done me good;
My soul, prepared in the mountains, absorbs your immortal
    strong nutriment;
Long had I walk'd my cities, my country roads, through farms,
    only half satisfied;
One doubt, nauseous, undulating like a snake, crawl'd on the
    ground before me,
Continually preceding my steps, turning upon me oft, ironically
    hissing low;
—The cities I loved so well, I abandon'd and left—I sped to the
    certainties suitable to me;
Hungering, hungering, hungering, for primal energies, and
    Nature's dauntlessness,
I refresh'd myself with it only, I could relish it only;
I waited the bursting forth of the pent fire—on the water and air
    I waited long;
—But now I no longer wait—I am fully satisfied—I am glutted;

I have witness'd the true lighting—I have witness'd my cities electric;
I have lived to behold man burst forth, and warlike America rise;
Hence I will seek no more the food of the northern solitary wilds,
No more on the mountains roam, or sail the stormy sea.

City of Ships

CITY of ships!
(O the black ships! O the fierce ships!
O the beautiful, sharp bow'd steam-ships and sail-ships!)
City of the world! (for all races are here;
All the lands of the earth make contributions here;)
City of the sea! city of hurried and glittering tides!
City whose gleeful tides continually rush or recede, whirling in and out,
    with eddies and foam!
City of wharves and stores! city of tall façades of marble and iron!
Proud and passionate city! mettlesome, mad, extravagant city!
Spring up, O city! not for peace alone, but be indeed yourself, warlike!
Fear not! submit to no models but your own, O city!
Behold me! incarnate me, as I have incarnated you!
I have rejected nothing you offer'd me—whom you adopted, I have
    adopted;
Good or bad, I never question you—I love all—I do not condemn
    anything;
I chant and celebrate all that is yours—yet peace no more;
In peace I chanted peace, but now the drum of war is mine;
War, red war, is my song through your streets, O city!

The Torch

ON my northwest coast in the midst of the night, a fishermen's group
    stands watching;
Out on the lake, expanding before them, others are spearing salmon;
The canoe, a dim and shadowy thing, moves across the black water,
Bearing a Torch a-blaze at the prow.

The Ship

LO! THE unbounded sea!
On its breast a Ship, spreading all her sails—an ample Ship,
    carrying even her moonsails;
The pennant is flying aloft, as she speeds, she speeds so stately—
    below, emulous waves press forward,
They surround the Ship, with shining curving motions, and foam.

Out of the Rolling Ocean, the Crowd

1

Out of the rolling ocean, the crowd, came a drop gently to me,
Whispering, *I love you, before long I die,*
I have travel'd a long way, merely to look on you, to touch you,
For I could not die till I once look'd on you,
For I fear'd I might afterward lose you.

2

(Now we have met, we have look'd, we are safe;
Return in peace to the ocean my love;
I too am part of that ocean, my love—we are not so much separated;
Behold the great rondure—the cohesion of all, how perfect!
But as for me, for you, the irresistible sea is to separate us,
As for an hour carrying us diverse—yet cannot carry us diverse for ever;
Be not impatient—a little space—know you, I salute the air, the ocean
    and the land,
Every day, at sundown, for your dear sake, my love.)

World, Take Good Notice

WORLD, take good notice, silver stars fading,
Milky hue ript, weft of white detaching,
Coals thirty-six, baleful and burning,
Scarlet, significant, hands off warning,
Now and henceforth flaunt from these shores.

from When Lilacs Last in the Door-Yard Bloom'd

10

O how shall I warble myself for the dead one there I loved?
And how shall I deck my song for the large sweet soul that has gone?
And what shall my perfume be, for the grave of him I love?
Sea-winds, blown from east and west,
Blown from the eastern sea, and blown from the western sea, till
  there on the prairies meeting:
These, and with these, and the breath of my chant,
I perfume the grave of him I love.

16

Come, lovely and soothing Death,
Undulate round the world, serenely arriving, arriving,
In the day, in the night, to all, to each,
Sooner or later, delicate Death.

Prais'd be the fathomless universe,
For life and joy, and for objects and knowledge curious;
And for love, sweet love—But praise! O praise and praise,
For the sure-enwinding arms of cool-enfolding Death.

Dark Mother, always gliding near, with soft feet,
Have none chanted for thee a chant of fullest welcome?
Then I chant it for thee—I glorify thee above all;
I bring thee a song that when thou must indeed come, come
  unfalteringly.

Approach, encompassing Death—strong Deliveress!
When it is so—when thou hast taken them, I joyously sing the dead,
Lost in the loving, floating ocean of thee,
Laved in the flood of thy bliss, O Death.

From me to thee glad serenades,
Dances for thee I propose, saluting thee—adornments and feastings
    for thee;
And the sights of the open landscape, and the high-spread sky,
    are fitting,
And life and the fields, and the huge and thoughtful night.

The night, in silence, under many a star;
The ocean shore, and the husky whispering wave, whose voice I know;
And the soul turning to thee, O vast and well-veil'd Death,
And the body gratefully nestling close to thee.

Over the tree-tops I float thee a song!
Over the rising and sinking waves—over the myriad fields, and
    the prairies wide;
Over the dense-pack'd cities all, and the teeming wharves and ways,
I float this carol with joy, with joy to thee, O Death!

O Captain! My Captain!

1

O CAPTAIN! my captain! our fearful trip is done;
The ship has weather'd every rack, the prize we sought is won;
The port is near, the bells I hear, the people all exulting,
While follow eyes the steady keel, the vessel grim and daring:
       But O heart! heart! heart!
          Leave you not the little spot,
             Where on the deck my captain lies.
             Fallen cold and dead.

2

O captain! my captain! rise up and hear the bells;
Rise up—for you the flag is flung—for you the bugle trills;
For you bouquets and ribbon'd wreaths—for you the shores
   a-crowding;
For you they call, the swaying mass, their eager faces turning;
       O captain! dear father!
          This arm I push beneath you;
             It is some dream that on the deck,
               You've fallen cold and dead.

3

My captain does not answer, his lips are pale and still;
My father does not feel my arm, he has no pulse nor will:
But the ship, the ship is anchor'd safe, its voyage closed and done;
From fearful trip, the victor ship, comes in with object won:
       Exult, O shores, and ring, O bells!
          But I, with silent tread,
             Walk the spot my captain lies,
             Fallen cold and dead.

from *Leaves of Grass* (1867)

But O the ship, the immortal ship! O ship aboard the ship!
O ship of the body—ship of the soul—voyaging, voyaging,
  voyaging.

— "Leaves of Grass," No. 3
(later titled "Aboard at a Ship's Helm")

from Starting from Paumanok

1

STARTING from fish-shape Paumanok, where I was born,
Well-begotten, and rais'd by a perfect mother;
After roaming many lands—lover of populous pavements;
Dweller in Mannahatta, city of ships, my city—or on southern
    savannas;
Or a soldier camp'd, or carrying my knapsack and gun—or a miner
    in California;
Or rude in my home in Dakotah's woods, my diet meat, my drink
    from the spring;
Or withdrawn to muse and meditate in some deep recess,
Far from the clank of crowds, intervals passing, rapt and happy;
Aware of the fresh free giver, the flowing Missouri—aware of
    mighty Niagara;
Aware of the buffalo herds, grazing the plains—the hirsute and
    strong-breasted bull;
Of earths, rocks, Fifth-month flowers, experienced—stars, rain, snow,
    my amaze;
Having studied the mocking-bird's tones, and the mountain hawk's,
And heard at dusk the unrival'd one, the hermit thrush from the
    swamp-cedars,
Solitary, singing in the West, I strike up for a New World.

15

Whoever you are! to you endless announcements.

Daughter of the lands, did you wait for your poet?
Did you wait for one with a flowing mouth and indicative hand?

Toward the male of The States, and toward the female of The States,
Live words—words to the lands.

O the lands! interlink'd, food-yielding lands!
Land of coal and iron! Land of gold! Lands of cotton, sugar, rice!
Land of wheat, beef, pork! Land of wool and hemp!
Land of the apple and grape!
Land of the pastoral plains, the grass-fields of the world! Land of
    those sweet-air'd interminable plateaus!
Land of the herd, the garden, the healthy house of adobie!
Lands where the northwest Columbia winds, and where the
    southwest Colorado winds!
Land of the eastern Chesapeake! Land of the Delaware!
Land of Ontario, Erie, Huron, Michigan!
Land of the Old Thirteen! Massachusetts land! Land of Vermont
    and Connecticut!
Land of the ocean shores! Land of sierras and peaks!
Land of boatmen and sailors! Fishermen's land!
Inextricable lands! the clutch'd together! the passionate ones!
The side by side! the elder and younger brothers! the bony-limb'd!
The great women's land! the feminine! the experienced sisters and
    the inexperienced sisters!
Far breath'd land! Arctic braced! Mexican breez'd! the diverse!
    the compact!
The Pennsylvanian! the Virginian! the double Carolinian!
O all and each well-loved by me! my intrepid nations!
O I at any rate include you all with perfect love!
I cannot be discharged from you! not from one, any sooner than
    another!
O Death! O for all that, I am yet of you, unseen, this hour, with
    irrepressible love,
Walking New England, a friend, a traveler,
Splashing my bare feet in the edge of the summer ripples, on
    Paumanok's sands,
Crossing the prairies—dwelling again in Chicago—dwelling in
    every town,
Observing shows, births, improvements, structures, arts,
Listening to the orators and the oratresses in public halls,

Of and through The States, as during life—each man and woman
my neighbor,
The Louisianian, the Georgian, as near to me, and I as near to him
and her,
The Mississippian and Arkansian yet with me—and I yet with any
of them;
Yet upon the plains west of the spinal river—yet in my house of adobie,
Yet returning eastward—yet in the Sea-Side State, or in Maryland,
Yet Kanadian, cheerily braving the winter—the snow and ice
welcome to me,
Yet a true son either of Maine, or of the Granite State, or of the
Narragansett Bay State, or of the Empire State;
Yet sailing to other shores to annex the same—yet welcoming every
new brother;
Hereby applying these leaves to the new ones, from the hour they
unite with the old ones;
Coming among the new ones myself, to be their companion and equal
—coming personally to you now;
Enjoining you to acts, characters, spectacles, with me.

from Children of Adam

From Pent-Up Aching Rivers

FROM pent-up, aching rivers;
From that of myself, without which I were nothing;
From what I am determin'd to make illustrious, even if I stand
  sole among men;
From my own voice resonant — singing the phallus,
Singing the song of procreation,
Singing the need of superb children, and therein superb grown people,
Singing the muscular urge and the blending,
Singing the bedfellow's song, (O resistless yearning!
O for any and each, the body correlative attracting!
O for you, whoever you are, your correlative body! O it, more than
  all else, you delighting!)
— From the hungry gnaw that eats me night and day;
From native moments — from bashful pains — singing them;
Singing something yet unfound, though I have diligently sought it,
  many a long year;
Singing the true song of the Soul, fitful, at random;
Singing what, to the Soul, entirely redeem'd her, the faithful one,
  even the prostitute, who detain'd me when I went to the city;
Singing the song of prostitutes;
Renascent with grossest Nature, or among animals;
Of that — of them, and what goes with them, my poems informing;
Of the smell of apples and lemons — of the pairing of birds,
Of the wet of woods — of the lapping of waves,
Of the mad pushes of waves upon the land — I them chanting;
The overture lightly sounding — the strain anticipating;
The welcome nearness — the sight of the perfect body;
The swimmer swimming naked in the bath, or motionless on his
  back lying and floating;
The female form approaching — I, pensive, love-flesh tremulous,
  aching;

—The slave's body for sale,—I, sternly, with harsh voice, auctioneering;
The divine list, for myself or you, or for any one, making;
The face—the limbs—the index from head to foot, and what it arouses;
The mystic deliria—the madness amorous—the utter abandonment;
(Hark close, and still, what I now whisper to you,
I love you—O you entirely possess me,
O I wish that you and I escape from the rest, and go utterly off—
    O free and lawless,
Two hawks in the air—two fishes swimming in the sea not more
    lawless than we;)
—The furious storm through me careering—I passionately trembling;
The oath of the inseparableness of two together—of the woman that
    loves me, and whom I love more than my life—that oath swearing;
(O I willingly stake all, for you!
O let me be lost, if it must be so!
O you and I—what is it to us what the rest do or think?
What is all else to us? only that we enjoy each other, and exhaust
    each other, if it must be so;)
—From the master—the pilot I yield the vessel to;
The general commanding me, commanding all—from him permission
    taking;
From time the programme hastening, (I have loiter'd too long, as it is;)
From sex—From the warp and from the woof;
(To talk to the perfect girl who understands me,
To waft to her these from my own lips—to effuse them from my
    own body;)
From privacy—from frequent repinings alone;
From plenty of persons near, and yet the right person not near;
From the soft sliding of hands over me, and thrusting of fingers
    through my hair and beard;
From the long sustain'd kiss upon the mouth or bosom;
From the close pressure that makes me or any man drunk, fainting
    with excess;
From what the divine husband knows—from the work of fatherhood;

From exultation, victory, and relief—from the bedfellow embrace
    in the night;
From the act-poems of eyes, hands, hips, and bosoms,
From the cling of the trembling arm,
From the bending curve and the clinch,
From side by side, the pliant coverlid off-throwing,
From the one so unwilling to have me leave—and me just as
    unwilling to leave,
(Yet a moment, O tender waiter, and I return;)
—From the hour of shining stars and dropping dews,
From the night, a moment, I, emerging, flitting out,
Celebrate you, act divine—and you, children prepared for,
And you, stalwart loins.

Facing West from California's Shores

FACING west, from California's shores,
Inquiring, tireless, seeking what is yet unfound,
I, a child, very old, over waves, towards the house of maternity,
    the land of migrations, look afar,
Look off the shores of my Western Sea—the circle almost circled;
For, starting westward from Hindustan, from the vales of Kashmere,
From Asia—from the north—from the God, the sage, and the hero,
From the south—from the flowery peninsulas, and the spice islands;
Long having wander'd since—round the earth having wander'd,
Now I face home again—very pleas'd and joyous;
(But where is what I started for, so long ago?
And why is it yet unfound?)

from Song of the Open Road

9

Allons! whoever you are, come travel with me!
Traveling with me, you find what never tires.

The earth never tires;
The earth is rude, silent, incomprehensible at first—
Nature is rude and incomprehensible at first;
Be not discouraged—keep on—there are divine things, well envelop'd;
I swear to you there are divine things more beautiful than words can tell.

Allons! We must not stop here!
However sweet these laid-up stores—however convenient this
    dwelling, we cannot remain here;
However shelter'd this port, and however calm these waters, we
    must not anchor here;
However welcome the hospitality that surrounds us, we are permitted
    to receive it but a little while.

10

Allons! The inducements shall be great to you;
We will sail pathless and wild seas;
We will go where winds blow, waves dash, and the Yankee clipper
    speeds by under full sail.
Allons! With power, liberty, the earth, the elements!
Health, defiance, gayety, self-esteem, curiosity;
Allons! from all formules!
From your formules, O bat-eyed and materialistic priests!

The stale cadaver blocks up the passage—the burial waits no longer.

Allons! Yet take warning!
He traveling with me needs the best blood, thews, endurance;
None may come to the trial, till he or she bring courage and health.

Come not here if you have already spent the best of yourself;
Only those may come, who come in sweet and determin'd bodies;
No diseas'd person—no rum-drinker or venereal taint is
    permitted here.

I and mine do not convince by arguments, similes, rhymes;
We convince by our presence.

Respondez!

RESPONDEZ! Respondez!

Let every one answer! let those who sleep be waked! let none evade!

(How much longer must we go on with our affectations and sneaking?

Let me bring this to a close—I pronounce openly for a new distribution
of roles;)

Let that which stood in front go behind! and let that which was behind
advance to the front and speak;

Let murderers, thieves, bigots, fools, unclean persons, offer new
propositions!

Let the old propositions be postponed!

Let faces and theories be turn'd inside out! Let meanings be freely
criminal, as well as results!

Let there be no suggestion above the suggestion of drudgery!

Let none be pointed toward his destination! (Say! do you know your
destination?)

Let trillions of men and women be mock'd with bodies and mock'd
with Souls!

Let the love that waits in them, wait! Let it die, or pass still-born to
other spheres!

Let the sympathy that waits in every man, wait! or let it also pass,
a dwarf, to other spheres!

Let contradictions prevail! Let one thing contradict another! and let
one line of my poems contradict another!

Let the people sprawl with yearning aimless hands!

Let their tongues be broken! Let their eyes be discouraged! Let none
descend into their hearts with the fresh lusciousness of love!

Let the theory of America be management, caste, comparison!
(Say! what other theory would you?)

Let them that distrust birth and death lead the rest!

(Say! why shall they not lead you?)

Let the crust of hell be near'd and trod on! Let the days be darker than
the nights! Let slumber bring less slumber than waking-time brings!

Let the world never appear to him or her for whom it was all made!

Let the heart of the young man exile itself from the heart of the
old man! and let the heart of the old man be exiled from that
of the young man!

Let the sun and moon go! Let scenery take the applause of the
audience! Let there be apathy under the stars!

Let freedom prove no man's inalienable right! Every one who can
tyrannize, let him tyrannize to his satisfaction!

Let none but infidels be countenanced!

Let the eminence of meanness, treachery, sarcasm, hate, greed,
indecency, impotence, lust, be taken for granted above all!
Let writers, judges, governments, households, religions,
philosophies, take such for granted above all!

Let the worst men beget children out of the worst women!

Let the priest still play at immortality!

Let death be inaugurated!

Let nothing remain but the ashes of teachers, artists, moralists,
lawyers, and learn'd and polite persons!

Let him who is without my poems be assassinated!

Let the cow, the horse, the camel, the garden-bee — Let the mud-fish,
the lobster, the mussel, eel, the stingfish — Let these, and the like
of these, be put on a perfect equality with man and woman!

Let churches accommodate serpents, vermin, and the corpses of
those who have died of the most filthy of diseases!

Let marriage slip down among fools, and be for none but fools!

Let men among themselves talk and think obscenely of women! and
let women among themselves talk and think obscenely of men!

Let every man doubt every woman! and let every woman trick
every man!

Let us all, without missing one, be exposed in public, naked, monthly,
at the peril of our lives! Let our bodies be freely handled and
examined by whoever chooses!

Let nothing but copies be permitted to exist upon the earth!

Let the earth desert God, nor let there never henceforth be mention'd
the name of God!

Let there be no God!

Let there be money, business, imports, exports, custom, authority,
   precedents, pallor, dyspepsia, smut, ignorance, unbelief!
Let judges and criminals be transposed! Let the prison-keepers be
   put in prison! Let those that were prisoners take the keys!
   (Say! why might they not just as well be transposed?)
Let the slaves be masters! Let the masters become slaves!
Let the reformers descend from the stands where they are forever
   bawling! Let an idiot or insane person appear on each of the stands!
Let the Asiatic, the African, the European, the American, and the
   Australian, go armed against the murderous stealthiness of
   each other! Let them sleep armed! Let none believe in good will!
Let there be no unfashionable wisdom! Let such be scorn'd and derided
   off from the earth!
Let a floating cloud in the sky—Let a wave of the sea—Let growing
   mint, spinach, onions, tomatoes—Let these be exhibited as shows
   at a great price for admission!
Let all the men of These States stand aside for a few smouchers! Let the
   few seize on what they choose! Let the rest gawk, giggle, starve, obey!
Let shadows be furnish'd with genitals! Let substances be deprived
   of their genitals!
Let there be wealthy and immense cities—but through any of them,
   not a single poet, savior, knower, lover!
Let the infidels of These States laugh all faith away!
If one man be found who has faith, let the rest set upon him! Let them
   affright faith! Let them destroy the power of breeding faith!
Let the she-harlots and the he-harlots be prudent!
Let them dance on, while seeming lasts! (O seeming! seeming! seeming!)
Let the preachers recite creeds! Let them teach only what they have
   been taught!
Let insanity have charge of sanity!
Let books take the place of trees, animals, rivers, clouds!
Let the daub'd portraits of heroes supersede heroes!
Let the manhood of man never take steps after itself!
Let it take steps after eunuchs, and after consumptive and genteel
   persons!

Let the white person tread the black person under his heel!
  (Say! which is trodden under heel, after all?)
Let the reflections of the things of the world be studied in mirrors!
  Let the things themselves continue unstudied!
Let a man seek pleasure everywhere except in himself! Let a woman
  seek happiness everywhere except in herself! (What real happiness
  have you had one single time through your whole life?)
Let the limited years of life do nothing for the limitless years of death!
  (What do you suppose death will do, then?)

As If a Phantom Caress'd Me

As if a phantom caress'd me,
I thought I was not alone, walking here by the shore;
But the one I thought was with me, as now I walk by the shore,
  the one I loved that caress'd me,
As I lean and look through the glimmering light — that one has
  utterly disappear'd,
And those appear that are hateful to me, and mock me.

from Songs Before Parting

from As I Sat Alone by Blue Ontario's Shores

6

Land of lands, and bards to corroborate!
Of them, standing among them, one lifts to the light his west-bred face,
To him the hereditary countenance bequeath'd, both mother's and
    father's,
His first parts substances, earth, water, animals, trees,
Built of the common stock, having room for far and near.
Used to dispense with other lands, incarnating this land,
Attracting it Body and Soul to himself, hanging on its neck with
    incomparable love,
Plunging his semitic muscle into its merits and demerits,
Making its cities, beginnings, events, diversities, wars, vocal in him,
Making its rivers, lakes, bays, embouchure in him,
Mississippi with yearly freshets and changing chutes —
Columbia, Niagara, Hudson, spending themselves lovingly in him,
If the Atlantic coast stretch, or the Pacific coast stretch, he stretching
    with them north or south,
Spanning between them east and west, and touching whatever is
    between them,
Growths growing from him to offset the growth of pine, cedar, hemlock,
    live-oak, locust, chestnut, hickory, cotton-wood, orange, magnolia,
Tangles as tangled in him as any cane-brake or swamp,
He likening sides and peaks of mountains, forests coated with northern
    transparent ice,
Off him pasturage sweet and natural as savanna, upland, prairie,
Through him flights, whirls, screams, answering those of the fish-hawk,
    mocking-bird, night-heron, and eagle;
His spirit surrounding his country's spirit, unclosed to good and evil,
Surrounding the essences of real things, old times and present times,
Surrounding just found shores, islands, tribes of red aborigines,
Weather-beaten vessels, landings, settlements, embryo stature
    and muscle,

The haughty defiance of the Year 1 — war, peace, the formation of
the Constitution,
The separate States, the simple, elastic scheme, the immigrants,
The Union, always swarming with blatherers, and always sure
and impregnable,
The unsurvey'd interior, log-houses, clearings, wild animals,
hunters, trappers;
Surrounding the multiform agriculture, mines, temperature,
the gestation of new States,
Congress convening every Twelfth-month, the members duly
coming up from the uttermost parts;
Surrounding the noble character of mechanics and farmers,
especially the young men,
Responding their manners, speech, dress, friendships — the gait
they have of persons who never knew how it felt to stand in the
presence of superiors,
The freshness and candor of their physiognomy, the copiousness
and decision of their phrenology,
The picturesque looseness of their carriage, their fierceness when
wrong'd,
The fluency of their speech, their delight in music, their curiosity,
good temper, and open-handedness — the whole composite make,
The prevailing ardor and enterprise, the large amativeness,
The perfect equality of the female with the male, the fluid movement
of the population,
The superior marine, free commerce, fisheries, whaling, gold-digging,
Wharf-hemm'd cities, railroad and steamboat lines, intersecting
all points,
Factories, mercantile life, labor-saving machinery, the north-east,
north-west, south-west,
Manhattan firemen, the Yankee swap, southern plantation life,
Slavery — the murderous, treacherous conspiracy to raise it upon
the ruins of all the rest;
On and on to the grapple with it — Assassin! then your life or ours
be the stake — and respite no more.

Song at Sunset

SPLENDOR of ended day, floating and filling me!
Hour prophetic—hour resuming the past!
Inflating my throat—you, divine average!
You, Earth and Life, till the last ray gleams, I sing.

Open mouth of my Soul, uttering gladness,
Eyes of my Soul, seeing perfection,
Natural life of me, faithfully praising things;
Corroborating forever the triumph of things.

Illustrious every one!
Illustrious what we name space—sphere of unnumber spirits;
Illustrious the mystery of motion, in all beings, even the tiniest insect;
Illustrious the attribute of speech—the senses—the body;
Illustrious the passing light! Illustrious the pale reflection on the
    new moon in the western sky!
Illustrious whatever I see, or hear, or touch, to the last.

Good in all,
In the satisfaction and aplomb of animals,
In the annual return of the seasons,
In the hilarity of youth,
In the strength and flush of manhood,
In the grandeur and exquisiteness of old age,
In the superb vistas of Death.

Wonderful to depart;
Wonderful to be here!
The heart, to jet the all-alike and innocent blood,
To breathe the air, how delicious!
To speak! to walk! to seize something by the hand!
To prepare for sleep, for bed—to look on my rose-color'd flesh,
To be conscious of my body, so happy, so large,

To be this incredible God I am,
To have gone forth among other Gods — those men and women
    I love.

Wonderful how I celebrate you and myself!
How my thoughts play subtly at the spectacles around!
How the clouds pass silently overhead!
How the earth darts on and on! and how the sun, moon, stars,
    dart on and on!
How the water sports and sings! (Surely it is alive!)
How the trees rise and stand up — with strong trunks — with
    branches and leaves!
(Surely there is something more in each of the trees — some
    living Soul.)

O amazement of things! even the least particle!
O spirituality of things!
O strain musical, flowing through ages and continents — now
    reaching me and America!
I take your strong chords — I intersperse them, and cheerfully
    pass them forward.

I too carol the sun, usher'd, or at noon, or, as now, setting,
I too throb to the brain and beauty of the earth, and of all the
    growths of the earth,
I too have felt the resistless call of myself.

As I sail'd down the Mississippi,
As I wander'd over the prairies,
As I have lived — As I have look'd through my windows, my eyes,
As I went forth in the morning — As I beheld the light breaking
    in the east;
As I bathed on the beach of the Eastern Sea, and again on the
    beach of the Western Sea;

As I roam'd the streets of inland Chicago—whatever streets I
    have roam'd;
Wherever I have been, I have charged myself with contentment
    and triumph.

I sing the Equalities;
I sing the endless finalés of things;
I say Nature continues—Glory continues;
I praise with electric voice;
For I do not see one imperfection in the universe;
And I do not see one cause or result lamentable at last in the universe.

O setting sun! though the time has come,
I still warble under you, unmitigated adoration.

from *Leaves of Grass* (1871–72), *Passage to India* (1871), and *As a Strong Bird on Pinions Free* (1872)

PASSAGE TO INDIA.—As in some ancient legend-play, to close the plot and the hero's career, there is a farewell gathering on ship's deck and on shore, a loosing of hawsers and ties, a spreading of sails to the wind—a starting out on unknown seas, to fetch up no one knows whither—to return no more—and the curtain falls, and there is the end of it.

— footnote in the preface to the two-volume
Centennial Edition of *Leaves of Grass* (1876)

A new race, a young and lusty generation, already sweeps in with oceanic currents, obliterating the war, and all its scars, its mounded graves, and all its reminiscences of hatred, conflict, death. So let it be obliterated.

— preface to *As a Strong Bird on Pinions Free* (1872)

from Inscriptions

In Cabin'd Ships at Sea

1

IN cabin'd ships, at sea,
The boundless blue on every side expanding,
With whistling winds and music of the waves — the large imperious
    waves — In such,
Or some lone bark, buoy'd on the dense marine,
Where, joyous, full of faith, spreading white sails,
She cleaves the ether, mid the sparkle and the foam of day, or under
    many a star at night,
By sailors young and old, haply will I, a reminiscence of the land,
    be read,
In full rapport at last.

2

Here are our thoughts — voyagers' thoughts,
Here not the land, firm land, alone appears, may then by them be said;
The sky o'erarches here — we feel the undulating deck beneath our feet,
We feel the long pulsation — ebb and flow of endless motion;
The tones of unseen mystery — the vague and vast suggestions of the
    briny world — the liquid-flowing syllables,
The perfume, the faint creaking of the cordage, the melancholy rhythm,
The boundless vista, and the horizon far and dim, are all here,
And this is Ocean's poem.

3

Then falter not, O book! fulfil your destiny!

You, not a reminiscence of the land alone,

You too, as a lone bark, cleaving the ether—purpos'd I know not
    whither—yet ever full of faith,

Consort to every ship that sails—sail you!

Bear forth to them, folded, my love—(Dear mariners! for you I
    fold it here, in every leaf;)

Speed on, my Book! spread your white sails, my little bark, athwart
    the imperious waves!

Chant on—sail on—bear o'er the boundless blue, from me, to
    every shore,

This song for mariners and all their ships.

from Songs of Insurrection

France, the 18th Year of These States

1

A GREAT year and place;
A harsh, discordant, natal scream out-sounding, to touch the
    mother's heart closer than any yet.

I walk'd the shores of my Eastern Sea,
Heard over the waves the little voice,
Saw the divine infant, where she woke, mournfully wailing, amid
    the roar of cannon, curses, shouts, crash of falling buildings;
Was not so sick from the blood in the gutters running—nor from
    the single corpses, nor those in heaps, nor those borne away
    in the tumbrils;
Was not so desperate at the battues of death—was not so shock'd
    at the repeated fusillades of the guns.

2

Pale, silent, stern, what could I say to that long-accrued retribution?
Could I wish humanity different?
Could I wish the people made of wood and stone?
Or that there be no justice in destiny or time?

3

O Liberty! O mate for me!
Here too the blaze, the grape-shot and the axe, in reserve, to fetch
    them out in case of need;
Here too, though long represt, can never be destroy'd;
Here too could rise at last, murdering and extatic;
Here too demanding full arrears of vengeance.

4

Hence I sign this salute over the sea,

And I do not deny that terrible red birth and baptism,

But remember the little voice that I heard wailing — and wait with
    perfect trust, no matter how long;

And from to-day, sad and cogent, I maintain the bequeath'd cause,
    as for all lands,

And I send these words to Paris with my love,

And I guess some chansonniers there will understand them,

For I guess there is latent music yet in France — floods of it;

O I hear already the bustle of instruments — they will soon be
    drowning all that would interrupt them;

O I think the east wind brings a triumphal and free march,

It reaches hither — it swells me to joyful madness,

I will run transpose it in words, to justify it,

I will yet sing a song for you, MA FEMME.

from *Passage to India*

Gliding o'er all, through all,
Through Nature, Time, and Space,
As a Ship on the waters advancing,
The Voyage of the Soul—not Life alone,
Death, —many Deaths I'll sing.

Passage to India

1

SINGING my days,
Singing the great achievements of the present,
Singing the strong light works of engineers,
Our modern wonders, (the antique ponderous Seven outvied,)
In the Old World, the east, the Suez canal,
The New by its mighty railroad spann'd,
The seas inlaid with eloquent, gentle wires,
I sound, to commence, the cry, with thee, O soul,
The Past! the Past! the Past!

The Past! the dark, unfathom'd retrospect!
The teeming gulf! the sleepers and the shadows!
The past! the infinite greatness of the past!
For what is the present, after all, but a growth out of the past?
(As a projectile, form'd, impell'd, passing a certain line, still keeps on,
So the present, utterly form'd, impell'd by the past.)

2

Passage, O soul, to India!
Eclaircise the myths Asiatic—the primitive fables.

Not you alone, proud truths of the world!
Nor you alone, ye facts of modern science!
But myths and fables of eld, Asia's, Africa's fables!
The far-darting beams of the spirit!—the unloos'd dreams!
The deep diving bibles and legends;
The daring plots of the poets—the elder religions;
—O you temples fairer than lilies, pour'd over by the rising sun!
O you fables, spurning the known, eluding the hold of the known,
    mounting to heaven!
You lofty and dazzling towers, pinnacled, red as roses, burnish'd
    with gold!
Towers of fables immortal, fashion'd from mortal dreams!
You too I welcome, and fully, the same as the rest;
You too with joy I sing.

3
Passage to India!
Lo, soul! seest thou not God's purpose from the first?
The earth to be spann'd, connected by net-work,
The people to become brothers and sisters,
The races, neighbors, to marry and be given in marriage,
The oceans to be cross'd, the distant brought near,
The lands to be welded together.

(A worship new, I sing;
You captains, voyagers, explorers, yours!
You engineers! you architects, machinists, yours!
You, not for trade or transportation only,
But in God's name, and for thy sake, O soul.

4
Passage to India!
Lo, soul, for thee, of tableaus twain,
I see, in one, the Suez canal initiated, open'd,

I see the procession of steamships, the Empress Eugenie's leading
 the van;
I mark, from on deck, the strange landscape, the pure sky, the level sand
 in the distance;
I pass swiftly the picturesque groups, the workmen gather'd,
The gigantic dredging machines.

In one, again, different, (yet thine, all thine, O soul, the same,)
I see over my own continent the Pacific Railroad surmounting
 every barrier;
I see continual trains of cars winding along the Platte, carrying
 freight and passengers;
I hear the locomotives rushing and roaring, and the shrill steam-whistle,
I hear the echoes reverberate through the grandest scenery in the world;
I cross the Laramie plains—I note the rocks in grotesque shapes—
 the buttes;
I see the plentiful larkspur and wild onions—the barren, colorless,
 sage-deserts;
I see in glimpses afar, or towering immediately above me, the great
 mountains—I see the Wind River and the Wahsatch mountains;
I see the Monument mountain and the Eagle's Nest—I pass the
 Promontory—I ascend the Nevadas;
I scan the noble Elk mountain, and wind around its base;
I see the Humboldt range—I thread the valley and cross the river,
I see the clear waters of Lake Tahoe—I see forests of majestic pines,
Or, crossing the great desert, the alkaline plains, I behold enchanting
 mirages of waters and meadows;
Marking through these, and after all, in duplicate slender lines,
Bridging the three or four thousand miles of land travel,
Tying the Eastern to the Western sea,
The road between Europe and Asia.

(Ah Genoese, thy dream! thy dream!
Centuries after thou art laid in thy grave,
The shore thou foundest verifies thy dream.)

5

Passage to India!
Struggles of many a captain — tales of many a sailor dead!
Over my mood, stealing and spreading they come,
Like clouds and cloudlets in the unreach'd sky.

Along all history, down the slopes,
As a rivulet running, sinking now, and now again to the surface rising,
A ceaseless thought, a varied train — Lo, soul! to thee, thy sight,
    they rise,
The plans, the voyages again, the expeditions:
Again Vasco de Gama sails forth;
Again the knowledge gain'd, the mariner's compass,
Lands found, and nations born — thou born, America, (a hemisphere
    unborn,)
For purpose vast, man's long probation fill'd,
Thou, rondure of the world, at last accomplish'd.

6

O, vast Rondure, swimming in space!
Cover'd all over with visible power and beauty!
Alternate light and day, and the teeming, spiritual darkness;
Unspeakable, high processions of sun and moon, and countless
    stars above;
Below, the manifold grass and waters, animals, mountains, trees;
With inscrutable purpose — some hidden, prophetic intention;
Now, first it seems, my thought begins to span thee.

Down from the gardens of Asia, descending, radiating,
Adam and Eve appear, then their myriad progeny after them,
Wandering, yearning, curious — with restless explorations,
With questionings, baffled, formless, feverish — with never-happy
    hearts,
With that sad, incessant refrain, *Wherefore, unsatisfied Soul?*
    and *Whither, O mocking Life?*

Ah, who shall soothe these feverish children?
Who justify these restless explorations?
Who speak the secret of impassive Earth?
Who bind it to us? What is this separate Nature, so unnatural?
What is this Earth to our affections? (unloving earth, without a throb
    to answer ours;
Cold earth, the place of graves.)

Yet, soul, be sure the first intent remains — and shall be carried out;
(Perhaps even now the time has arrived.)

After the seas are all cross'd, (as they seem already cross'd,)
After the great captains and engineers have accomplish'd their work,
After the noble inventors — after the scientists, the chemist, the
    geologist, ethnologist,
Finally shall come the Poet worthy that name;
The true Son of God shall come, singing his songs.

Then, not your deeds only, O voyagers, O scientists and inventors,
    shall be justified,
All these hearts, as of fretted children, shall be sooth'd,
All affection shall be fully responded to — the secret shall be told;
All these separations and gaps shall be taken up, and hook'd and
    link'd together;
The whole Earth — this cold, impassive, voiceless Earth, shall be
    completely justified;
Trinitas divine shall be gloriously accomplish'd and compacted by
    the true Son of God, the poet,
(He shall indeed pass the straits and conquer the mountains,
He shall double the Cape of Good Hope to some purpose;)
Nature and Man shall be disjoin'd and diffused no more,
The true Son of God shall absolutely fuse them.

7

Year at whose open'd, wide-flung door I sing!
Year of the purpose accomplish'd!
Year of the marriage of continents, climates and oceans!
(No mere Doge of Venice now, wedding the Adriatic;)
I see, O year, in you, the vast terraqueous globe, given, and giving all,
Europe to Asia, Africa join'd, and they to the New World;
The lands, geographies, dancing before you, holding a festival
    garland,
As brides and bridegrooms hand in hand.

8

Passage to India!
Cooling airs from Caucasus far, soothing cradle of man,
The river Euphrates flowing, the past lit up again.

Lo, soul, the retrospect, brought forward;
The old, most populous, wealthiest of Earth's lands,
The streams of the Indus and the Ganges, and their many affluents;
(I, my shores of America walking to-day, behold, resuming all,)
The tale of Alexander, on his warlike marches, suddenly dying,
On one side China, and on the other side Persia and Arabia,
To the south the great seas, and the Bay of Bengal;
The flowing literatures, tremendous epics, religions, castes,
Old occult Brahma, interminably far back—the tender and junior
    Buddha,
Central and southern empires, and all their belongings, possessors,
The wars of Tamerlane, the reign of Aurungzebe,
The traders, rulers, explorers, Moslems, Venetians, Byzantium,
    the Arabs, Portuguese,
The first travelers, famous yet, Marco Polo, Batouta the Moor,
Doubts to be solv'd, the map incognita, blanks to be fill'd,
The foot of man unstay'd, the hands never at rest,
Thyself, O soul, that will not brook a challenge.

9

The medieval navigators rise before me,
The world of 1492, with its awaken'd enterprise;
Something swelling in humanity now like the sap of the earth in spring,
The sunset splendor of chivalry declining.

And who art thou, sad shade?
Gigantic, visionary, thyself a visionary,
With majestic limbs, and pious, beaming eyes,
Spreading around, with every look of thine, a golden world,
Enhuing it with gorgeous hues.

As the chief histrion,
Down to the footlights walks, in some great scena,
Dominating the rest, I see the Admiral himself,
(History's type of courage, action, faith;)
Behold him sail from Palos, leading his little fleet;
His voyage behold—his return—his great fame,
His misfortunes, calumniators—behold him a prisoner, chain'd,
Behold his dejection, poverty, death.

(Curious, in time, I stand, noting the efforts of heroes;
Is the deferment long? bitter the slander, poverty, death?
Lies the seed unreck'd for centuries in the ground? Lo! to God's
    due occasion,
Uprising in the night, it sprouts, blooms,
And fills the earth with use and beauty.)

10

Passage indeed, O soul, to primal thought!
Not lands and seas alone—thy own clear freshness,
The young maturity of brood and bloom;
To realms of budding bibles.

O soul, repressless, I with thee, and thou with me,
Thy circumnavigation of the world begin;
Of man, the voyage of his mind's return,
To reason's early paradise,
Back, back to wisdom's birth, to innocent intuitions,
Again with fair Creation.

11
O we can wait no longer!
We too take ship, O soul!
Joyous, we too launch out on trackless seas!
Fearless, for unknown shores, on waves of extasy to sail,
Amid the wafting winds, (thou pressing me to thee, I thee to me,
    O soul,)
Caroling free — singing our song of God,
Chanting our chant of pleasant exploration.

With laugh, and many a kiss,
(Let others deprecate — let others weep for sin, remorse,
    humiliation;)
O soul, thou pleasest me — I thee.

Ah, more than any priest, O soul, we too believe in God;
But with the mystery of God we dare not dally.

O soul, thou pleasest me — I thee,
Sailing these seas, or on the hills, or waking in the night,
Thoughts, silent thoughts, of Time, and Space, and Death, like
    waters flowing,
Bear me, indeed, as through the regions infinite,
Whose air I breathe, whose ripples hear — lave me all over;
Bathe me, O God, in thee — mounting to thee,
I and my soul to range in range of thee.

O Thou transcendent!
Nameless—the fibre and the breath!
Light of the light—shedding forth universes—thou centre of them!
Thou mightier centre of the true, the good, the loving!
Thou moral, spiritual fountain! affection's source! thou reservoir,
(O pensive soul of me! O thirst unsatisfied! waitest not there?
Waitest not haply for us, somewhere there, the Comrade perfect?)
Thou pulse! thou motive of the stars, suns, systems,
That, circling, move in order, safe, harmonious,
Athwart the shapeless vastnesses of space!
How should I think—how breathe a single breath—how speak—
    if, out of myself,
I could not launch, to those, superior universes?

Swiftly I shrivel at the thought of God,
At Nature and its wonders, Time and Space and Death,
But that I, turning, call to thee, O soul, thou actual Me,
And lo! thou gently masterest the orbs,
Thou matest Time, smilest content at Death,
And fillest, swellest full, the vastnesses of Space.

Greater than stars or suns,
Bounding, O soul, thou journeyest forth;
—What love, than thine and ours could wider amplify?
What aspirations, wishes, outvie thine and ours, O soul?
What dreams of the ideal? what plans of purity, perfection, strength?
What cheerful willingness, for others' sake, to give up all?
For others' sake to suffer all?

Reckoning ahead, O soul, when thou, the time achiev'd,
(The seas all cross'd, weather'd the capes, the voyage done,)
Surrounded, copest, frontest God, yieldest, the aim attain'd,
As, fill'd with friendship, love complete, the Elder Brother found,
The Younger melts in fondness in his arms.

12

Passage to more than India!
Are thy wings plumed indeed for such far flights?
O Soul, voyagest thou indeed on voyages like these?
Disportest thou on waters such as these?
Soundest below the Sanscrit and the Vedas?
Then have thy bent unleash'd.

Passage to you, your shores, ye aged fierce enigmas!
Passage to you, to mastership of you, ye strangling problems!
You, strew'd with the wrecks of skeletons, that, living, never
    reach'd you.

13

Passage to more than India!
O secret of the earth and sky!
Of you, O waters of the sea! O winding creeks and rivers!
Of you, O woods and fields! Of you, strong mountains of my land!
Of you, O prairies! Of you, gray rocks!
O morning red! O clouds! O rain and snows!
O day and night, passage to you!

O sun and moon, and all you stars! Sirius and Jupiter!
Passage to you!

Passage—immediate passage! the blood burns in my veins!
Away, O soul! hoist instantly the anchor!
Cut the hawsers—haul out—shake out every sail!
Have we not stood here like trees in the ground long enough?
Have we not grovel'd here long enough, eating and drinking like
    mere brutes?
Have we not darken'd and dazed ourselves with books long enough?

Sail forth! steer for the deep waters only!
Reckless, O soul, exploring, I with thee, and thou with me;
For we are bound where mariner has not yet dared to go,
And we will risk the ship, ourselves and all.

O my brave soul!
O farther, farther sail!
O daring joy, but safe! Are they not all the seas of God?
O farther, farther, farther sail!

from Whispers of Heavenly Death

Whispers of Heavenly Death

WHISPERS of heavenly death, murmur'd I hear;
Labial gossip of night—sibilant chorals;
Footsteps gently ascending—mystical breezes, wafted soft and low;
Ripples of unseen rivers—tides of a current, flowing, forever
   flowing;
(Or is it the plashing of tears? the measureless waters of human
   tears?)

I see, just see, skyward, great cloud-masses;
Mournfully, slowly they roll, silently swelling and mixing,
With, at times, a half-dimm'd, sadden'd, far-off star,
Appearing and disappearing.

(Some parturition, rather—some solemn, immortal birth:
On the frontiers, to eyes impenetrable,
Some Soul is passing over.)

from Leaves of Grass

Warble for Lilac-Time

WARBLE me now, for joy of Lilac-time,
Sort me, O tongue and lips, for Nature's sake, and sweet life's sake —
and death's the same as life's,
Souvenirs of earliest summer — birds' eggs, and the first berries;
Gather the welcome signs, (as children, with pebbles, or stringing
shells;)
Put in April and May — the hylas croaking in the ponds — the
elastic air,
Bees, butterflies, the sparrow with its simple notes,
Blue-bird, and darting swallow — nor forget the high-hole flashing his
golden wings,
The tranquil sunny haze, the clinging smoke, the vapor,
Spiritual, airy insects, humming on gossamer wings,
Shimmer of waters, with fish in them — the cerulean above;
All that is jocund and sparkling — the brooks running,
The maple woods, the crisp February days, and the sugar-making;
The robin, where he hops, bright-eyed, brown-breasted,
With musical clear call at sunrise, and again at sunset,
Or flitting among the trees of the apple-orchard, building the nest
of his mate;
The melted snow of March — the willow sending forth its yellow-
green sprouts;
— For spring-time is here! the summer is here! and what is this in it
and from it?
Thou, Soul, unloosen'd — the restlessness after I know not what;
Come! let us lag here no longer — let us be up and away!
O for another world! O if one could but fly like a bird!
O to escape — to sail forth, as in a ship!
To glide with thee, O Soul, o'er all, in all, as a ship o'er the waters!
— Gathering these hints, the preludes — the blue sky, the grass,
the morning drops of dew;

(With additional songs — every spring will I now strike up
   additional songs,
Nor ever again forget, these tender days, the chants of Death
   as well as Life;)
The lilac-scent, the bushes, and the dark green, heart-shaped leaves,
Wood-violets, the little delicate pale blossoms called innocence,
Samples and sorts not for themselves alone, but for their
   atmosphere,
To tally, drench'd with them, tested by them,
Cities and artificial life, and all their sights and scenes,
My mind henceforth, and all its meditations — my recitatives,
My land, my age, my race, for once to serve in songs,
(Sprouts, tokens ever of death indeed the same as life,)
To grace the bush I love — to sing with the birds,
A warble for joy of Lilac-time.

from Now Finale to the Shore

Now Finale to the Shore

NOW finale to the shore!
Now, land and life, finale, and farewell!
Now Voyager depart! (much, much for thee is yet in store;)
Often enough hast thou adventur'd o'er the seas,
Cautiously cruising, studying the charts,
Duly again to port, and hawser's tie, returning:
— But now obey thy cherish'd, secret wish,
Embrace thy friends — leave all in order;
To port, and hawser's tie, no more returning,
Depart upon thy endless cruise, old Sailor!

The Untold Want

THE untold want, by life and land ne'er granted,
Now, Voyager, sail thou forth, to seek and find.

Joy, Shipmate, Joy!

JOY, shipmate — joy!
(Pleas'd to my Soul at death I cry;)
Our life is closed — our life begins;
The long, long anchorage we leave,
The ship is clear at last — she leaps!
She swiftly courses from the shore;
Joy! shipmate — joy!

from *As a Strong Bird on Pinions Free*

As a Strong Bird on Pinions Free

1

AS a strong bird, on pinions free,
Joyous, the amplest spaces heavenward cleaving,
Such be the thought I'd think to-day of thee, America;
Such be the recitative I'd bring to-day for thee.

The conceits of the poets of other lands I bring thee not,
Nor the compliments that have served their turn so long,
Nor rhyme—nor the classics—nor perfume of foreign court or
    indoor library;
But an odor I'd bring to-day as from forests of pine in the north,
    in Maine—or breath of an Illinois prairie,
With open airs of Virginia, or Georgia or Tennessee—or from
    Texas uplands or Florida's glades;
With presentment of Yellowstone's scenes or Yosemite;
And murmuring under, pervading all, I'd bring the rustling
    sea sound,
That endlessly sounds from the two great seas of the world.

And for thy subtler sense, subtler refrains, O Union!
Preludes of intellect tallying these and thee—mind-formulas
    fitted for thee—real and sane and large as these and thee;
Thou, mounting higher, diving deeper than we knew—thou
    transcendental Union!
By thee Fact to be justified—blended with Thought;
Thought of Man justified—blended with God:
Through thy Idea—lo! the immortal Reality!
Through thy Reality—lo! the immortal Idea!

2

Brain of the New World! what a task is thine!
To formulate the Modern. . . . . Out of the peerless grandeur of
    the modern,
Out of Thyself—comprising Science—to recast Poems, Churches, Art,
(Recast—may-be discard them, end them—May-be their work is done
    —who knows?)
By vision, hand, conception, on the background of the mighty past,
    the dead,
To limn, with absolute faith, the mighty living present.

And yet, thou living, present brain! heir of the dead, the Old World brain!
Thou that lay folded, like an unborn babe, within its folds so long!
Thou carefully prepared by it so long!—haply thou but unfoldest it—
    only maturest it;
It to eventuate in thee—the essence of the by-gone time contained
    in thee;
Its poems, churches, arts, unwitting to themselves, destined with
    reference to thee,
The fruit of all the Old, ripening to-day in thee.

3

Sail, sail thy best, ship of Democracy!
Of value is thy freight—'tis not the present only,
The Past is also stored in thee!
Thou holdest not the venture of thyself alone—not of thy western
    continent alone;
Earth's *résumé* entire floats on thy keel, O ship—is steadied by thy spars;
With thee Time voyages in trust—the antecedent nations sink or swim
    with thee;
With all their ancient struggles, martyrs, heroes, epics, wars, though
    bear'st the other continents;
Theirs, theirs as much as thine, the destination-port triumphant:
—Steer, steer with good strong hand and wary eye, O helmsman—
    thou carryest great companions,

from *As a Strong Bird on Pinions Free* (1872)   **157**

Venerable, priestly Asia sails this day with thee,
And royal, feudal Europe sails with thee.

4

Beautiful World of new, superber Birth, that rises to my eyes,
Like a limitless, golden cloud, filling the western sky;
Emblem of general Maternity, lifted above all;
Sacred shape of the bearer of daughters and sons;
Out of thy teeming womb, thy giant babes in ceaseless procession
    issuing,
Acceding from such gestation, taking and giving continual strength
    and life;
World of the Real! world of the twain in one!
World of the Soul—born by the world of the real alone—led to
    identity, body, by it alone;
Yet in beginning only—incalculable masses of composite,
    precious materials,
By history's cycles forwarded—by every nation, language,
    hither sent,
Ready, collected here—a freer, vast, electric World, to be
    constructed here,
(The true New World—the world of orbic Science, Morals,
    Literatures to come,)
Thou Wonder World, yet undefined, unform'd—neither do I
    define thee;
How can I pierce the impenetrable blank of the future?
I feel thy ominous greatness, evil as well as good;
I watch thee, advancing, absorbing the present, transcending
    the past;
I see thy light lighting and thy shadow shadowing, as if the entire
    globe;
But I do not undertake to define thee—hardly to comprehend thee;
I but thee name—thee prophecy—as now!
I merely thee ejaculate!

Thee in thy future!
Thee in thy only permanent life, career—thy own unloosen'd mind—
thy soaring spirit;
Thee as another equally needed sun, America—radiant, ablaze,
swift-moving, fructifying all;
Thee! risen in thy potent cheerfulness and joy—thy endless,
great hilarity
(Scattering for good the cloud that hung so long—that weighed so long,
upon the mind of man,
The doubt, suspicion, dread, of gradual, certain decadence of man;)
Thee in thy larger, saner breeds of Female, Male—thee in thy athletes,
moral spiritual, South, North, West, East,
(To thy immortal breasts, Mother of All, thy every daughter, son,
endear'd alike, forever equal;)
Thee in thy own musicians, singers, artists, unborn yet, but certain;
Thee in thy moral wealth and civilization, (until which thy proudest
material wealth and civilization must remain in vain;)
Thee in thy all-supplying, all-enclosing Worship—thee in no single
bible, saviour, merely,
Thy saviours countless, latent within thyself—thy bibles incessant,
within thyself, equal to any, divine as any;
Thee in an education grown of thee—in teachers, studies, students,
born of thee;
Thee in thy democratic fêtes, en masse—thy high original festivals,
operas, lecturers, preachers;
Thee in thy ultimata, (the preparations only now completed—the
edifice on sure foundations tied,)
Thee in thy pinnacles, intellect, thought—thy top-most rational joys—
thy love and godlike aspiration,
In thy resplendent coming literati—thy full-lung'd orators—thy
sacerdotal bards—kosmic savans,
These! these in thee, (certain to come), to-day I prophecy.

5

Land tolerating all — accepting all — not for the good alone —
   all good for thee;
Land in the realms of God to be a realm unto thyself;
Under the rule of God to be a rule unto thyself.

(Lo! where arise three peerless stars,
To be thy natal stars, my country — Ensemble — Evolution — Freedom,
Set in the sky of Law.)
Land of unprecedented faith — God's faith!
Thy soil, thy very subsoil, all upheav'd;
The general inner earth, so long, so sedulously draped over, now
   and hence for what it is boldly laid bare,
Open'd by thee to heaven's light, for benefit or bale.

Not for success alone;
Not to fair-sail unintermitted always;
The storm shall dash thy face — the murk of war, and worse than war,
   shall cover thee all over;
(Wert capable of war — its tug and trials? Be capable of peace,
   its trials;
For the tug and mortal strain of nations come at last in peace —
   not war;)
In many a smiling mask death shall approach, beguiling thee —
   thou in disease shalt swelter;
The livid cancer spread its hideous claws, clinging upon thy breasts,
   seeking to strike thee deep within;
Consumption of the worst — moral consumption — shall rouge
   thy face with hectic;
But thou shalt face thy fortunes, thy diseases, and surmount them all,
Whatever they are to-day, and whatever through time they may be,
They each and all shall lift, and pass away, and cease from thee;
While thou, Time's spirals rounding — out of thyself, thyself still
   extricating, fusing,

Equable, natural, mystical Union thou—(the mortal with
    immortal blent,)
Shalt soar toward the fulfilment of the future—the spirit of the body
    and the mind,
The Soul—its destinies.

The Soul, its destinies—the real real,
(Purport of all these apparitions of the real;)
In thee, America, the Soul, its destinies;
Thou globe of globes! thou wonder nebulous!
By many a throe of heat and cold convuls'd—(by these thyself
    solidifying;)
Thou mental, moral orb! thou New, indeed new, Spiritual World!
The Present holds thee not—for such vast growth as thine—
    for such unparalleled flight as thine,
The Future only holds thee, and can hold thee.

O Star of France!
1870–71

1

O STAR of France!
The brightness of thy hope and strength and fame,
Like some proud ship that led the fleet so long,
Beseems to-day a wreck, driven by the gale—a mastless hulk;
And 'mid its teeming, madden'd, half-drown'd crowds,
Nor helm nor helmsman.

2

Dim smitten star!
Orb not of France alone—pale symbol of my soul, its dearest hopes,
The struggle and the daring—rage divine for liberty,
Of aspirations toward the far ideal—enthusiast's dreams of
    brotherhood,
Of terror to the tyrant and the priest.

3

Star crucified! by traitors sold!
Star panting o'er a land of death—heroic land!
Strange, passionate, mocking, frivolous land.

Miserable! yet for thy errors, vanities, sins, I will not now rebuke thee,
Thy unexampled woes and pangs have quell'd them all,
And left thee sacred.

In that amid thy many faults, thou ever aimedst highly,
In that thou wouldst not really sell thyself, however great the price,
In that thou surely wakedst weeping from thy drugg'd sleep,
In that alone, among thy sisters, thou, Giantess, didst rend the ones
    that shamed thee,
In that thou couldst not, wouldst not, wear the usual chains,
This cross, thy livid face, thy pierced hands and feet,
The spear thrust in thy side.

4

O star! O ship of France, beat back and baffled long!
Bear up O smitten orb! O ship, continue on!

Sure, as the ship of all, the Earth itself,
Product of deathly fire and turbulent chaos,
Forth from its spasms of fury and its poisons,
Issuing at last in perfect power and beauty,
Onward, beneath the sun, following its course,
So thee, O ship of France!

Finish'd the days, the clouds dispel'd,
The travail o'er, the long-sought extrication,
When lo! reborn, high o'er the European world,
(In gladness, answering thence, as face afar to face, reflecting ours,
    Columbia,)
Again thy star, O France — fair, lustrous star,
In heavenly peace, clearer, more bright than ever,
Shall beam immortal.

By Broad Potomac's Shore

1

BY broad Potomac's shore—again, old tongue!
(Still uttering—still ejaculating—canst never cease this babble?)
Again, old heart so gay—again to you, your sense, the full flush
    spring returning;
Again the freshness and the odors—again Virginia's summer sky,
    pellucid blue and silver,
Again the forenoon purple of the hills,
Again the deathless grass, so noiseless, soft and green,
Again the blood-red roses blooming.

2

Perfume this book of mine, O blood-red roses!
Lave subtly with your waters every line, Potomac!
Give me of you, O spring, before I close, to put between its pages!
O forenoon purple of the hills, before I close, of you!
O smiling earth—O summer sun, give me of you!
O deathless grass, of you!

from *Leaves of Grass* (1876) and *Two Rivulets* (1876)

Indirectly, but surely, goodness, virtue, law, (of the very best,) follow freedom. These, to democracy, are what the keel is to the ship, or saltness to the ocean.

—*Democratic Vistas* (1871)

For some reason—not explainable or definite to my own mind, yet secretly pleasing and satisfactory to it—I have not hesitated to embody in, and run through the Volume, two altogether distinct veins, or strata—Politics for one, and for the other, the pensive thought of Immortality. Thus, too, the prose and poetic, the dual forms for the present book.

—preface to *Two Rivulets*

The Beauty of the Ship

WHEN, staunchly entering port,
After long ventures, hauling up, worn and old,
Batter'd by sea and wind, torn by many a fight,
With the original sails all gone, replaced, or mended,
I only saw, at last, the beauty of the Ship.

from *Two Rivulets*

For the Eternal Ocean bound,
These ripples, passing surges, streams of Death and Life.

Two Rivulets

TWO Rivulets side by side,
Two blended, parallel, strolling tides,
Companions, travelers, gossiping as they journey.

For the Eternal Ocean bound,
These ripples, passing surges, streams of Death and Life,
Object and Subject hurrying, whirling by,
The Real and Ideal,

Alternate ebb and flow the Days and Nights,
(Strands of a Trio twining, Present, Future, Past.)

In You, whoe'er you are, my book perusing,
In I myself — in all the World — these ripples flow,
All, all, toward the mystic Ocean tending.

(O yearnful waves! the kisses of your lips!
Your breast so broad, with open arms, O firm, expanded shore!)

THOUGHTS FOR THE CENTENNIAL. — Thoughts even for America's first Centennial, (as for others, certainly waiting folded in hidden train, to duly round and complete their circles, mightier and mightier in the future,) do not need to be, and probably cannot be, literally originated, (for all thoughts are old,) so much as they need to escape from too vehement temporary coloring, and from all narrow and merely local influences — and also from the coloring and shaping through European feudalism — and still need to be averaged by the scale of the Centuries, from their point of view entire, and presented thence, comformably to the freedom and vastness of modern science. . . . . . And even out of a Hundred Years, and on their scale, how small were the best thoughts, poems, conclusions and products, except for a certain invariable resemblance and uniform standard in the final thoughts, theology, poems, &c., of all nations, all civilizations, all centuries and times.

Those precious legacies—accumulations! They come to us from the far-off—from all eras, and all lands—from Egypt, and India, and Greece and Rome—and along through the middle and later ages, in the grand monarchies of Europe—born under far different institutes and conditions from ours—but out of the insight and inspiration of the same old Humanity—the same old heart and brain—the same old countenance yearningly, pensively, looking forth. . . . . . Strictly speaking, they are indeed none of them new, and are indeed not ours originally—ours, however, by inheritance. What we have to do to-day is to receive them cheerfully, and to give them ensemble, and a modern American and Democratic physiognomy.

Or from That Sea of Time

1

OR, from that Sea of Time,
Spray, blown by the wind—a double winrow-drift of weeds and shells;
(O little shells, so curious-convolute! so limpid-cold and voiceless!
Yet will you not, to the tympanus of temples held,
Murmurs and echoes still bring up—Eternity's music, faint and far,
Wafted inland, sent from Atlantica's rim—strains for the Soul of
    the Prairies,
Whisper'd reverberations—chords for the ear of the West, joyously
    sounding
Your tidings old, yet ever new and untranslatable;)
Infinitessimals out of my life, and many a life,
(For not my life and years alone I give—all, all I give;)
These thoughts and Songs—waifs from the deep—here, cast high
    and dry,
Wash'd on America's shores.

2

Currents of starting a Continent new,
Overtures sent to the solid out of the liquid,
Fusion of ocean and land—tender and pensive waves,
(Not safe and peaceful only—waves rous'd and ominous too,
Out of the depths, the storm's abysms—Who knows whence?
    Death's waves,
Raging over the vast, with many a broken spar and tatter'd sail.)

~~~~~~

IN THOUGHTS for the Centennial, I need not add to the multiform and swelling paeans, the self-laudation, the congratulatory voices, and the bringing to the front, and domination to-day, of Material Wealth, Products, Goods, Inventive Smartness, &c., (all very well, may-be.) But, just for a change, I feel like presenting these two reflections:

1. Of most foreign countries, small or large, from the remotest times known, down to our own, each has contributed after its kind, directly or indirectly, at least one great undying Song, to help vitalize and increase the valor, wisdom, and elegance of Humanity, from the points of view attain'd

by it up to date. The stupendous epics of India, the holy Bible itself, the Homeric canticles, the Nibe-lungen, the Cid Campeador, the Inferno, Shakspere's dramas of the passions and of the feudal lords, Burns's songs, Goethe's in Germany, Tennyson's poems in England, Victor Hugo's in France, and many more, are the widely various yet integral signs or land-marks, (in certain respects the highest set up by the human mind and soul, beyond science, invention, political amelioration, &c.,) narrat-ing in subtlest, best ways, the long, long routes of History, and giving identity to the stages arrived at by aggregate Humanity, and the conclusions assumed in its progressive and varied civilizations. . . . . Where is America's art-rendering, in any thing like the spirit worthy of herself and the modern, to these characteristic immortal monuments?

Eidólons

I MET a Seer,
Passing the hues and objects of the world,
The fields of art and learning, pleasure, sense,
　　To glean Eidólons.

Put in thy chants, said he,
No more the puzzling hour, nor day—nor segments, parts, put in,
Put first before the rest, as light for all, and entrance-song of all,
　　That of Eidólons.

Ever the dim beginning;
Ever the growth, the rounding of the circle;
Ever the summit and the merge at last, (to surely start again,)
　　Eidólons! Eidólons!

Ever the mutable!
Ever materials, changing, crumbling, re-cohering;
Ever the ateliers, the factories divine,
　　Issuing Eidólons.

Lo! I or you!
Or woman, man, or State, known or unknown;
We seeming solid wealth, strength, beauty build,
　　But really build Eidólons.

The ostent evanescent;
The substance of an artist's mood, or savan's studies long,
Or warrior's, martyr's, hero's toils,
　　To fashion his Eidólon.

~~~~~~~~~~~~~~~~~~~~~~~~~~~~~~

2. So far, in America, our Democratic Society, (estimating its various strata, in the mass, as one,) possesses nothing—nor have we contributed any characteristic music, the finest tie of Nationality

—to make up for that glowing, blood-throbbing, religious, social, emotional, artistic, indefinable, indescribably beautiful charm and hold which fused the separate parts of the old Feudal societies together, in their wonderful interpenetration, in Europe and Asia, of love, belief and loyalty, running one way like a living weft—and picturesque responsibility, duty, and blessedness, running like a warp the other way. (In the Southern States, under Slavery, much of the same.) . . . . In coincidence, and as things now exist in The States, what is more terrible, more alarming, than the total want of any such fusion and mutuality of love, belief and rapport of interest, between the comparatively few successful rich, and the great masses of the unsuccessful, the poor? . . . . . . As a mixed political and social question, is not this full of dark significance? Is it not worth considering as a problem and puzzle in our Democracy—an indispensable want to be supplied?

Of every human life,
(The units gather'd, posted—not a thought, emotion, deed, left out;)
The whole, or large or small, summ'd, added up,
    In its Eidólon.

The old, old urge;
Based on the ancient pinnacles, lo! newer, higher pinnacles;
From Science and the Modern still impell'd,
    The old, old urge, Eidólons.

The present, now and here,
America's busy, teeming, intricate whirl,
Of aggregate and segregate, for only thence releasing,
    To-day's Eidólons.

These, with the past,
Of vanish'd lands—of all the reigns of kings across the sea,
Old conquerors, old campaigns, old sailors' voyages,
    Joining Eidólons.

Densities, growth, façades,
Strata of mountains, soils, rocks, giant trees,
Far-born, far-dying, living long, to leave,
    Eidólons everlasting.

Exaltè, rapt, extatic,
The visible but their womb of birth,
Of orbic tendencies to shape, and shape, and shape,
    The mighty Earth-Eidólon.

～～～～～～～～～～～～～～～～～～～～～～～～～～

DEMOCRACY in the New World, estimated and summ'd-up to-day, having thoroughly justified itself the past hundred years, (as far as growth, vitality and power are concern'd,) by severest and most varied trials of peace and war, and having establish'd itself for good, with all its necessities and benefits, for time to come, is now to be seriously consider'd also in its pronounc'd and already developt dangers. While the battle was raging, and the result suspended, all defections and criticisms were to be hush'd, and every thing bent with vehemence unmitigated toward the urge of victory. But that victory settled, new responsibilities advance. I can conceive of no better service in the United States, henceforth, by Democrats of thorough and heart-felt faith, than boldly exposing the weakness, liabilities and infinite corruptions of Democracy. . . . . . By the unprecedented opening-up of humanity en-masse in the United States, the last hundred years, under our institutions, not only the good qualities of the race, but just as much the bad ones, are prominently brought forward. Man is about the same, in the main, whether with despotism, or whether with freedom.

"The ideal form of human society," Canon Kingsley declares, "is democracy. A nation—and were it even possible, a whole world—of free men, lifting free foreheads to God and Nature; calling no man master, for One is their master, even God; knowing and doing their duties toward the Maker of the Universe, and therefore to each other; not from fear, nor calculation of profit or loss, but because they have seen the beauty of righteousness, and trust, and peace; because the law of God is in their hearts. Such a nation—such a society—what nobler conception of moral existence can we form? Would not that, indeed, be the kingdom of God come on earth?"

To this faith, founded in the Practical as well as the Ideal, let us hold—and never abandon or lose it! . . . . . . Then what a spectacle is practically exhibited by our American Democracy to-day!

All space, all time,
(The stars, the terrible perturbations of the suns,
Swelling, collapsing, ending, serving their longer, shorter use,)
Fill'd with Eidólons only.

The noiseless myriads!
The infinite oceans where the rivers empty!
The separate, countless free identities, like eyesight;
The true realities, Eidólons.

Not this the World,
Nor these the Universes — they the Universes,
Purport and end — ever the permanent life of life,
Eidólons, Eidólons.

Beyond thy lectures learn'd professor,
Beyond thy telescope or spectroscope, observer keen — beyond
all mathematics,
Beyond the doctor's surgery, anatomy — beyond the chemist with
his chemistry,
The entities of entities, Eidólons.

Unfix'd yet fix'd,
Ever shall be — ever have been, and are,
Sweeping the present to the infinite future,
Eidólons, Eidólons, Eidólons.

The prophet and the bard,
Shall yet maintain themselves — in higher stages yet,
Shall mediate to the Modern, to Democracy — interpret yet to them,
God, and Eidólons.

~~~~~~~~~~~~~~~~~~~~~~~~~~~~~~~~~~~~~

THOUGH I think I fully comprehend the absence of moral tone in our current politics and business, and the almost entire futility of absolute and simple honor as a counterpoise against the enormous greed for worldly wealth, with the trickeries of gaining it, all through society our day, I still do not share the depression and despair on the subject which I find possessing many good people. The advent of America, the history of the past century, has been the first general aperture and opening-up to the average Human Commonalty, on the broadest scale, of the eligibilities to wealth and worldly success and eminence, and has been fully taken advantage of; and the example has spread hence, in ripples, to all nations. To these eligibilities—to this limitless aperture, the race has tended, en-masse, roaring and rushing and crude, and fiercely, turbidly hastening—and we have seen the first stages, and are now in the midst of the result of it all, so far. . . . But there will certainly ensue other stages, and entirely different ones. In nothing is there more evolution than the American mind. Soon, it will be fully realized that ostensible wealth and money-making, show, luxury, &c., imperatively necessitate something beyond—namely, the sane, eternal moral and spiritual-esthetic attributes, elements. (We cannot have even that realization on any less terms than the price we are now paying for it.) Soon, it will be understood clearly, that the State cannot flourish, (nay, cannot exist,) without those elements. They will gradually enter into the chyle of sociology and literature. They will finally make the blood and brawn of the best American Individualities of both sexes—and thus, with them, to a certainty, (through these very processes of to-day,) dominate the New World.

And thee, My Soul!
Joys, ceaseless exercises, exaltations!
Thy yearning amply fed at last, prepared to meet,
    Thy mates, Eidólons.

Thy Body permanent,
The Body lurking there within thy Body,
The only purport of the Form thou art—the real I myself,
    An image, an Eidólon.

Thy very songs, not in thy songs;
No special strains to sing—none for itself;
But from the whole resulting, rising at last and floating,
    A round, full-orb'd Eidólon.

Spain, 1873–74

OUT of the murk of heaviest clouds,
Out of the feudal wrecks, and heap'd-up skeletons of kings,
Out of that old entire European debris—the shatter'd mummeries,
Ruin'd cathedrals, crumble of palaces, tombs of priests,
Lo! Freedom's features, fresh, undimm'd look forth—the same
    immortal face looks forth;
(A glimpse as of thy Mother's face, Columbia,
A flash significant as of a sword,
Beaming towards thee.)

Nor think we forget thee, Maternal;
Lag'd'st thou so long? Shall the clouds close again upon thee?
Ah, but thou hast Thyself now appear'd to us—we know thee;
Thou hast given us a sure proof, the glimpse of Thyself;
Thou waitest there, as everywhere, thy time.

Prayer of Columbus

It was near the close of his indomitable and pious life—on his last voyage, when nearly 70 years of age—that Columbus, to save his two remaining ships from foundering in the Caribbean Sea in a terrible storm, had to run them ashore on the Island of Jamaica—where, laid up for a long and miserable year—1503—he was taken very sick, had several relapses, his men revolted, and death seem'd daily imminent; though he was eventually rescued, and sent home to Spain to die, unrecognized, neglected and in want......It is only ask'd, as preparation and atmosphere for the following lines, that the bare authentic facts be recall'd and realized, and nothing contributed by the fancy. See, the Antilliean Island, with its florid skies and rich foliage and scenery, the waves beating the solitary sands, and the hulls of the ships in the distance. See, the figure of the great Admiral, walking the beach, as a stage, in this sublimest tragedy—for what tragedy, what poem, so piteous and majestic as the real scene?—and hear him uttering—as his mystical and religious soul surely utter'd, the ideas following—perhaps, in their equivalents, the very words.

A BATTER'D, wreck'd old man,
Thrown on this savage shore, far, far from home,
Pent by the sea, and dark rebellious brows, twelve dreary months,
Sore, stiff with many toils, sicken'd, and nigh to death,
I take my way along the island's edge,
Venting a heavy heart.

I am too full of woe!
Haply I may not live another day;
I can not rest, O God—I can not eat or drink or sleep,
Till I put forth myself, my prayer, once more to Thee,
Breathe, bathe myself once more in Thee—commune with Thee,
Report myself once more to Thee.

Thou knowest my years entire, my life,
(My long and crowded life of active work—not adoration merely;)
Thou knowest the prayers and vigils of my youth;
Thou knowest my manhood's solemn and visionary meditations;

~~~~~~

IF YOU GO to Europe, (to say nothing of Asia, more ancient and massive still,) you cannot stir without meeting venerable mementos—cathedrals, ruins of temples, castles, monuments of the great, statues and paintings, (far, far beyond anything America can ever expect to produce,) haunts of heroes long dead, saints, poets, divinities, with deepest associations of ages. . . . . .But here in the New World, while those we can never emulate, we have more than those to build, and far more greatly to build. (I am not sure but the day for conventional monuments, statues, memorials, &c., has pass'd away—and that they are henceforth superfluous and vulgar.). . . . . .An enlarged general superior Humanity, (partly indeed resulting from those,) we are to build. European, Asiatic greatness are in the past. Vaster and subtler, America, combining, justifying the past, yet works for a grander future, in living Democratic forms. (Here too are indicated the paths for our National bards.). . . . . . Other times, other lands, have had their missions—Art, War, Ecclesiasticism, Literature, Discovery, Trade, Architecture, &c., &c.—but *that* is the enclosing purport of the United States.

Thou knowest how, before I commenced, I devoted all to come to
Thee;Thou knowest I have in age ratified all those vows, and strictly
    kept them;
Thou knowest I have not once lost nor faith nor ecstasy in Thee;
(In shackles, prison'd, in disgrace, repining not,
Accepting all from Thee—as duly come from Thee.)

All my emprises have been fill'd with Thee,
My speculations, plans, begun and carried on in thoughts of Thee,
Sailing the deep, or journeying the land for Thee;
Intentions, purports, aspirations mine—leaving results to Thee.

O I am sure they really came from Thee!
The urge, the ardor, the unconquerable will,
The potent, felt, interior command, stronger than words,
A message from the Heavens, whispering to me even in sleep,
These sped me on.

By me, and these, the work so far accomplish'd, (for what has been,
    has been;)
By me Earth's elder, cloy'd and stifled lands, uncloy'd, unloos'd;
By me the hemispheres rounded and tied—the unknown to the
    known.

The end I know not—it is all in Thee;
Or small, or great, I know not—haply, what broad fields, what lands;
Haply, the brutish, measureless, human undergrowth I know,
Transplanted there, may rise to stature, knowledge worthy Thee;

THOUGH These States are to have their own Individuality, and show it forth with courage in all their expressions, it is to be a large, tolerant, and all-inclusive Individuality. Ours is to be the Nation of the Kosmos: we want nothing small—nothing unfriendly or crabbed here—But rather to become the friend and well-wisher of all—as we derive our sources from all, and are in continual communications with all.

OF a grand and universal Nation, when one appears, perhaps it ought to have morally what Nature has physically, the power to take in and assimilate all the human strata, all kinds of experience, and all theories, and whatever happens or occurs, or offers itself, or fortune, or what is call'd misfortune.

Haply the swords I know may there indeed be turn'd to reaping tools;
Haply the lifeless cross I know—Europe's dead cross—may bud
and blossom there.

One effort more—my altar this bleak sand:
That Thou, O God, my life hast lighted,
With ray of light, steady, ineffable, vouchsafed of Thee,
(Light rare, untellable—lighting the very light!
Beyond all signs, descriptions, languages!)
For that, O God—be it my latest word—here on my knees,
Old, poor, and paralyzed—I thank Thee.

My terminus near,
The clouds already closing in upon me,
The voyage balk'd—the course disputed, lost,
I yield my ships to Thee.

Steersman unseen! henceforth the helms are Thine;
Take Thou command—what to my petty skill Thy navigation?

My hands, my limbs grow nerveless;
My brain feels rack'd, bewilder'd;
Let the old timbers part—I will not part!
I will cling fast to Thee, O God, though the waves buffet me;
Thee, Thee, at least, I know.

Is it the prophet's thought I speak, or am I raving?
What do I know of life? what of myself?
I know not even my own work, past or present;
Dim, ever-shifting guesses of it spread before me,
Of newer, better worlds, their mighty parturition,
Mocking, perplexing me.

And these things I see suddenly—what mean they?
As if some miracle, some hand divine unseal'd my eyes,
Shadowy, vast shapes, smile through the air and sky,
And on the distant waves sail countless ships,
And anthems in new tongues I hear saluting me.

***

NATIONALITY—(AND YET.)—It is more and more clear to me that the main sustenance for highest separate Personality, These States, is to come from that general sustenance of the aggregate, (as air, earth, rains, give sustenance to a tree)—and that such Personality, by Democratic standards, will only be fully coherent, grand and free, through the cohesion, grandeur and freedom of the common aggregate, the Union. . . . . . . Thus the existence of the true American, Continental Solidarity of the future, depending on myriads of superb, large-sized, emotional and physically perfect Individualities, of one sex just as much as the other, the supply vices, habits, appetites, under which nearly every man of us, (often the greatest brawler for freedom,) is enslaved.

from *Leaves of Grass* (1881–82)

I would inaugurate from America, for this purpose, new formulas — international poems. . . . All serves our New World progress, even the bafflers, headwinds, cross-tides. Through many perturbations and squalls, and much backing and filling, the ship, upon the whole, makes unmistakably for her destination.

— "Poetry To-day in America — Shakspere — the Future,"
North American Review (February 1881)

Sea-Drift

Out of the Cradle Endlessly Rocking

OUT of the cradle endlessly rocking,
Out of the mocking-bird's throat, the musical shuttle,
Out of the Ninth-month midnight,
Over the sterile sands and the fields beyond, where the child leaving
    his bed wander'd alone, bareheaded, barefoot,
Down from the shower'd halo,
Up from the mystic play of shadows twining and twisting as if they
    were alive,
Out from the patches of briers and blackberries,
From the memories of the bird that chanted to me,
From your memories sad brother, from the fitful risings and fallings
    I heard,
From under that yellow half-moon late-risen and swollen as if
    with tears,
From those beginning notes of yearning and love there in the mist,
From the thousand responses of my heart never to cease,
From the myriad thence-arous'd words,
From the word stronger and more delicious than any,
From such as now they start the scene revisiting,
As a flock, twittering, rising, or overhead passing,
Borne hither, ere all eludes me, hurriedly,
A man, yet by these tears a little boy again,
Throwing myself on the sand, confronting the waves,
I, chanter of pains and joys, uniter of here and hereafter,
Taking all hints to use them, but swiftly leaping beyond them,
A reminiscence sing.

Once Paumanok,
When the lilac-scent was in the air and Fifth-month grass was growing,
Up this seashore in some briers,
Two feather'd guests from Alabama, two together,

And their nest, and four light-green eggs spotted with brown,
And every day the he-bird to and fro near at hand,
And every day the she-bird crouch'd on her nest, silent, with
    bright eyes,
And every day I, a curious boy, never too close, never disturbing
    them,
Cautiously peering, absorbing, translating.

Shine! shine! shine!
Pour down your warmth, great sun!
While we bask, we two together.

Two together!
Winds blow south, or winds blow north,
Day come white, or night come black,
Home, or rivers and mountains from home,
Singing all time, minding no time,
While we two keep together.

Till of a sudden,
May-be kill'd, unknown to her mate,
One forenoon the she-bird crouch'd not on the nest,
Nor return'd that afternoon, nor the next,
Nor ever appear'd again.

And thenceforward all summer in the sound of the sea,
And at night under the full of the moon in calmer weather,
Over the hoarse surging of the sea,
Or flitting from brier to brier by day,
I saw, I heard at intervals the remaining one, the he-bird,
The solitary guest from Alabama.

Blow! blow! blow!
Blow up sea-winds along Paumanok's shore;
I wait and I wait till you blow my mate to me.

Yes, when the stars glisten'd,
All night long on the prong of a moss-scallop'd stake,
Down almost amid the slapping waves,
Sat the lone singer wonderful causing tears.

He call'd on his mate,
He pour'd forth the meanings which I of all men know.

Yes my brother I know,
The rest might not, but I have treasur'd every note,
For more than once dimly down to the beach gliding,
Silent, avoiding the moonbeams, blending myself with the shadows,
Recalling now the obscure shapes, the echoes, the sounds and sights
    after their sorts,
The white arms out in the breakers tirelessly tossing,
I, with bare feet, a child, the wind wafting my hair,
Listen'd long and long.

Listen'd to keep, to sing, now translating the notes,
Following you my brother.

Soothe! soothe! soothe!
Close on its wave soothes the wave behind,
And again another behind embracing and lapping, every one close,
But my love soothes not me, not me.

Low hangs the moon, it rose late,
It is lagging—O I think it is heavy with love, with love.

O madly the sea pushes upon the land,
With love, with love.

O night! do I not see my love fluttering out among the breakers?
What is that little black thing I see there in the white?

Loud! loud! loud!
Loud I call to you, my love!
High and clear I shoot my voice over the waves,
Surely you must know who is here, is here,
You must know who I am, my love.

Low-hanging moon!
What is that dusky spot in your brown yellow?
O it is the shape, the shape of my mate!
O moon do not keep her from me any longer.

Land! land! O land!
Whichever way I turn, O I think you could give me my mate
     back again if you only would,
For I am almost sure I see her dimly whichever way I look.

O rising stars!
Perhaps the one I want so much will rise, will rise with some of you.

O throat! O trembling throat!
Sound clearer through the atmosphere!
Pierce the woods, the earth,
Somewhere listening to catch you must be the one I want.

Shake out carols!
Solitary here, the night's carols!
Carols of lonesome love! death's carols!
Carols under that lagging, yellow, waning moon!
O under that moon where she droops almost down into the sea!
O reckless despairing carols.

But soft! sink low!
Soft! let me just murmur,
And do you wait a moment you husky-nois'd sea,
For somewhere I believe I heard my mate responding to me,

So faint, I must be still, be still to listen,
But not altogether still, for then she might not come immediately to me.

Hither my love!
Here I am! here!
With this just-sustain'd note I announce myself to you,
This gentle call is for you my love, for you.

Do not be decoy'd elsewhere,
That is the whistle of the wind, it is not my voice,
That is the fluttering, the fluttering of the spray,
Those are the shadows of leaves.

O darkness! O in vain!
O I am very sick and sorrowful.

O brown halo in the sky near the moon, drooping upon the sea!
O troubled reflection in the sea!
O throat! O throbbing heart!
And I singing uselessly, uselessly all the night.

O past! O happy life! O songs of joy!
In the air, in the woods, over fields,
Loved! loved! loved! loved! loved!
But my mate no more, no more with me!
We two together no more.

The aria sinking,
All else continuing, the stars shining,
The winds blowing, the notes of the bird continuous echoing,
With angry moans the fierce old mother incessantly moaning,
On the sands of Paumanok's shore gray and rustling,
The yellow half-moon enlarged, sagging down, drooping, the face of
    the sea almost touching,
The boy ecstatic, with his bare feet the waves, with his hair the
    atmosphere dallying,

The love in the heart long pent, now loose, now at last tumultuously
    bursting,
The aria's meaning, the ears, the soul, swiftly depositing,
The strange tears down the cheeks coursing,
The colloquy there, the trio, each uttering,
The undertone, the savage old mother incessantly crying,
To the boy's soul's questions sullenly timing, some drown'd secret
    hissing,
To the outsetting bard.

Demon or bird! (said the boy's soul,)
Is it indeed toward your mate you sing? or is it really to me?
For I, that was a child, my tongue's use sleeping, now I have heard you,
Now in a moment I know what I am for, I awake,
And already a thousand singers, a thousand songs, clearer, louder
    and more sorrowful than yours,
A thousand warbling echoes have started to life within me, never to die.
O you singer solitary, singing by yourself, projecting me,
O solitary me listening, never more shall I cease perpetuating you,
Never more shall I escape, never more the reverberations,
Never more the cries of unsatisfied love be absent from me,
Never again leave me to be the peaceful child I was before what
    there in the night,
By the sea under the yellow and sagging moon,
The messenger there arous'd, the fire, the sweet hell within,
The unknown want, the destiny of me.

O give me the clew! (it lurks in the night here somewhere,)
O if I am to have so much, let me have more!

A word then, (for I will conquer it,)
The word final, superior to all,
Subtle, sent up—what is it?—I listen;
Are you whispering it, and have been all the time, you sea-waves?
Is that it from your liquid rims and wet sands?

Whereto answering, the sea,
Delaying not, hurrying not,
Whisper'd me through the night, and very plainly before day-break,
Lisp'd to me the low and delicious word death,
And again death, death, death, death,
Hissing melodious, neither like the bird nor like my arous'd
    child's heart,
But edging near as privately for me rustling at my feet,
Creeping thence steadily up to my ears and laving me softly all over,
Death, death, death, death, death.

Which I do not forget,
But fuse the song of my dusky demon and brother,
That he sang to me in the moonlight on Paumanok's gray beach,
With the thousand responsive songs at random,
My own songs awaked from that hour,
And with them the key, the word up from the waves,
The word of the sweetest song and all songs,
That strong and delicious word which, creeping to my feet,
(Or like some old crone rocking the cradle, swathed in sweet garments,
    bending aside,)
The sea whisper'd me.

As I Ebb'd with the Ocean of Life

As I ebb'd with the ocean of life,
As I wended the shores I know,
As I walk'd where the ripples continually wash you Paumanok,
Where they rustle up hoarse and sibilant,
Where the fierce old mother endlessly cries for her castaways,
I musing late in the autumn day, gazing off southward,
Held by this electric self out of the pride of which I utter poems,
Was seiz'd by the spirit that trails in the lines underfoot,
The rim, the sediment that stands for all the water and all the land
   of the globe.

Fascinated, my eyes reverting from the south, dropt, to follow those
   slender windrows,
Chaff, straw, splinters of wood, weeds, and the sea-gluten,
Scum, scales from shining rocks, leaves of salt-lettuce, left by the tide,
Miles walking, the sound of breaking waves the other side of me,
Paumanok there and then as I thought the old thought of likenesses,
These you presented to me you fish-shaped island,
As I wended the shores I know,
As I walk'd with that electric self seeking types.

As I wend to the shores I know not,
As I list to the dirge, the voices of men and women wreck'd,
As I inhale the impalpable breezes that set in upon me,
As the ocean so mysterious rolls toward me closer and closer,
I too but signify at the utmost a little wash'd-up drift,
A few sands and dead leaves to gather,
Gather, and merge myself as part of the sands and drift.

O baffled, balk'd, bent to the very earth,
Oppress'd with myself that I have dared to open my mouth,
Aware now that amid all that blab whose echoes recoil upon me
   I have not once had the least idea who or what I am,

But that before all my arrogant poems the real Me stands yet untouch'd,
    untold, altogether unreach'd,
Withdrawn far, mocking me with mock-congratulatory signs and bows,
With peals of distant ironical laughter at every word I have written,
Pointing in silence to these songs, and then to the sand beneath.

I perceive I have not really understood any thing, not a single object,
    and that no man ever can,
Nature here in sight of the sea taking advantage of me to dart upon me
    and sting me,
Because I have dared to open my mouth to sing at all.

You oceans both, I close with you,
We murmur alike reproachfully rolling sands and drift, knowing
    not why,
These little shreds indeed standing for you and me and all.

You friable shore with trails of debris,
You fish-shaped island, I take what is underfoot,
What is yours is mine my father.

I too Paumanok,
I too have bubbled up, floated the measureless float, and been wash'd
    on your shores,
I too am but a trail of drift and debris,
I too leave little wrecks upon you, you fish-shaped island.

I throw myself upon your breast my father,
I cling to you so that you cannot unloose me,
I hold you so firm till you answer me something.

Kiss me my father,
Touch me with your lips as I touch those I love,
Breathe to me while I hold you close the secret of the murmuring I envy.

Ebb, ocean of life, (the flow will return,)
Cease not your moaning you fierce old mother,
Endlessly cry for your castaways, but fear not, deny not me,
Rustle not up so hoarse and angry against my feet as I touch you
or gather from you.

I mean tenderly by you and all,
I gather for myself and for this phantom looking down where
we lead, and following me and mine.

Me and mine, loose windrows, little corpses,
Froth, snowy white, and bubbles,
(See, from my dead lips the ooze exuding at last,
See, the prismatic colors glistening and rolling,)
Tufts of straw, sands, fragments,
Buoy'd hither from many moods, one contradicting another,
From the storm, the long calm, the darkness, the swell,
Musing, pondering, a breath, a briny tear, a dab of liquid or soil,
Up just as much out of fathomless workings fermented and thrown,
A limp blossom or two, torn, just as much over waves floating,
drifted at random,
Just as much for us that sobbing dirge of Nature,
Just as much whence we come that blare of the cloud-trumpets,
We, capricious, brought hither we know not whence, spread out
before you,
You up there walking or sitting,
Whoever you are, we too lie in drifts at your feet.

Tears

TEARS! tears! tears!
In the night, in solitude, tears,
On the white shore dripping, dripping, suck'd in by the sand,
Tears, not a star shining, all dark and desolate,
Moist tears from the eyes of a muffled head;
O who is that ghost? that form in the dark, with tears?
What shapeless lump is that, bent, crouch'd there on the sand?
Streaming tears, sobbing tears, throes, choked with wild cries;
O storm, embodied, rising, careering with swift steps along the beach!
O wild and dismal night storm, with wind—O belching and desperate!
O shade so sedate and decorous by day, with calm countenance and
   regulated pace,
But away at night as you fly, none looking—O then the unloosen'd
   ocean,
Of tears! tears! tears!

To the Man-of-War-Bird

THOU who hast slept all night upon the storm,
Waking renew'd on thy prodigious pinions,
(Burst the wild storm? above it thou ascended'st,
And rested on the sky, thy slave that cradled thee,)
Now a blue point, far, far in heaven floating,
As to the light emerging here on deck I watch thee,
(Myself a speck, a point on the world's floating vast.)

Far, far at sea,
After the night's fierce drifts have strewn the shore with wrecks,
With re-appearing day as now so happy and serene,
The rosy and elastic dawn, the flashing sun,
The limpid spread of air cerulean,
Thou also re-appearest.

Thou born to match the gale, (thou art all wings,)
To cope with heaven and earth and sea and hurricane,
Thou ship of air that never furl'st thy sails,
Days, even weeks untired and onward, through spaces, realms
    gyrating,
At dusk that look'st on Senegal, at morn America,
That sport'st amid the lightning-flash and thunder-cloud,
In them, in thy experiences, had'st thou my soul,
What joys! what joys were thine!

Aboard at a Ship's Helm

ABOARD at a ship's helm,
A young steersman steering with care.

Through fog on a sea-coast dolefully ringing,
An ocean-bell—O a warning bell, rock'd by the waves.

O you give good notice indeed, you bell by the sea-reefs ringing,
Ringing, ringing, to warn the ship from its wreck-place.

For as on the alert O steersman, you mind the loud admonition,
The bows turn, the freighted ship tacking speeds away under her
    gray sails,
The beautiful and noble ship with all her precious wealth speeds away
    gayly and safe.

But O the ship, the immortal ship! O ship aboard the ship!
Ship of the body, ship of the soul, voyaging, voyaging, voyaging.

On the Beach at Night

ON the beach at night,
Stands a child with her father,
Watching the east, the autumn sky.

Up through the darkness,
While ravening clouds, the burial clouds, in black masses spreading,
Lower sullen and fast athwart and down the sky,
Amid a transparent clear belt of ether yet left in the east,
Ascends large and calm the lord-star Jupiter,
And nigh at hand, only a very little above,
Swim the delicate sisters the Pleiades.

From the beach the child holding the hand of her father,
Those burial-clouds that lower victorious soon to devour all,
Watching, silently weeps.

Weep not, child,
Weep not, my darling,
With these kisses let me remove your tears,
The ravening clouds shall not long be victorious,
They shall not long possess the sky, they devour the stars only in
    apparition,
Jupiter shall emerge, be patient, watch again another night, the
    Pleiades shall emerge,
They are immortal, all those stars both silvery and golden shall
    shine out again,
The great stars and the little ones shall shine out again, they endure,
The vast immortal suns and the long-enduring pensive moons
    shall again shine.

Then dearest child mournest thou only for Jupiter?
Considerest thou alone the burial of the stars?

Something there is,
(With my lips soothing thee, adding I whisper,
I give thee the first suggestion, the problem and indirection,)
Something there is more immortal even than the stars,
(Many the burials, many the days and night, passing away,)
Something that shall endure longer even than lustrous Jupiter,
Longer than sun or any revolving satellite,
Or the radiant sisters the Pleiades.

The World Below the Brine

THE world below the brine,
Forests at the bottom of the sea, the branches and leaves,
Sea-lettuce, vast lichens, strange flowers and seeds, the thick tangle,
    openings, and pink turf,
Different colors, pale gray and green, purple, white, and gold, the
    play of light through the water,
Dumb swimmers there among the rocks, coral, gluten, grass, rushes,
    and the aliment of the swimmers,
Sluggish existences grazing there suspended, or slowly crawling
    close to the bottom,
The sperm-whale at the surface blowing air and spray, or disporting
    with his flukes,
The leaden-eyed shark, the walrus, the turtle, the hairy sea-leopard,
    and the sting-ray,
Passions there, wars, pursuits, tribes, sight in those ocean-depths,
    breathing that thick-breathing air, as so many do,
The change thence to the sight here, and to the subtle air breathed
    by beings like us who walk this sphere,
The change onward from ours to that of beings who walk other spheres.

On the Beach at Night Alone

ON the beach at night alone,
As the old mother sways her to and fro singing her husky song,
As I watch the bright stars shining, I think a thought of the clef of
    the universes and of the future.

A vast similitude interlocks all,
All spheres, grown, ungrown, small, large, suns, moons, planets,
All distances of place however wide,
All distances of time, all inanimate forms,
All souls, all living bodies though they be ever so different, or in
    different worlds,
All gaseous, watery, vegetable, mineral processes, the fishes, the
    brutes,
All nations, colors, barbarisms, civilizations, languages,
All identities that have existed or may exist on this globe, or any
    globe,
All lives and deaths, all of the past, present, future,
This vast similitude spans them, and always has spann'd,
And shall forever span them and compactly hold and enclose them.

Song for All Seas, All Ships

TO-DAY a rude brief recitative,
Of ships sailing the seas, each with its special flag or ship-signal,
Of unnamed heroes in the ships— of waves spreading and spreading
  far as the eye can reach,
Of dashing spray, and the winds piping and blowing,
And out of these a chant for the sailors of all nations,
Fitful, like a surge.

Of sea-captains young or old, and the mates, and of all intrepid sailors,
Of the few, very choice, taciturn, whom fate can never surprise nor
  death dismay,
Pick'd sparingly without noise by thee old ocean, chosen by thee,
Thou sea that pickest and cullest the race in time, and unitest nations,
Suckled by thee, old husky nurse, embodying thee,
Indomitable, untamed as thee.

(Ever the heroes on water or on land, by ones or twos appearing,
Ever the stock preserv'd and never lost, though rare, enough for
  seed preserv'd.)

Flaunt out O sea your separate flags of nations!
Flaunt out visible as ever the various ship-signals!
But do you reserve especially for yourself and for the soul of man
  one flag above all the rest,
A spiritual woven signal for all nations, emblem of man elate
  above death,
Token of all brave captains and all intrepid sailors and mates,
And all that went down doing their duty,
Reminiscent of them, twined from all intrepid captains young or old,
A pennant universal, subtly waving all time, o'er all brave sailors,
All seas, all ships.

Patroling Barnegat

WILD, wild the storm, and the sea high running,
Steady the roar of the gale, with incessant undertone muttering,
Shouts of demoniac laughter fitfully piercing and pealing,
Waves, air, midnight, their savagest trinity lashing,
Out in the shadows there milk-white combs careering,
On beachy slush and sand spirts of snow fierce slanting,
Where through the murk the easterly death-wind breasting,
Through cutting swirl and spray watchful and firm advancing,
(That in the distance! is that a wreck? is the red signal flaring?)

Slush and sand of the beach tireless till daylight wending,
Steadily, slowly, through hoarse roar never remitting,
Along the midnight edge by those milk-white combs careering,
A group of dim, weird forms, struggling, the night confronting,
That savage trinity warily watching.

After the Sea-Ship

AFTER the sea-ship, after the whistling winds,
After the white-gray sails taut to their spars and ropes,
Below, a myriad myriad waves hastening, lifting up their necks,
Tending in ceaseless flow toward the track of the ship,
Waves of the ocean bubbling and gurgling, blithely prying,
Waves, undulating waves, liquid, uneven, emulous waves,
Toward that whirling current, laughing and buoyant, with curves,
Where the great vessel sailing and tacking displaced the surface,
Larger and smaller waves in the spread of the ocean yearnfully
    flowing,
The wake of the sea-ship after she passes, flashing and frolicsome
    under the sun,
A motley procession with many a fleck of foam and many fragments,
Following the stately and rapid ship, in the wake following.

from Autumn Rivulets

As Consequent, *Etc.*

AS consequent from store of summer rains,
Or wayward rivulets in autumn flowing,
Or many a herb-lined brook's reticulations,
Or subterranean sea-rills making for the sea,
Songs of continued years I sing.

Life's ever-modern rapids first, (soon, soon to blend,
With the old streams of death.)

Some threading Ohio's farm-fields or the woods,
Some down Colorado's cañons from sources of perpetual snow,
Some half-hid in Oregon, or away southward in Texas,
Some in the north finding their way to Erie, Niagara, Ottawa,
Some to Atlantica's bays, and so to the great salt brine.

In you whoe'er you are my book perusing,
In I myself, in all the world, these currents flowing,
All, all toward the mystic ocean tending.

Currents for starting a continent new,
Overtures sent to the solid out of the liquid,
Fusion of ocean and land, tender and pensive waves,
(Not safe and peaceful only, waves rous'd and ominous too,
Out of the depths the storm's abysmic waves, who knows whence?
Raging over the vast, with many a broken spar and tatter'd sail.)

Or from the sea of Time, collecting vasting all, I bring,
A windrow-drift of weeds and shells.

O little shells, so curious-convolute, so limpid-cold and voiceless,
Will you not little shells to the tympans of temples held,
Murmurs and echoes still call up, eternity's music faint and far,
Wafted inland, sent from Atlantica's rim, strains for the soul of
    the prairies,
Whisper'd reverberations, chords for the ear of the West joyously
    sounding,
Your tidings old, yet ever new and untranslatable,
Infinitesimals out of my life, and many a life,
(For not my life and years alone I give—all, all I give,)
These waifs from the deep, cast high and dry,
Wash'd on America's shores?

from *Specimen Days & Collect* (1882–83)

Even as a boy, I had the fancy, the wish, to write a piece, perhaps a poem, about the sea-shore—that suggesting, dividing line, contact, junction, the solid marrying the liquid—that curious, lurking something, (as doubtless every objective form finally becomes to the subjective spirit,) which means far more than its mere first sight, grand as that is—blending the real and ideal, and each made portion of the other.

—"Sea-Shore Fancies"

Paumanok, and My Life on It
as Child and Young Man

Worth fully and particularly investigating indeed this Pauma-
nok, (to give the spot its aboriginal name,*) stretching east through
Kings, Queens and Suffolk counties, 120 miles altogether—on the
north Long Island sound, a beautiful, varied and picturesque se-
ries of inlets, "necks" and sea-like expansions, for a hundred miles
to Orient point. On the ocean side the great south bay dotted with
countless hummocks, mostly small, some quite large, occasion-
ally long bars of sand out two hundred rods to a mile-and-a-
half from the shore. While now and then, as at Rockaway and far
east along the Hamptons, the beach makes right on the island,
the sea dashing up without intervention. Several light-houses on
the shores east; a long history of wrecks tragedies, some even of
late years. As a youngster, I was in the atmosphere and traditions
of many of these wrecks—of one or two almost an observer. Off
Hempstead beach for example, was the loss of the ship "Mexico"
in 1840, (alluded to in "the Sleepers" in L. of G.) And at Hampton,
some years later, the destruction of the brig "Elizabeth," a fearful
affair, in one of the worst winter gales, where Margaret Fuller went
down, with her husband and child.

Inside the outer bars or beach this south bay is everywhere
comparatively shallow; of cold winters all thick ice on the sur-
face. As a boy I often went forth with a chum or two, on those
frozen fields, with hand-sled, axe and eel-spear, after messes of
eels. We would cut holes in the ice, sometimes striking quite an
eel-bonanza, and filling our baskets with great, fat, sweet, white-

*[Author's footnote]: "Paumanok, (or Paumanake, or Paumanack, the Indian name of Long
Island,) over a hundred miles long; shaped like a fish—plenty of sea shore, sandy, stormy,
uninviting, the horizon boundless, the air too strong for invalids, the bays a wonderful resort
for aquatic birds, the south-side meadows cover'd with salt hay, the soil of the island gen-
erally tough, but good for the locust-tree, the apple orchard, and the blackberry, and with
numberless springs of the sweetest water in the world. Years ago, among the bay-men—a
strong, wild race, now extinct, or rather entirely changed—a native of Long Island was called
a *Paumanacker,* or *Creole-Paumanacker.*" —*John Burroughs.*

meated fellows. The scenes, the ice, drawing the hand-sled, cutting holes, spearing the eels, &c., were of course just such fun as is dearest to boyhood. The shores of this bay, winter and summer, and my doings there in early life, are woven all through L. of G. One sport I was very fond of was to go on a bay-party in summer to gather sea-gull's eggs. (The gulls lay two or three eggs, more than half the size of hen's eggs, right on the sand, and leave the sun's heat to hatch them.)

The eastern end of Long Island, the Peconic bay region, I knew quite well too — sail'd more than once around Shelter Island, and down to Montauk — spent many an hour on Turtle hill by the old light-house, on the extreme point, looking out over the ceaseless roll of the Atlantic. I used to like to go down there and fraternize with the blue-fishers, or the annual squads of sea-bass takers. Sometimes, along Montauk peninsula, (it is some 15 miles long, and good grazing,) met the strange, unkempt, half-barbarous herdsmen, at that time living there entirely aloof from society or civilization, in charge, on those rich pasturages, of vast droves of horses, kine or sheep, own'd by farmers of the eastern towns. Sometimes, too, the few remaining Indians, or half-breeds, at that period left on Montauk peninsula, but now I believe altogether extinct.

More in the middle of the island were the spreading Hempstead plains, then (1830-'40) quite prairie-like, open, uninhabited, rather sterile, cover'd with kill-calf and huckleberry bushes, yet plenty of fair pasture for the cattle, mostly milch-cows, who fed there by hundreds, even thousands, and at evening, (the plains too were own'd by the towns, and this was the use of them in common,) might be seen taking their way home, branching off regularly in the right places. I have often been out on the edges of these plains toward sundown, and can yet recall in fancy the interminable cow processions, and hear the music of the tin or copper bells clanking far or near, and breathe the cool of the sweet and slightly aromatic evening air, and note the sunset.

Through the same region of the island, but further east, extended wide central tracts of pine and scrub-oak, (charcoal was largely made here,) monotonous and sterile. But many a good day or half-day did I have, wandering through those solitary cross-roads, inhaling the peculiar and wild aroma. Here, and all along the island and its shores, I spent intervals many years, all seasons, sometimes riding, sometimes boating, but generally afoot, (I was always then a good walker,) absorbing fields, shores, marine incidents, characters, the bay-men, farmers, pilots—always had a plentiful acquaintance with the latter, and with fishermen—went every summer on sailing trips—always liked the bare sea-beach, south side, and have some of my happiest hours on it to this day.

As I write, the whole experience comes back to me after the lapse of forty and more years—the soothing rustle of the waves, and the saline smell—boyhood's times, the clam-digging, barefoot, and with trowsers roll'd up—hauling down the creek—the perfume of the sedge-meadows—the hay-boat, and the chowder and fishing excursions;—or, of later years, little voyages down and out New York bay, in the pilot boats. Those same later years, also, while living in Brooklyn, (1836–'50) I went regularly every week in the mild seasons down to Coney island, at that time a long, bare unfrequented shore, which I had all to myself, and where I loved, after bathing, to race up and down the hard sand, and declaim Homer or Shakspere to the surf and sea-gulls by the hour. But I am getting ahead too rapidly, and must keep more in my traces.

My Passion for Ferries

Living in Brooklyn or New York city from this time forward, my life, then, and still more the following years, was curiously identified with Fulton ferry, already becoming the greatest of its sort in the world for general importance, volume, variety, rapidity, and picturesqueness. Almost daily, later, ('50 to '60,) I cross'd on the boats, often up in the pilot-houses where I could get a full sweep, absorbing shows, accompaniments, surroundings. What oceanic currents, eddies, underneath—the great tides of humanity also, with ever-shifting movements. Indeed, I have always had a passion for ferries; to me they afford inimitable, streaming, never-failing, living poems. The river and bay scenery, all about New York island, any time of a fine day—the hurrying, splashing sea-tides—the changing panorama of steamers, all sizes, often a string of big ones outward bound to distant ports—the myriads of white-sail'd schooners, sloops, skiffs, and the marvellously beautiful yachts—the majestic sound boats as they rounded the Battery and came along towards 5, afternoon, eastward bound—the prospect off towards Staten island, or down the Narrows, or the other way up the Hudson—what refreshment of spirit such sights and experiences gave me years ago (and many a time since.) My old pilot friends, the Balsirs, Johnny Cole, Ira Smith, William White, and my young ferry friend, Tom Gere—how well I remember them all.

An Interregnum Paragraph

Several years now elapse before I resume my diary. I continued at Washington working in the Attorney-General's department through '66 and '67, and some time afterward. In February '73 I was stricken down by paralysis, gave up my desk, and migrated to Camden, New Jersey, where I lived during '74 and '75, quite unwell—but after that began to grow better; commenc'd going for weeks at a time, even for months, down in the country, to a charmingly recluse and rural spot along Timber creek, twelve or thirteen miles from where it enters the Delaware river. Domicil'd at the farm-house of my friends, the Staffords, near by, I lived half the time along this creek and its adjacent fields and lanes. And it is to my life here that I, perhaps, owe partial recovery (a sort of second wind, or semi-renewal of the lease of life) from the prostration of 1874-'75. If the notes of that outdoor life could only prove as glowing to you, reader dear, as the experience itself was to me. Doubtless in the course of the following, the fact of invalidism will crop out, (I call myself *a half-Paralytic* these days, and reverently bless the Lord it is no worse,) between some of the lines — but I get my share of fun and healthy hours, and shall try to indicate them. (The trick is, I find, to tone your wants and tastes low down enough, and make much of negatives, and of mere daylight and the skies.)

To the Spring and the Brook

So, still sauntering on, to the spring under the willows — musical as soft clinking glasses — pouring a sizeable stream, thick as my neck, pure and clear, out from its vent where the bank arches over like a great brown shaggy eyebrow or mouth-roof — gurgling, gurgling ceaselessly — meaning, saying something, of course (if one could only translate it) — always gurgling there, the whole year through — never giving out — oceans of mint, blackberries in summer — choice of light and shade — just the place for my July sun-baths and water-baths too — but mainly the inimitable soft sound-gurgles of it, as I sit there hot afternoons. How they and all grow into me, day after day — everything in keeping — the wild, just-palpable perfume, and the dapple of leaf-shadows, and all the natural-medicinal, elemental-moral influences of the spot.

Babble on, O brook, with that utterance of thine! I too will express what I have gather'd in my days and progress, native, subterranean, past — and now thee. Spin and wind thy way — I with thee, a little while, at any rate. As I haunt thee so often, season by season, thou knowest reckest not me, (yet why be so certain? who can tell?) — but I will learn from thee, and dwell on thee — receive, copy, print from thee.

A July Afternoon by the Pond

The fervent heat, but so much more endurable in this pure air — the white and pink pond-blossoms, with great heart-shaped leaves; the glassy waters of the creek, the banks, with dense bushery, and the picturesque beeches and shade and turf; the tremulous, reedy call of some bird from recesses, breaking the warm, indolent, half-voluptuous silence; an occasional wasp, hornet, honey-bee or bumble (they hover near my hands or face, yet annoy me not, nor I them, as they appear to examine, find nothing, and away they go)—the vast space of the sky overhead so clear, and the buzzard up there sailing his slow whirl in majestic spirals and discs; just over the surface of the pond, two large slate-color'd dragon-flies, with wings of lace, circling and darting and occasionally balancing themselves quite still, their wings quivering all the time, (are they not showing off for my amusement?)—the pond itself, with the sword-shaped calamus; the water snakes—occasionally a flitting blackbird, with red dabs on his shoulders, as he darts slantingly by—the sounds that bring out the solitude, warmth, light and shade—the quawk of some pond duck—(the crickets and grasshoppers are mute in the noon heat, but I hear the song of the first cicadas;)—then at some distance the rattle and whirr of a reaping machine as the horses draw it on a rapid walk through a rye field on the opposite side of the creek —(what was the yellow or light-brown bird, large as a young hen, with short neck and long-stretch'd legs I just saw, in flapping and awkward flight over there through the trees?)—the prevailing delicate, yet palpable, spicy, grassy, clovery perfume to my nostrils; and over all, encircling all, to my sight and soul, the free space of the sky, transparent and blue—and hovering there in the west, a mass of white-gray fleecy clouds the sailors call "shoals of mackerel"—the sky, with silver swirls like locks of toss'd hair, spreading, expanding—a vast voiceless, formless simulacrum—yet may-be the most real reality and formulator of everything—who knows?

from Autumn Side-Bits

Another Day.—The ground in all directions strew'd with *debris* from a storm. Timber creek, as I slowly pace its banks, has ebb'd low, and shows reaction from the turbulent swell of the late equinoctial. As I look around, I take account of stock—weeds and shrubs, knolls, paths, occasional stumps, some with smooth'd tops, (several I use as seats of rest, from place to place, and from one I am now jotting these lines,)—frequent wild-flowers, little white, star-shaped things, or the cardinal red of the lobelia, or the cherry-ball seeds of the perennial rose, or the many-threaded vines winding up and around trunks of trees.

A Winter Day on the Sea-Beach

One bright December mid-day lately I spent down on the New Jersey sea-shore, reaching it by a little more than an hour's railroad trip over the old Camden and Atlantic. I had started betimes, fortified by nice strong coffee and a good breakfast (cook'd by the hands I love, my dear sister Lou's—how much better it makes the victuals taste, and then assimilate, strengthen you, perhaps make the whole day comfortable afterwards.) Five or six miles at the last, our track enter'd a broad region of salt grass meadows, intersected by lagoons, and cut up everywhere by watery runs. The sedgy perfume, delightful to my nostrils, reminded me of "the mash" and south bay of my native island. I could have journey'd contentedly till night through these flat and odorous sea-prairies. From half-past 11 till 2 I was nearly all the time along the beach, or in sight of the ocean, listening to its hoarse murmur, and inhaling the bracing and welcome breezes. First, a rapid five-mile drive over the hard sand—our carriage wheels hardly made dents in it. Then after dinner (as there were nearly two hours to spare) I walk'd off in another direction, (hardly met or saw a person,) and taking possession of what appear'd to have been the reception-room of an old bath-house range, had a broad expanse of view all to myself—quaint, refreshing, unimpeded—a dry area of sedge and Indian grass immediately before and around me—space, simple, unornamented space. Distant vessels, and the far-off, just visible trailing smoke of an inward bound steamer; more plainly, ships, brigs, schooners, in sight, most of them with every sail set to the firm and steady wind.

The attractions, fascinations there are in sea and shore! How one dwells on their simplicity, even vacuity! What is it in us, arous'd by those indirections and directions? That spread of waves and gray-white beach, salt, monotonous, senseless — such an entire absence of art, books, talk, elegance — so indescribably comforting, even this winter day — grim, yet so delicate-looking, so spiritual — striking emotional, impalpable depths, subtler than all the poems, paintings, music, I have ever read, seen, heard. (Yet let me be fair, perhaps it is because I have read those poems and heard that music.)

Sea-Shore Fancies

Even as a boy, I had the fancy, the wish, to write a piece, per-haps a poem, about the sea-shore — that suggesting, dividing line, contact, junction, the solid marrying the liquid — that curi-ous, lurking something, (as doubtless every objective form finally becomes to the subjective spirit,) which means far more than its mere first sight, grand as that is — blending the real and ideal, and each made portion of the other. Hours, days, in my Long Island youth and early manhood, I haunted the shores of Rockaway or Coney island, or away east to the Hamptons or Montauk. Once, at the latter place, (by the old lighthouse, nothing but sea-tossings in sight in every direction as far as the eye could reach,) I remem-ber well, I felt that I must one day write a book expressing this liquid, mystic theme. Afterward, I recollect, how it came to me that instead of any special lyrical or epical or literary attempt, the sea-shore should be an invisible *influence*, a pervading gauge and tally for me, in my composition. (Let me give a hint here to young writers. I am not sure but I have unwittingly follow'd out the same rule with other powers besides sea and shores — avoiding them,

in the way of any dead set at poetizing them, as too big for for-
mal handling—quite satisfied if I could indirectly show that we
have met and fused, even if only once, but enough—that we have
really absorb'd each other and understand each other.)

There is a dream, a picture, that for years at intervals, (some-
times quite long ones, but surely again, in time,) has come
noiselessly up before me, and I really believe, fiction as it is, has
enter'd largely into my practical life—certainly into my writings,
and shaped and color'd them. It is nothing more or less than a
stretch of interminable white-brown sand, hard and smooth and
broad, with the ocean perpetually, grandly, rolling in upon it, with
slow-measured sweep, with rustle and hiss and foam, and many
a thump as of low bass drums. This scene, this picture, I say, has
risen before me at times for years. Sometimes I wake at night and
can hear and see it plainly.

A Two-Hours' Ice-Sail

Feb. 3, '77.—From 4 to 6 P.M. crossing the Delaware, (back
again at my Camden home,) unable to make our landing, through
the ice; our boat stanch and strong and skilfully piloted, but old
and sulky, and poorly minding her helm. (*Power,* so important
in poetry and war, is also first point of all in a winter steamboat,
with long stretches of ice-packs to tackle.) For over two hours we
bump'd and beat about, the invisible ebb, sluggish but irresist-
ible, often carrying us long distances against our will. In the first
tinge of dusk, as I look'd around, I thought there could not be pre-
sented a more chilling, arctic, grim-extended, depressing scene.
Everything was yet plainly visible; for miles north and south, ice,
ice, ice, mostly broken, but some big cakes, and no clear water
in sight. The shores, piers, surfaces, roofs, shipping, mantled with
snow. A faint winter vapor hung a fitting accompaniment around
and over the endless whitish spread, and gave it just a tinge of
steel and brown.

Feb. 6. — As I cross home in the 6 P.M. boat again, the transparent shadows are filled everywhere with leisurely falling, slightly slanting, curiously sparse but very large, flakes of snow. On the shores, near and far, the glow of just-lit gas-clusters at intervals. The ice, sometimes in hummocks, sometimes floating fields, through which our boat goes crunching. The light permeated by that peculiar evening haze, right after sunset, which sometimes renders quite distant objects so distinctly.

An Afternoon Scene

Feb. 22. — Last night and to-day rainy and thick, till midafternoon, when the wind chopp'd round, the clouds swiftly drew off like curtains, the clear appear'd, and with it the fairest, grandest, most wondrous rainbow I ever saw, all complete, very vivid at its earth-ends, spreading vast effusions of illuminated haze, violet, yellow, drab-green, in all directions overhead, through which the sun beam'd — an indescribable utterance of color and light, so gorgeous yet so soft, such as I had never witness'd before. Then its continuance: a full hour pass'd before the last of those earth-ends disappear'd. The sky behind was all spread in translucent blue, with many little white clouds and edges. To these a sunset, filling, dominating the esthetic and soul senses, sumptuously, tenderly, full. I end this note by the pond, just light enough to see, through the evening shadows, the western reflections in its water-mirror surface, with inverted figures of trees. I hear now and then the *flup* of a pike leaping out, and rippling the water.

A Sun-Bath — Nakedness

Sunday, Aug. 27. — Another day quite free from mark'd prostration and pain. It seems indeed as if peace and nutriment from heaven subtly filter into me as I slowly hobble down these country lanes and across fields, in the good air—as I sit here in solitude with Nature—open, voiceless, mystic, far removed, yet palpable, eloquent Nature. I merge myself in the scene, in the perfect day. Hovering over the clear brook-water, I am sooth'd by its soft gurgle in one place, and the hoarser murmurs of its three-foot fall in another. Come, ye disconsolate, in whom any latent eligibility is left —come get the sure virtues of creek-shore, and wood and field. Two months (July and August, '77,) have I absorb'd them, and they begin to make a new man of me. Every day, seclusion—every day at least two or three hours of freedom, bathing, no talk, no bonds, no dress, no books, no *manners*.

Shall I tell you, reader, to what I attribute my already much-restored health? That I have been almost two years, off and on, without drugs and medicines, and daily in the open air. Last summer I found a particularly secluded little dell off one side by my creek, originally a large dug-out marl-pit, now abandon'd, fill'd with bushes, trees, grass, a group of willows, a straggling bank, and a spring of delicious water running right through the middle of it, with two or three little cascades. Here I retreated every hot day, and follow it up this summer. Here I realize the meaning of that old fellow who said he was seldom less alone than when alone. Never before did I get so close to Nature; never before did she come so close to me. By old habit, I pencill'd down from to time to time, almost automatically, moods, sights, hours, tints and outlines, on the spot. Let me specially record the satisfaction of this current forenoon, so serene and primitive, so conventionally exceptional, natural.

An hour or so after breakfast I wended my way down to the recesses of the aforesaid dell, which I and certain thrushes, cat-birds, &c., had all to ourselves. A light south-west wind was blowing through the tree-tops. It was just the place and time for my Adamic air-bath and flesh-brushing from head to foot. So hanging clothes on a rail near by, keeping old broadbrim straw on head and easy shoes on feet, havn't I had a good time the last two hours! First with the stiff-elastic bristles rasping arms, breast, sides, till they turn'd scarlet—then partially bathing in the clear waters of the running brook—taking everything very leisurely, with many rests and pauses—stepping about barefooted every few minutes now and then in some neighboring black ooze, for unctuous mud-bath to my feet—a brief second and third rinsing in the crystal running waters—rubbing with the fragrant towel—slow negligent promenades on the turf up and down in the sun, varied with occasional rests, and further frictions of the bristle-brush—sometimes carrying my portable chair with me from place to place, as my range is quite extensive here, nearly a hundred rods, feeling quite secure from intrusion, (and that indeed I am not at all nervous about, if it accidentally happens.)

As I walk'd slowly over the grass, the sun shone out enough to show the shadow moving with me. Somehow I seem'd to get identity with each and every thing around me, in its condition. Nature was naked, and I was also. It was too lazy, soothing, and joyous-equable to speculate about. Yet I might have thought somehow in this vein: Perhaps the inner never lost rapport we hold with earth, light, air, trees, &c., is not to be realized through eyes and mind only, but through the whole corporeal body, which I will not have blinded or bandaged any more than the eyes. Sweet, sane, still Nakedness in Nature!—ah if poor, sick, prurient humanity in cities might really know you once more! Is not nakedness then indecent? No, not inherently. It is your thought, your sophistication, your fear, your respectability, that is indecent. There come moods when these clothes of ours are not only too irksome to wear, but are themselves indecent. Perhaps indeed he or she to whom the free exhilarating extasy of nakedness in Nature has never been eligible (and how many thousands there are!) has not really known what purity is—nor what faith or art or health really is. (Probably the whole curriculum of first-class philosophy, beauty, heroism, form, illustrated by the old Hellenic race—the highest height and deepest depth known to civilization in those departments—came from their natural and religious idea of Nakedness.)

Many such hours, from time to time, the last two summers—I

attribute my partial rehabilitation largely to them. Some good people may think it a feeble or half-crack'd way of spending one's time and thinking. May-be it is.

A Jaunt Up the Hudson

June 20th. — On the "Mary Powell," enjoy'd everything beyond precedent. The delicious tender summer day, just warm enough — the constantly changing but ever beautiful panorama on both sides of the river — (went up near a hundred miles) — the high straight walls of the stony Palisades — beautiful Yonkers, and beautiful Irvington — the never-ending hills, mostly in rounded lines, swathed with verdure, — the distant turns, like great shoulders in blue veils — the frequent gray and brown of the tall-rising rocks — the river itself, now narrowing, now expanding — the white sails of the many sloops, yachts, &c., some near, some in the distance — the rapid succession of handsome villages and cities, (our boat is a swift traveler, and makes few stops) — the Race — picturesque West Point, and indeed all along — the costly and often turreted mansions forever showing in some cheery light color, through the woods — make up the scene.

Manhattan from the Bay

June 25. — Returned to New York last night. Out to-day on the waters for a sail in the wide bay, southeast of Staten island — a rough, tossing ride, and a free sight — the long stretch of Sandy Hook, the highlands of Navesink, and the many vessels outward and inward bound. We came up through the midst of all, in the full sun. I especially enjoy'd the last hour or two. A moderate sea-breeze had set in; yet over the city, and the waters adjacent, was a thin haze, concealing nothing, only adding to the beauty. From my point of view, as I write amid the soft breeze, with a sea-temperature, surely nothing on earth of its kind can go beyond this show. To the left the North river with its far vista —nearer, three or four war-ships, anchor'd peacefully—the Jersey side, the banks of Weehawken, the Palisades, and the gradually receding blue, lost in the distance—to the right the East river —the mast-hemm'd shores—the grand obelisk-like towers of the bridge, one on either side, in haze, yet plainly defin'd, giant brothers twain, throwing free graceful interlinking loops high across the tumbled tumultuous current below—(the tide is just changing to its ebb)—the broad water-spread everywhere crowded—no, not crowded, but thick as stars in the sky—with all sorts and sizes of sail and steam vessels, plying ferry-boats, arriving and departing coasters, great ocean Dons, iron-black, modern, magnificent in size and power, fill'd with their incalculable value of human life and precious merchandise—with here and there, above all, those daring, careening things of grace and wonder, those white and shaded swift-darting fish-birds, (I wonder if shore or sea elsewhere can outvie them,) ever with their slanting spars, and fierce, pure, hawk-like beauty and motion—first-class New York sloop or schooner yachts, sailing, this fine day, the free sea in a good wind. And rising out of the midst, tall-topt, ship-hemm'd, modern, American, yet strangely oriental, V-shaped Manhattan, with its compact mass, its spires, its cloud-touching edifices group'd at the centre—the green of the trees, and all the white, brown and gray of the architecture well blended, as I see it, under a miracle of limpid sky, delicious light of heaven above, and June haze on the surface below.

A Night Remembrance

Aug. 25, 9–10 a. m.—I sit by the edge of the pond, everything quiet, the broad polish'd surface spread before me—the blue of the heavens and the white clouds reflected from it—and flitting across, now and then, the reflection of some flying bird. Last night I was down here with a friend till after midnight; everything a miracle of splendor — the glory of the stars, and the completely rounded moon — the passing clouds, silver and luminous-tawny — now and then masses of vapory illuminated scud — and silently by my side my dear friend. The shades of the trees, and patches of moonlight on the grass — the softly blowing breeze, and just-palpable odor of the neighboring ripening corn — the indolent and spiritual night, inexpressibly rich, tender, suggestive — something altogether to filter through one's soul, and nourish and feed and soothe the memory long afterwards.

Delaware River — Days and Nights

April 5, 1879. — With the return of spring to the skies, airs, waters of the Delaware, return the sea-gulls. I never tire of watching their broad and easy flight, in spirals, or as they oscillate with slow unflapping wings, or look down with curved beak, or dipping to the water after food. The crows, plenty enough all through the winter, have vanish'd with the ice. Not one of them now to be seen. The steamboats have again come forth — bustling up, handsome, freshly painted, for summer work — the Columbia, the Edwin Forrest, (the Republic not yet out,) the Reybold, the Nelly White, the Twilight, the Ariel, the Warner, the Perry, the Taggart, the Jersey Blue — even the hulky old Trenton — not forgetting those saucy little bull-pups of the current, the steamtugs.

But let me bunch and catalogue the affair — the river itself, all the way from the sea — Cape Island on one side and Henlopen light on the other — up the broad bay north, and so to Philadelphia, and on further to Trenton; — the sights I am most familiar with, (as I live a good part of the time in Camden, I view matters from that outlook) — the great arrogant, black, full-freighted ocean steamers, inward or outward bound — the ample width here between the two cities, intersected by Windmill island — an occasional man-of-war, sometimes a foreigner, at anchor, with her guns and port-holes, and the boats, and the brown-faced sailors, and the regular oar-strokes, and the gay crowds of "visiting day" — the frequent large and handsome three-masted schooners, (a favorite style of marine build, hereabout of late years,) some of them new and very jaunty, with their white-gray sails and yellow pine spars—the sloops dashing along in a fair wind—(I see one now, coming up, under broad canvas, her gaff-topsail shining in the sun, high and picturesque—what a thing of beauty amid the sky and waters!)—the crowded wharf-slips along the city—the flags of different nationalities, the sturdy English cross on its ground of blood, the French tricolor, the banner of the great North German empire, and the Italian and the Spanish colors—sometimes, of an afternoon, the whole scene enliven'd by a fleet of yachts, in a half calm, lazily returning from a race down at Gloucester; — the neat, rakish, revenue steamer "Hamilton" in mid-stream, with her perpendicular stripes flaunting aft—and, turning the eyes north, the long ribands of fleecy-white steam, or dingy-black smoke, stretching far, fan-shaped, slanting diagonally across from the Kensington or Richmond shores, in the west-by-south-west wind.

Scenes on Ferry and River—Last Winter's Nights

Then the Camden ferry. What exhilaration, change, people, business, by day. What soothing, silent, wondrous hours, at night, crossing on the boat, most all to myself—pacing the deck, alone, forward or aft. What communion with the waters, the air, the exquisite *chiaroscuro*—the sky and stars, that speak no word, nothing to the intellect, yet so eloquent, so communicative to the soul. And the ferry men—little they know how much they have been to me, day and night—how many spells of listlessness, ennui, debility, they and their hardy ways have dispell'd. And the pilots—captains Hand, Walton, and Giberson by day, and captain Olive at night; Eugene Crosby, with his strong young arm so often supporting, circling, convoying me over the gaps of the bridge, through impediments, safely aboard. Indeed all my ferry friends—captain Frazee the superintendent, Lindell, Hiskey, Fred Rauch, Price, Watson, and a dozen more. And the ferry itself, with its queer scenes—sometimes children suddenly born in the waiting-houses (an actual fact—and more than once)—sometimes a masquerade party, going over at night, with a band of music, dancing and whirling like mad on the broad deck, in their fantastic dresses; sometimes the astronomer, Mr. Whitall, (who posts me up in points about the stars by a living lesson there and then, and answering every question)—sometimes a prolific family group, eight, nine, ten, even twelve! (Yesterday, as I cross'd, a mother, father, and eight children, waiting in the ferry-house, bound westward somewhere.)

I have mention'd the crows. I always watch them from the boats. They play quite a part in the winter scenes on the river, by day. Their black splatches are seen in relief against the snow and ice everywhere at that season—sometimes flying and flapping—sometimes on little or larger cakes, sailing up or down the stream. One day the river was mostly clear—only a single long ridge of broken ice making a narrow stripe by itself, running along down the current for over a mile, quite rapidly. On this white stripe the crows were congregated, hundreds of them—a funny procession—("half mourning" was the comment of some one.)

Then the reception room, for passengers waiting—life illustrated thoroughly. Take a March picture I jotted there two or three weeks since. Afternoon, about 3½ o'clock, it begins to snow. There has been a matinee performance at the theater—from 4¼ to 5 comes a stream of homeward bound ladies. I never knew the spacious room to present a gayer, more lively scene—handsome, well-drest Jersey women and girls, scores of them, streaming in for nearly an hour—the bright eyes and glowing faces, coming in from the air—a sprinkling of snow on bonnets or dresses as they enter—the five or ten minutes' waiting—the chatting and laughing—(women can have capital times among themselves, with plenty of wit, lunches, jovial abandon)—Lizzie, the pleasant-manner'd waiting room woman—for sound, the bell-taps and steam-signals of the departing boats with their rhythmic break and undertone—the domestic pictures, mothers with bevies of daughters, (a charming sight)—children, countrymen—the railroad men in their blue clothes and caps—all the various characters of city and country represented or suggested. Then outside some belated passenger frantically running, jumping after the boat. Towards six o'clock the human stream gradually thickening—now a pressure of vehicles, drays, piled railroad crates —now a drove of cattle, making quite an excitement, the drovers with heavy sticks, belaboring the steaming sides of the frighten'd brutes. Inside the reception room, business bargains, flirting, love-making, *eclaircissements*, proposals—pleasant, sober-faced Phil coming in with his burden of afternoon papers—or Jo, or Charley (who jump'd in the dock last week, and saved a stout lady from drowning,) to replenish the stove, after clearing it with long crow-bar poker.

Besides all this "comedy human," the river affords nutriment of a higher order. Here are some of my memoranda of the past winter, just as pencill'd down on the spot.

A January Night.—Fine trips across the wide Delaware tonight. Tide pretty high, and a strong ebb. River, a little after 8, full of ice, mostly broken, but some large cakes making our strong-timber'd steamboat hum and quiver as she strikes them. In the clear moonlight they spread, strange, unearthly, silvery, faintly glistening, as far as I can see. Bumping, trembling, sometimes hissing like a thousand snakes, the tide-procession, as we wend with or through it, affording a grand undertone, in keeping with the scene. Overhead, the splendor indescribable; yet something haughty, almost supercilious, in the night. Never did I realize more latent sentiment, almost *passion*, in those silent interminable stars up there. One can understand, such a night, why, from the days of the Pharaohs or Job, the dome of heaven, sprinkled with planets, has supplied the subtlest, deepest criticism on human pride, glory, ambition.

Another Winter Night. — I don't know anything more *filling* than to be on the wide firm deck of a powerful boat, a clear, cool, extra-moonlight night, crushing proudly and resistlessly through this thick, marbly, glistening ice. The whole river is now spread with it—some immense cakes. There is such weirdness about the scene—partly the quality of the light, with its tinge of blue, the lunar twilight—only the large stars holding their own in the radiance of the moon. Temperature sharp, comfortable for motion, dry, full of oxygen. But the sense of power—the steady, scornful, imperious urge of our strong new engine, as she ploughs her way through the big and little cakes.

Another. — For two hours I cross'd and recross'd, merely for pleasure—for a still excitement. Both sky and river went through several changes. The first for awhile held two vast fan-shaped echelons of light clouds, through which the moon waded, now radiating, carrying with her an aureole of tawny transparent brown, and now flooding the whole vast with clear vapory light-green, through which, as through an illuminated veil, she moved with measur'd womanly motion. Then, another trip, the heavens would be absolutely clear, and Luna in all her effulgence. The big Dipper in the north, with the double star in the handle much plainer than common. Then the sheeny track of light in the water, dancing and rippling. Such transformations; such pictures and poems, inimitable.

Another. — I am studying the stars, under advantages, as I cross to-night. (It is late in February, and again extra clear.) High toward the west, the Pleiades, tremulous with delicate sparkle, in the soft heavens. Aldebaran, leading the V-shaped Hyades—and overhead Capella and her kids. Most majestic of all, in full display in the high south, Orion, vast-spread, roomy, chief histrion of the stage, with his shiny yellow rosette on his shoulder, and his three Kings—and a little to the east, Sirius, calmly arrogant, most wondrous single star. Going late ashore, (I couldn't give up the beauty and soothingness of the night,) as I staid around, or slowly wander'd, I heard the echoing calls of the railroad men in the West

Jersey depot yard, shifting and switching trains, engines, &c.; amid the general silence otherways, and something in the acoustic quality of the air, musical, emotional effects, never thought of before. I linger'd long and long, listening to them.

Night of March 18, '79. — One of the calm, pleasantly cool, exquisitely clear and cloudless, early spring nights — the atmosphere again that rare vitreous blue-black, welcom'd by astronomers. Just at 8, evening, the scene overhead of certainly solemnest beauty, never surpass'd. Venus nearly down in the west, of a size and lustre as if trying to outshow herself, before departing. Teeming, maternal orb — I take you again to myself. I am reminded of that spring preceding Abraham Lincoln's murder, when I, restlessly haunting the Potomac banks, around Washington city, watch'd you, off there, aloof, moody as myself:

As we walk'd up and down in the dark blue so mystic,
As we walk'd in silence the transparent shadowy night,
As I saw you had something to tell, as you bent to me night
    after night,
As you droop from the sky low down, as if to my side, (while
    the other stars all look'd on,)
As we wander'd together the solemn night.

With departing Venus, large to the last, and shining even to the edge of the horizon, the vast dome presents at this moment, such a spectacle! Mercury was visible just after sunset — a rare sight. Arcturus is now risen, just north of east. In calm glory all the stars of Orion hold the place of honor, in meridian, to the south — with the Dog-star a little to the left. And now, just rising, Spica, late, low, and slightly veil'd. Castor, Regulus and the rest, all shining unusually clear, (no Mars or Jupiter or moon till morning.) On the edges of the river, many lamps twinkling — with two or three huge chimneys, a couple of miles up, belching forth molten, steady flames, volcano-like, illuminating all around — and sometimes an electric or calcium, its Dante-Inferno gleams, in far shafts, terrible, ghastly-powerful. Of later May nights, crossing, I like to watch the fishermen's little buoy-lights—so pretty, so dreamy—like corpse candles—undulating delicate and lonesome on the surface of the shadowy waters, floating with the current.

Up the Hudson to Ulster County

April 23. — Off to New York on a little tour and visit. Leaving the hospitable, home-like quarters of my valued friends, Mr. and Mrs. J. H. Johnston—took the 4 P. M. boat, bound up the Hudson, 100 miles or so. Sunset and evening fine. Especially enjoy'd the hour after we passed Cozzens's landing—the night lit by the crescent moon and Venus, now swimming in tender glory, and now hid by the high rocks and hills of the western shore, which we hugg'd close. (Where I spend the next ten days is in Ulster county and its neighborhood, with frequent morning and evening drives, observations of the river, and short rambles.)

April 24—Noon. — A little more and the sun would be oppressive. The bees are out gathering their bread from willows and other trees. I watch them returning, darting through the air or lighting on the hives, their thighs covered with the yellow forage. A solitary robin sings near. I sit in my shirt sleeves and gaze from an open bay-window on the indolent scene—the thin haze, the Fishkill hills in the distance—off on the river, a sloop with slanting mainsail, and two or three little shad-boats. Over on the railroad opposite, long freight trains, sometimes weighted by cylinder-tanks of petroleum, thirty, forty, fifty cars in a string, panting and rumbling along in full view, but the sound soften'd by distance.

An Ulster County Waterfall

I jot this mem. in a wild scene of woods and hills, where we have come to visit a waterfall. I never saw finer or more copious hemlocks, many of them large, some old and hoary. Such a sentiment to them, secretive, shaggy—what I call weather-beaten and let-alone—a rich underlay of ferns, yew sprouts and mosses, beginning to be spotted with the early summer wild-flowers. Enveloping all, the monotone and liquid gurgle from the hoarse impetuous copious fall—the greenish-tawny, darkly transparent waters, plunging with velocity down the rocks, with patches of milk-white foam—a stream of hurrying amber, thirty feet wide, risen far back in the hills and woods, now rushing with volume—every hundred rods a fall, and sometimes three or four in that distance. A primitive forest, druidical, solitary and savage—not ten visitors a year broken rocks everywhere—shade overhead, thick underfoot with leaves—a just palpable wild and delicate aroma.

Hudson River Sights

It was a happy thought to build the Hudson river railroad right along the shore. The grade is already made by nature; you are sure of ventilation one side—and you are in nobody's way. I see, hear, the locomotives and cars, rumbling, roaring, flaming, smoking, constantly, away off there, night and day—less than a mile distant, and in full view by day. I like both sight and sound. Express trains thunder and lighten along; of freight trains, most of them very long, there cannot be less than a hundred a day. At night far down you see the headlight approaching, coming steadily on like a meteor. The river at night has its special character-beauties. The shad fishermen go forth in their boats and pay out their nets—one sitting forward, rowing, and one standing up aft dropping it properly—marking the line with little floats bearing candles, conveying, as they glide over the water, an indescribable sentiment and doubled brightness. I like to watch the tows at night, too, with their twinkling lamps, and hear the husky panting of the steamers; or catch the sloops' and schooners' shadowy forms, like phantoms, white, silent, indefinite, out there. Then the Hudson of a clear moon-light night.

But there is one sight the very grandest. Sometimes in the fiercest driving storm of wind, rain, hail or snow, a great eagle will appear over the river, now soaring with steady and now overhended wings—always confronting the gale, or perhaps cleaving into, or at times literally *sitting* upon it. It is like reading some first-class natural tragedy or epic, or hearing martial trumpets. The splendid bird enjoys the hubbub—is adjusted and equal to it—finishes it so artistically. His pinions just oscillating—the position of his head and neck—his resistless, occasionally varied flight—now a swirl, now an upward movement—the black clouds driving—the angry wash below—the hiss of rain, the wind's piping (perhaps the ice colliding, grunting)—he tacking or jibing—now, as it were, for a change, abandoning himself to the gale, moving with it with such velocity—and now, resuming control, he comes up against it, lord of the situation and the storm—lord, amid it, of power and savage joy.

Sometimes (as at present writing,) middle of sunny afternoon, the old "Vanderbilt" steamer stalking ahead—I plainly hear her rhythmic, slushing paddles—drawing by long hawsers an immense and varied following string, ("an old sow and pigs," the river folks call it.) First comes a big barge, with a house built on it, and spars towering over the roof; then canal boats, a lengthen'd, clustering train, fasten'd and link'd together—the one in the middle, with high staff, flaunting a broad and gaudy flag—others with the almost invariable lines of new-wash'd clothes, drying; two sloops and a schooner aside the tow—little wind, and that adverse—with three long, dark, empty barges bringing up the rear. People are on the boats: men lounging, women in sun-bonnets, children, stovepipes with streaming smoke.

Departing of the Big Steamers

May 15.—A three hours' bay-trip from 12 to 3 this afternoon, accompanying "the City of Brussels" down as far as the Narrows, in behoof of some Europe-bound friends, to give them a good send off. Our spirited little tug, the "Seth Low," kept close to the great black "Brussels," sometimes one side, sometimes the other, always up to her, or even pressing ahead, (like the blooded pony accompanying the royal elephant.) The whole affair, from the first, was an animated, quick-passing, characteristic New York scene; the large, good-looking, well-dress'd crowd on the wharf-end — men and women come to see their friends depart, and bid them God-speed — the ship's sides swarming with passengers — groups of bronze-faced sailors, with uniform'd officers at their posts — the quiet directions, as she quickly unfastens and moves out, prompt to a minute — the emotional faces, adieus and fluttering handkerchiefs, and many smiles and some tears on the wharf — the answering faces, smiles, tears and fluttering handkerchiefs, from the ship — (what can be subtler and finer than this play of faces on such occasions in these responding crowds? — what go more to one's heart?) — the proud, steady, noiseless cleaving of the grand oceaner down the bay — we speeding by her side a few miles, and then turning, wheeling, amid a babel of wild hurrahs, shouted partings, ear-splitting steam whistles, kissing of hands and waving of handkerchiefs.

This departing of the big steamers, noons or afternoons — there is no better medicine when one is listless or vapory. I am fond of going down Wednesdays and Saturdays — their more special days — to watch them and the crowds on the wharves, the arriving passengers, the general bustle and activity, the eager looks from the faces, the clear-toned voices, (a travel'd foreigner, a musician, told me the other day she thinks an American crowd has the finest voices in the world,) the whole look of the great, shapely black ships themselves, and their groups and lined sides — in the setting of our bay with the blue sky overhead. Two days after the above I saw the "Britannic," the "Donau," the "Helvetia" and the "Schiedam" steam out, all off for Europe — a magnificent sight.

Swallows on the River

Sept. 3. — Cloudy and wet, and wind due east; air without palpable fog, but very heavy with moisture — welcome for a change. Forenoon, crossing the Delaware, I noticed unusual numbers of swallows in flight, circling, darting, graceful beyond description, close to the water. Thick, around the bows of the ferry-boat as she lay tied in her slip, they flew; and as we went out I watch'd beyond the pier-heads, and across the broad stream, their swift-winding loop-ribands of motion, down close to it, cutting and intersecting. Though I had seen swallows all my life, seem'd as though I never before realized their peculiar beauty and character in the landscape. (Some time ago, for an hour, in a huge old country barn, watching these birds flying, recall'd the 22d book of the Odyssey, where Ulysses slays the suitors, bringing things to *eclaircissement*, and Minerva, swallow-bodied, darts up through the spaces of the hall, sits high on a beam, looks complacently on the show of slaughter, and feels in her element, exulting, joyous.)

New Senses — New Joys

We follow the stream of amber and bronze brawling along its bed, with its frequent cascades and snow-white foam. Through the cañon we fly — mountains not only each side, but seemingly, till we get near, right in front of us — every rood a new view flashing, and each flash defying description — on the almost perpendicular sides, clinging pines, cedars, spruces, crimson sumach bushes, spots of wild grass — but dominating all, those towering rocks, rocks, rocks, bathed in delicate vari-colors, with the clear sky of autumn overhead. New senses, new joys, seem develop'd. Talk as you like, a typical Rocky Mountain cañon, or a limitless sea-like stretch of the great Kansas or Colorado plains, under favoring circumstances, tallies, perhaps expresses, certainly awakes, those grandest and subtlest element-emotions in the human soul, that all the marble temples and sculptures from Phidias to Thorwald-sen — all paintings, poems, reminiscences, or even music, probably never can.

Unfulfilled Wants — the Arkansas River

I had wanted to go to the Yellowstone river region — wanted specially to see the National Park, and the geysers and the "hoo-doo" or goblin land of that country; indeed, hesitated a little at Pueblo, the turning point — wanted to thread the Veta pass — wanted to go over the Santa Fe trail away southwestward to New Mexico — but turn'd and set my face eastward — leaving behind me whetting glimpse-tastes of southeastern Colorado, Pueblo, Bald mountain, the Spanish peaks, Sangre de Christos, Mile-Shoe-curve (which my veteran friend on the locomotive told me was "the boss railroad curve of the universe,") fort Garland on the plains, Veta, and the three great peaks of the Sierra Blancas.

The Arkansas river plays quite a part in the whole of this region — I see it, or its high-cut rocky northern shore, for miles, and cross and recross it frequently, as it winds and squirms like a snake. The plains vary here even more than usual — sometimes a long sterile stretch of scores of miles — then green, fertile and grassy, an equal length. Some very large herds of sheep. (One wants new words in writing about these plains, and all the inland American West — the terms, *far*, *large*, *vast*, &c., are insufficient.)

Earth's Most Important Stream

The valley of the Mississippi river and its tributaries, (this stream and its adjuncts involve a big part of the question,) comprehends more than twelve hundred thousand square miles, the greater part prairies. It is by far the most important stream on the globe, and would seem to have been marked out by design, slow-flowing from north to south, through a dozen climates, all fitted for man's healthy occupancy, its outlet unfrozen all the year, and its line forming a safe, cheap continental avenue for commerce and passage from the north temperate to the torrid zone. Not even the mighty Amazon (though larger in volume) on its line of east and west—not the Nile in Africa, nor the Danube in Europe, nor the three great rivers of China, compare with it. Only the Mediterranean sea has play'd some such part in history, and all through the past, as the Mississippi is destined to play in the future. By its demesnes, water'd and welded by its branches, the Missouri, the Ohio, the Arkansas, the Red, the Yazoo, the St. Francis and others, it already compacts twenty-five millions of people, not merely the most peaceful and money-making, but the most restless and warlike on earth. Its valley, or reach, is rapidly concentrating the political power of the American Union. One almost thinks it *is* the Union—or soon will be. Take it out, with its radiations, and what would be left? From the car windows through Indiana, Illinois, Missouri, or stopping some days along the Topeka and Santa Fe road, in southern Kansas, and indeed wherever I went, hundreds and thousands of miles through this region, my eyes feasted on primitive and rich meadows, some of them partially inhabited, but far, immensely far more untouch'd, unbroken—and much of it more lovely and fertile in its unplough'd innocence than the fair and valuable fields of New York's, Pennsylvania's, Maryland's or Virginia's richest farms.

Nights on the Mississippi

Oct. 29th, 30th, and 31st.—Wonderfully fine, with the full harvest moon, dazzling and silvery. I have haunted the river every night lately, where I could get a look at the bridge by moon-light. It is indeed a structure of perfection and beauty unsurpassable, and I never tire of it. The river at present is very low; I noticed today it had much more of a blue-clear look than usual. I hear the slight ripples, the air is fresh and cool, and the view, up or down, wonderfully clear, in the moonlight. I am out pretty late: it is so fascinating, dreamy. The cool night-air, all the influences, the silence, with those far-off eternal stars, do me good. I have been quite ill of late. And so, well-near the centre of our national demesne, these night views of the Mississippi.

A Hint of Wild Nature

Feb. 13. — As I was crossing the Delaware to-day, saw a large flock of wild geese, right overhead, not very high up, ranged in V-shape, in relief against the noon clouds of light smoke-color. Had a capital though momentary view of them, and then of their course on and on southeast, till gradually fading — (my eyesight yet first rate for the open air and its distances, but I use glasses for reading.) Queer thoughts melted into me the two or three minutes, or less, seeing these creatures cleaving the sky — the spacious, airy realm — even the prevailing smoke-gray color everywhere, (no sun shining) — the waters below — the rapid flight of the birds, appearing just for a minute — flashing to me such a hint of the whole spread of Nature, with her eternal unsophisticated freshness, her never-visited recesses of sea, sky, shore — and then disappearing in the distance.

Seeing Niagara to Advantage

June 4, '80. — For really seizing a great picture or book, or piece of music, or architecture, or grand scenery — or perhaps for the first time even the common sunshine, or landscape, or may-be even the mystery of identity, most curious mystery of all — there comes some lucky five minutes of a man's life, set amid a fortuitous concurrence of circumstances, and bringing in a brief flash the culmination of years of reading and travel and thought. The present case about two o'clock this afternoon, gave me Niagara, its superb severity of action and color and majestic grouping, in one short, indescribable show. We were very slowly crossing the Suspension bridge—not a full stop anywhere, but next to it—the day clear, sunny, still—and I out on the platform. The falls were in plain view about a mile off, but very distinct, and no roar—hardly a murmur. The river tumbling green and white, far below me; the dark high banks, the plentiful umbrage, many bronze cedars, in shadow; and tempering and arching all the immense materiality, a clear sky overhead, with a few white clouds, limpid, spiritual, silent. Brief, and as quiet as brief, that picture—a remembrance always afterwards. Such are the things, indeed, I lay away with my life's rare and blessed bits of hours, reminiscent, past—the wild sea-storm I once saw one winter day, off Fire island—the elder Booth in Richard, that famous night forty years ago in the old Bowery—or Alboni in the children's scene in Norma—or night-views, I remember, on the field, after battles in Virginia—or the peculiar sentiment of moonlight and stars over the great Plains, western Kansas—or scooting up New York bay, with a stiff breeze and a good yacht, off Navesink. With these, I say, I henceforth place that view, that afternoon, that combination complete, that five minutes' perfect absorption of Niagara—not the great majestic gem alone by itself, but set complete in all its varied, full, indispensable surroundings.

The St. Lawrence Line

August 20.—Premising that my three or four months in Canada were intended, among the rest, as an exploration of the line of the St. Lawrence, from lake Superior to the sea, (the engineers here insist upon considering it as one stream, over 2000 miles long, including lakes and Niagara and all)—that I have only partially carried out my programme; but for the seven or eight hundred miles so far fulfill'd, I find that the *Canada question* is absolutely control'd by this vast water line, with its first-class features and points of trade, humanity, and many more—here I am writing this nearly a thousand miles north of my Philadelphia starting-point (by way of Montreal and Quebec) in the midst of regions that go to a further extreme of grimness, wildness of beauty, and a sort of still and pagan *scaredness*, while yet Christian, inhabitable, and partially fertile, than perhaps any other on earth. The weather remains perfect; some might call it a little cool, but I wear my old gray overcoat and find it just right. The days are full of sunbeams and oxygen. Most of the forenoons and afternoons I am on the forward deck of the steamer.

The Savage Saguenay

Up these black waters, over a hundred miles—always strong, deep, (hundreds of feet, sometimes thousands,) ever with high, rocky hills for banks, green and gray—at times a little like some parts of the Hudson, but much more pronounc'd and defiant. The hills rise higher—keep their ranks more unbroken. The river is straighter and of more resolute flow, and its hue, though dark as ink, exquisitely polish'd and sheeny under the August sun. Different, indeed, this Saguenay from all other rivers—different effects—a bolder, more vehement play of lights and shades. Of a rare charm of singleness and simplicity. (Like the organ-chant at midnight from the old Spanish convent, in "Favorita"—one strain only, simple and monotonous and unornamented—but indescribably penetrating and grand and masterful.) Great place for echoes: while our steamer was tied at the wharf at Tadousac (taj-oo-sac) waiting, the escape-pipe letting off steam, I was sure I heard a band at the hotel up in the rocks—could even make out some of the tunes. Only when our pipe stopp'd, I knew what caused it. Then at cape Eternity and Trinity rock, the pilot with his whistle producing similar marvellous results, echoes indescribably weird, as we lay off in the still bay under their shadows.

Chicoutimi and Ha-Ha Bay

No indeed—life and travel and memory have offer'd and will preserve to me no deeper-cut incidents, panorama, or sights to cheer my soul, than these at Chicoutimi and Ha-ha bay, and my days and nights up and down this fascinating savage river—the rounded mountains, some bare and gray, some dull red, some draped close all over with matted green verdure or vines—the ample, calm, eternal rocks everywhere—the long streaks of motley foam, a milk-white curd on the glistening breast of the stream—the little two-masted schooner, dingy yellow, with patch'd sails, set wing-and-wing, nearing us, coming saucily up the water with a couple of swarthy, black-hair'd men aboard—the strong shades falling on the light gray or yellow outlines of the hills all through the forenoon, as we steam within gunshot of them—while ever the pure and delicate sky spreads over all. And the splendid sunsets, and the sights of evening—the same old stars, (relatively a little different, I see, so far north) Arcturus and Lyra, and the Eagle, and great Jupiter like a silver globe, and the constellation of the Scorpion. Then northern lights nearly every night.

My Native Sand and Salt Once More

July 25, '81. —Far Rockaway, L. I.—A good day here, on a jaunt, amid the sand and salt, a steady breeze setting in from the sea, the sun shining, the sedge-odor, the noise of the surf, a mixture of hissing and booming, the milk-white crests curling over. I had a leisurely bath and naked ramble as of old, on the warm-gray shore-sands, my companions off in a boat in deeper water—(I shouting to them Jupiter's menaces against the gods, from Pope's Homer.)

July 28—to Long Branch.—8½ A. M., on the steamer "Plymouth Rock," foot of 23d street, New York, for Long Branch. Another fine day, fine sights, the shores, the shipping and bay—everything comforting to the body and spirit of me. (I find the human and objective atmosphere of New York city and Brooklyn more affiliative to me than any other.) *An hour later*—Still on the steamer, now sniffing the salt very plainly—the long pulsating *swash* as our boat steams seaward—the hills of Navesink and many passing vessels—the air the best part of all. At Long Branch the bulk of the day, stopt at a good hotel, took all very leisurely, had an excellent dinner, and then drove for over two hours about the place, especially Ocean avenue, the finest drive one can imagine, seven or eight miles right along the beach. In all directions costly villas, palaces, millionaires—(but few among them I opine like my friend George W. Childs, whose personal integrity, generosity, unaffected simplicity, go beyond all worldly wealth.)

An Ossianic Night—Dearest Friends

Nov., '81.—Again back in Camden. As I cross the Delaware in long trips to-night, between 9 and 11, the scene overhead is a peculiar one—swift sheets of flitting vapor-gauze, follow'd by dense clouds throwing an inky pall on everything. Then a spell of that transparent steel-gray black sky I have noticed under similar circumstances, on which the moon would beam for a few moments with calm lustre, throwing down a broad dazzle of highway on the waters; then the mists careering again. All silently, yet driven as if by the furies they sweep along, sometimes quite thin, sometimes thicker—a real Ossianic night—amid the whirl, absent or dead friends, the old, the past, somehow tenderly suggested—while the Gael-strains chant themselves from the mists—["Be thy soul blest, O Carril! in the midst of thy eddying winds. O that thou woulds't come to my hall when I am alone by night! And thou dost come, my friend. I hear often thy light hand on my harp, when it hangs on the distant wall, and the feeble sound touches my ear. Why dost thou not speak to me in my grief, and tell me when I shall behold my friends? But thou passest away in thy murmuring blast; the wind whistles through the gray hairs of Ossian."]

But most of all, those changes of moon and sheets of hurrying vapor and black clouds, with the sense of rapid action in weird silence, recall the far-back Erse belief that such above were the preparations for receiving the wraiths of just-slain warriors— ["We sat that night in Selma, round the strength of the shell. The wind was abroad in the oaks. The spirit of the mountain roar'd. The blast came rustling through the hall, and gently touch'd my harp. The sound was mournful and low, like the song of the tomb. Fingal heard it the first. The crowded sighs of his bosom rose. Some of my heroes are low, said the gray-hair'd king of Morven. I hear the sound of death on the harp. Ossian, touch the trembling string. Bid the sorrow rise, that their spirits may fly with joy to Morven's woody hills. I touch'd the harp before the king; the sound was mournful and low. Bend forward from your clouds, I said, ghosts of my fathers! bend. Lay by the red terror of your course. Receive the falling chief; whether he comes from a distant land, or rises from the rolling sea. Let his robe of mist be near; his spear that is form'd of a cloud. Place a half-extinguish'd meteor by his side, in the form of a hero's sword. And oh! let his countenance be lovely, that his friends may delight in his presence. Bend from your clouds, I said, ghosts of my fathers, bend. Such was my song in Selma, to the lightly trembling harp."]

How or why I know not, just at the moment, but I too muse and think of my best friends in their distant homes—of William O'Connor, of Maurice Bucke, of John Burroughs, and of Mrs. Gilchrist—friends of my soul—stanchest friends of my other soul, my poems.

Only a New Ferry Boat

Jan. 12, '82.—Such a show as the Delaware presented an hour before sundown yesterday evening, all along between Philadelphia and Camden, is worth weaving into an item. It was full tide, a fair breeze from the southwest, the water of a pale tawny color, and just enough motion to make things frolicsome and lively. Add to these an approaching sunset of unusual splendor, a broad tumble of clouds, with much golden haze and profusion of beaming shaft and dazzle. In the midst of all, in the clear drab of the afternoon light, there steam'd up the river the large, new boat, "the Wenonah," as pretty an object as you could wish to see, lightly and swiftly skimming along, all trim and white, cover'd with flags, transparent red and blue, streaming out in the breeze. Only a new ferry-boat, and yet in its fitness comparable with the prettiest product of Nature's cunning, and rivaling it. High up in the transparent ether gracefully balanced and circled four or five great sea hawks, while here below, amid the pomp and picturesqueness of sky and river, swam this creation of artificial beauty and motion and power, in its way no less perfect.

The Great Unrest of Which We Are a Part

My thoughts went floating on vast and mystic currents as I sat to-day in solitude and half-shade by the creek returning mainly to two principal centres. One of my cherish'd themes for a never-achiev'd poem has been the two impetuses of man and the universe—in the latter, creation's incessant unrest,* exfoliation, (Darwin's evolution, I suppose.) Indeed, what is Nature but change, in all its visible, and still more its invisible processes? Or what is humanity in its faith, love, heroism, poetry, even morals, but *emotion*?

*[Author's footnote]: "Fifty thousand years ago the constellation of the Great Bear or Dipper was a starry cross; a hundred thousand years hence the imaginary Dipper will be upside down, and the stars which form the bowl and handle will have changed places. The misty nebulae are moving, and besides are whirling around in great spirals, some one way, some another. Every molecule of matter in the whole universe is swinging to and fro; every particle of ether which fills space is in jelly-like vibration. Light is one kind of motion, heat another, electricity another, magnetism another, sound another. Every human sense is the result of motion; every perception, every thought is but motion of the molecules of the brain translated by that incomprehensible thing we call 'mind.' The processes of growth, of existence, of decay, whether in worlds, or in the minutest organisms, are but motion."

from *Leaves of Grass* (1891–92)

COME, said my Soul,
Such verses for my Body let us write, (for we are one,)
That should I after death invisibly return,
Or, long, long hence, in other spheres,
There to some group of mates the chants resuming,
(Tallying Earth's soil, trees, winds, tumultuous waves,)
Ever with pleas'd smile I may keep on,
Ever and ever yet the verse owning — as, first, I here and now,
Signing for Soul and Body, set to them my name,

Walt Whitman

—epigraph to the "Deathbed Edition"

from *Sands at Seventy*

Paumanok

Sea-beauty! stretch'd and basking!
One side thy inland ocean laving, broad, with copious commerce,
    steamers, sails,
And one the Atlantic's wind caressing, fierce or gentle—mighty hulls
    dark-gliding in the distance.
Isle of sweet brooks of drinking-water—healthy air and soil!
Isle of the salty shore and breeze and brine!

From Montauk Point

I stand as on some mighty eagle's beak,
Eastward the sea absorbing, viewing, (nothing but sea and sky,)
The tossing waves, the foam, the ships in the distance,
The wild unrest, the snowy, curling caps—that inbound urge and
    urge of waves,
Seeking the shores forever.

A Font of Type

This latent mine—these unlaunch'd voices—passionate powers,
Wrath, argument, or praise, or comic leer, or prayer devout,
(Not nonpareil, brevier, bourgeois, long primer merely,)
These ocean waves arousable to fury and to death,
Or sooth'd to ease and sheeny sun and sleep,
Within the pallid slivers slumbering.

Fancies at Navesink

The Pilot in the Mist

Steaming the northern rapids—(an old St. Lawrence reminiscence,
A sudden memory-flash comes back, I know not why,
Here waiting for the sunrise, gazing from this hill;)*
Again 'tis just at morning—a heavy haze contends with day-break,
Again the trembling, laboring vessel veers me—I press through
　　foam-dash'd rocks that almost touch me,
Again I mark where aft the small thin Indian helmsman
Looms in the mist, with brow elate and governing hand.

Had I the Choice

Had I the choice to tally greatest bards,
To limn their portraits, stately, beautiful, and emulate at will,
Homer with all his wars and warriors—Hector, Achilles, Ajax,
Or Shakspere's woe-entangled Hamlet, Lear, Othello—Tennyson's
　　fair ladies,
Metre or wit the best, or choice conceit to wield in perfect rhyme,
　　delight of singers;
These, these, O sea, all these I'd gladly barter,
Would you the undulation of one wave, its trick to me transfer,
Or breathe one breath of yours upon my verse,
And leave its odor there.

*[Author's footnote]: Navesink—a sea-side mountain, lower entrance of New York Bay.

You Tides with Ceaseless Swell

You tides with ceaseless swell! you power that does this work!
You unseen force, centripetal, centrifugal, through space's spread,
Rapport of sun, moon, earth, and all the constellations,
What are the messages by you from distant stars to us? what Sirius'?
    what Capella's?
What central heart—and you the pulse—vivifies all? what boundless
    aggregate of all?
What subtle indirection and significance in you? what clue to all in you?
    what fluid, vast identity,
Holding the universe with all its parts as one—as sailing in a ship?

Last of Ebb, and Daylight Waning

Last of ebb, and daylight waning,
Scented sea-cool landward making, smells of sedge and salt incoming,
With many a half-caught voice sent up from the eddies,
Many a muffled confession—many a sob and whisper'd word,
As of speakers far or hid.

How they sweep down and out! how they mutter!
Poets unnamed—artists greatest of any, with cherish'd lost designs,
Love's unresponse—a chorus of age's complaints—hope's last words,
Some suicide's despairing cry, *Away to the boundless waste, and
    never again return.*

On to oblivion then!
On, on, and do your part, ye burying, ebbing tide!
On for your time, ye furious debouché!

And Yet Not You Alone

And yet not you alone, twilight and burying ebb,
Nor you, ye lost designs alone—nor failures, aspirations;
I know, divine deceitful ones, your glamour's seeming;
Duly by you, from you, the tide and light again—duly the hinges
    turning,
Duly the needed discord-parts offsetting, blending,
Weaving from you, from Sleep, Night, Death itself,
The rhythmus of Birth eternal.

Proudly the Flood Comes In

Proudly the flood comes in, shouting, foaming, advancing,
Long it holds at the high, with bosom broad outswelling,
All throbs, dilates—the farms, woods, streets of cities—workmen
    at work,
Mainsails, topsails, jibs, appear in the offing—steamers' pennants
    of smoke—and under the forenoon sun,
Freighted with human lives, gaily the outward bound, gaily the
    inward bound,
Flaunting from many a spar the flag I love.

By That Long Scan of Waves

By that long scan of waves, myself call'd back, resumed upon myself,
In every crest some undulating light or shade — some retrospect,
Joys, travels, studies, silent panoramas — scenes ephemeral,
The long past war, the battles, hospital sights, the wounded and
  the dead,
Myself through every by-gone phase — my idle youth — old age at hand,
My three-score years of life summ'd up, and more, and past,
By any grand ideal tried, intentionless, the whole a nothing,
And haply yet some drop within God's scheme's ensemble —
  some wave, or part of wave,
Like one of yours, ye multitudinous ocean.

Then Last of All

Then last of all, caught from these shores, this hill,
Of you O tides, the mystic human meaning:
Only by law of you, your swell and ebb, enclosing me the same,
The brain that shapes, the voice that chants this song.

With Husky-Haughty Lips, O Sea!

With husky-haughty lips, O sea!
Where day and night I wend thy surf-beat shore,
Imaging to my sense thy varied strange suggestions,
(I see and plainly list thy talk and conference here,)
Thy troops of white-maned racers racing to the goal,
Thy ample, smiling face, dash'd with the sparkling dimples of the sun,
Thy brooding scowl and murk — thy unloos'd hurricanes,
Thy unsubduedness, caprices, wilfulness;
Great as thou art above the rest, thy many tears — a lack from all
    eternity in thy content,
(Naught but the greatest struggles, wrongs, defeats, could make
    thee greatest — no less could make thee,)
Thy lonely state — something thou ever seek'st and seek'st, yet
    never gain'st,
Surely some right withheld — some voice, in huge monotonous rage,
    of freedom-lover pent,
Some vast heart, like a planet's, chain'd and chafing in those
    breakers,
By lengthen'd swell, and spasm, and panting breath,
And rhythmic rasping of thy sands and waves,
And serpent hiss, and savage peals of laughter,
And undertones of distant lion roar,
(Sounding, appealing to the sky's deaf ear — but now, rapport
    for once,
A phantom in the night thy confidant for once,)
The first and last confession of the globe,
Outsurging, muttering from thy soul's abysms,
The tale of cosmic elemental passion,
Thou tellest to a kindred soul.

Of That Blithe Throat of Thine

[More than eighty-three degrees north—about a good day's steaming distance
to the Pole by one of our fast oceaners in clear water—Greely the explorer
heard the song of a single snow-bird merrily sounding over the desolation.]

Of that blithe throat of thine from arctic bleak and blank,
I'll mind the lesson, solitary bird—let me too welcome chilling drifts,
E'en the profoundest chill, as now—a torpid pulse, a brain unnerv'd,
Old age land-lock'd within its winter bay—(cold, cold, O cold!)
These snowy hairs, my feeble arm, my frozen feet,
For them thy faith, thy rule I take, and grave it to the last;
Not summer's zones alone—not chants of youth, or south's warm
    tides alone,
But held by sluggish floes, pack'd in the northern ice, the cumulus
    of years,
These with gay heart I also sing.

Yonnondio

[The sense of the word is *lament for the aborigines*. It is an Iroquois term;
and has been used for a personal name.]

A song, a poem of itself—the word itself a dirge,
Amid the wilds, the rocks, the storm and wintry night,
To me such misty, strange tableaux the syllables calling up;
Yonnondio—I see, far in the west or north, a limitless ravine, with
    plains and mountains dark,
I see swarms of stalwart chieftains, medicine-men, and warriors,
As flitting by like clouds of ghosts, they pass and are gone in the twilight,
(Race of the woods, the landscapes free, and the falls!
No picture, poem, statement, passing them to the future:)
Yonnondio! Yonnondio!—unlimn'd they disappear;
To-day gives place, and fades—the cities, farms, factories fade;
A muffled sonorous sound, a wailing word is borne through the air
    for a moment,
Then blank and gone and still, and utterly lost.

The Voice of the Rain

And who art thou? said I to the soft-falling shower,
Which, strange to tell, gave me an answer, as here translated:
I am the Poem of Earth, said the voice of the rain,
Eternal I rise impalpable out of the land and the bottomless sea,
Upward to heaven, whence, vaguely form'd, altogether changed,
    and yet the same,
I descend to lave the drouths, atomies, dust-layers of the globe,
And all that in them without me were seeds only, latent, unborn;
And forever, by day and night, I give back life to my own origin,
    and make pure and beautify it;
(For song, issuing from its birth-place, after fulfilment, wandering,
Reck'd or unreck'd. duly with love returns.)

Twenty Years

Down on the ancient wharf, the sand, I sit, with a new-comer
    chatting:
He shipp'd as green-hand boy, and sail'd away, (took some sudden,
    vehement notion;)
Since, twenty years and more have circled round and round,
While he the globe was circling round and round, — and now returns:
How changed the place — all the old land-marks gone — the parents
    dead;
(Yes, he comes back *to lay in port for good — to settle* — has a
    well-fill'd purse — no spot will do but this;)
The little boat that scull'd him from the sloop, now held in leash I see,
I hear the slapping waves, the restless keel, the rocking in the sand,
I see the sailor kit, the canvas bag, the great box bound with brass,
I scan the face all berry-brown and bearded — the stout-strong frame,
Dress'd in its russet suit of good Scotch cloth:
(Then what the told-out story of those twenty years? What of the
    future?)

The Dismantled Ship

In some unused lagoon, some nameless bay,
On sluggish, lonesome waters, anchor'd near the shore,
An old, dismasted, gray and batter'd ship, disabled, done,
After free voyages to all the seas of earth, haul'd up at last and
    hawser'd tight,
Lies rusting, mouldering.

from *Good-Bye My Fancy*

Last droplets of and after spontaneous rain,
From many limpid distillations and past showers;
(Will they germinate anything? mere exhalations as they all are—
    the land's and sea's—America's;
Will they filter to any deep emotion? any heart and brain?)
                    —from "Preface Note to 2d Annex"

Sail Out for Good, Eidólon Yacht!

HEAVE the anchor short!
Raise main-sail and jib—steer forth,
O little white-hull'd sloop, now speed on really deep waters,
(I will not call it our concluding voyage,
But outset and sure entrance to the truest, best, maturest;)
Depart, depart from solid earth—no more returning to these shores,
Now on for aye our infinite free venture wending,
Spurning all yet tried ports, seas, hawsers, densities, gravitation,
Sail out for good, eidólon yacht of me!

Lingering Last Drops

AND whence and why come you?

We know not whence, (was the answer,)
We only know that we drift here with the rest,
That we linger'd and lagg'd—but were wafted at last, and are
    now here,
To make the passing shower's concluding drops.

An Ended Day

THE soothing sanity and blitheness of completion,
The pomp and hurried contest-glare and rush are done;
Now triumph! transformation! jubilate!*

Old Age's Ship & Crafty Death's

FROM east and west across the horizon's edge,
Two mighty masterful vessels sailers steal upon us:
But we'll make race a-time upon the seas — a battle-contest yet!
  bear lively there!
(Our joys of strife and derring-do to the last!)
Put on the old ship all her power to-day!
Crowd top-sail, top-gallant and royal studding-sails,
Out challenge and defiance — flags and flaunting pennants added,
As we take to the open — take to the deepest, freest waters.

---

*[Author's footnote]: NOTE. — *Summer country life.* — *Several years.* — In my rambles and
explorations I found a woody place near the creek, where for some reason the birds in happy
mood seem'd to resort in unusual numbers. Especially at the beginning of the day, and
again at the ending, I was sure to get there the most copious bird-concerts. I repair'd there
frequently at sunrise — and also at sunset, or just before . . . Once the question arose in me:
Which is the best singing, the first or the lattermost? The first always exhilarated, and per-
haps seem'd more joyous and stronger; but I always felt the sunset or late afternoon sounds
more penetrating and sweeter — seem'd to touch the soul — often the evening thrushes, two
or three of them, responding and perhaps blending. Though I miss'd some of the mornings,
I found myself getting to be quite strictly punctual at the evening utterances.

ANOTHER NOTE. — "He went out with the tide and the sunset," was a phrase I heard from
a surgeon describing an old sailor's death under peculiarly gentle conditions.

During the Secession War, 1863 and '4, visiting the Army Hospitals around Washington, I
form'd the habit, and continued it to the end, whenever the ebb or flood tide began the latter
part of day, of punctually visiting those at that time populous wards of suffering men. Some-
how (or I thought it so) the effect of the hour was palpable. The badly wounded would get
some ease, and would like to talk a little, or be talk'd to. Intellectual and emotional natures
would be at their best: Deaths were always easier; medicines seem'd to have better effect
when given then, and a lulling atmosphere would pervade the wards.

Similar influences, similar circumstances and hours, day-close, after great battles, even
with all their horrors. I had more than once the same experience on the fields cover'd with
fallen or dead.

Shakspere-Bacon's Cipher

I DOUBT it not—then more, far more;
In each old song bequeath'd—in every noble page or text,
(Different—something unreck'd before—some unsuspected author,)
In every object, mountain, tree, and star—in every birth and life,
As part of each—evolv'd from each—meaning, behind the ostent,
A mystic cipher waits infolded.

To the Sun-set Breeze

AH, whispering, something again, unseen,
Where late this heated day thou enterest at my window, door,
Thou, laving, tempering all, cool-freshing, gently vitalizing
Me, old, alone, sick, weak-down, melted-worn with sweat;
Thou, nestling, folding close and firm yet soft, companion better
    than talk, book, art,
(Thou hast, O Nature! elements! utterance to my heart beyond
    the rest—and this is of them,)
So sweet thy primitive taste to breathe within—thy soothing fingers
    on my face and hands,
Thou, messenger-magical strange bringer to body and spirit of me,
(Distances balk'd—occult medicines penetrating me from head
    to foot,)
I feel the sky, the prairies vast—I feel the mighty northern lakes,
I feel the ocean and the forest—somehow I feel the globe itself
    swift-swimming in space;
Thou blown from lips so loved, now gone—haply from endless
    store, God-sent,
(For thou art spiritual, Godly, most of all known to my sense,)
Minister to speak to me, here and now, what word has never told,
    and cannot tell,
Art thou not universal concrete's distillation? Law's, all Astronomy's
    last refinement?
Hast thou no soul? Can I not know, identify thee?

A Twilight Song

AS I sit in twilight late alone by the flickering oak-flame,
Musing on long-pass'd war-scenes—of the countless buried unknown
    soldiers,
Of the vacant names, as unindented air's and sea's—the unreturn'd,
The brief truce after battle, with grim burial-squads, and the deep-fill'd
    trenches
Of gather'd dead from all America, North, South, East, West, whence
    they came up,
From wooded Maine, New-England's farms, from fertile Pennsylvania,
    Illinois, Ohio,
From the measureless West, Virginia, the South, the Carolinas, Texas,
(Even here in my room-shadows and half-lights in the noiseless
    flickering flames,
Again I see the stalwart ranks on-filing, rising—I hear the rhythmic
    tramp of the armies;)
You million unwrit names all, all—you dark bequest from all the war,
A special verse for you—a flash of duty long neglected—your mystic
    roll strangely gather'd here,
Each name recall'd by me from out the darkness and death's ashes,
Henceforth to be, deep, deep within my heart recording, for many
    a future year,
Your mystic roll entire of unknown names, or North or South,
Embalm'd with love in this twilight song.

A Voice from Death
(The Johnstown, Penn., cataclysm, May 31, 1889.)

A VOICE from Death, solemn and strange, in all his sweep and
    power,
With sudden, indescribable blow—towns drown'd—humanity by
    thousands slain,
The vaunted work of thrift, goods, dwellings, forge, street, iron
    bridge,
Dash'd pell-mell by the blow—yet usher'd life continuing on,
(Amid the rest, amid the rushing, whirling, wild debris,
A suffering woman saved—a baby safely born!)

Although I come and unannounc'd, in horror and in pang,
In pouring flood and fire, and wholesale elemental crash, (this
    voice so solemn, strange,)
I too a minister of Deity.

Yea, Death, we bow our faces, veil our eyes to thee,
We mourn the old, the young untimely drawn to thee,
The fair, the strong, the good, the capable,
The household wreck'd, the husband and the wife, the engulf'd
    forger in his forge,
The corpses in the whelming waters and the mud,
The gather'd thousands to their funeral mounds, and thousands
    never found or gather'd.

Then after burying, mourning the dead,
(Faithful to them found or unfound, forgetting not, bearing the past,
    here new musing,)
A day—a passing moment or an hour—America itself bends low,
Silent, resign'd, submissive.

War, death, cataclysm like this, America,
Take deep to thy proud prosperous heart.

E'en as I chant, lo! out of death, and out of ooze and slime,
The blossoms rapidly blooming, sympathy, help, love,
From West and East, from South and North and over sea,
Its hot-spurr'd hearts and hands humanity to human aid moves on;
And from within a thought and lesson yet.

Thou ever-darting Globe! through Space and Air!
Thou waters that encompass us!
Thou that in all the life and death of us, in action or in sleep!
Thou laws invisible that permeate them and all,
Thou that in all, and over all, and through and under all, incessant!
Thou! thou! the vital, universal, giant force resistless, sleepless, calm,
Holding Humanity as in thy open hand, as some ephemeral toy,
How ill to e'er forget thee!

For I too have forgotten,
(Wrapt in these little potencies of progress, politics, culture, wealth,
    inventions, civilization,)
Have lost my recognition of your silent ever-swaying power, ye mighty,
    elemental throes,
In which and upon which we float, and every one of us is buoy'd.

A Persian Lesson

FOR his o'erarching and last lesson the greybeard sufi,
In the fresh scent of the morning in the open air,
On the slope of a teeming Persian rose-garden,
Under an ancient chestnut-tree wide spreading its branches,
Spoke to the young priests and students.

"Finally my children, to envelop each word, each part of the rest,
Allah is all, all, all—is immanent in every life and object,
May-be at many and many-a-more removes—yet Allah, Allah,
    Allah is there.

"Has the estray wander'd far? Is the reason-why strangely hidden?
Would you sound below the restless ocean of the entire world?
Would you know the dissatisfaction? the urge and spur of every life;
The something never still'd—never entirely gone? the invisible
    need of every seed?

"It is the central urge in every atom,
(Often unconscious, often evil, downfallen,)
To return to its divine source and origin, however distant,
Latent the same in subject and in object, without one exception."

Grand Is the Seen

GRAND is the seen, the light, to me — grand are the sky and stars,
Grand is the earth, and grand are lasting time and space,
And grand their laws, so multiform, puzzling, evolutionary;
But grander far the unseen soul of me, comprehending, endowing
    all those,
Lighting the light, the sky and stars, delving the earth, sailing the sea,
(What were all those, indeed, without thee, unseen soul? of what
    amount without thee?)
More evolutionary, vast, puzzling, O my soul!
More multiform far — more lasting thou than they.

from A Backward Glance O'er Travel'd Roads

Later, at intervals, summers and falls, I used to go off, sometimes for a week at a stretch, down in the country, or to Long Island's sea-shores — there, in the presence of outdoor influences, I went over thoroughly the Old and New Testaments, and absorb'd (probably to better advantage for me than in any library or indoor room — it makes such difference *where* you read,) Shakspere, Ossian, the best translated versions I could get of Homer, Eschylus, Sopho-cles, the old German Nibelungen, the ancient Hindoo poems, and one or two other masterpieces, Dante's among them. As it hap-pen'd, I read the latter mostly in an old wood. The Iliad (Buckley's prose version,) I read first thoroughly on the peninsula of Orient, northeast end of Long Island, in a shelter'd hollow of rocks and sand, with the sea on each side. (I have wonder'd since why I was not overwhelm'd by those mighty masters. Likely because I read them, as described, in the full presence of Nature, under the sun, with the far-spreading landscape and vistas, or the sea rolling in.)

"There is a river . . ."
[Date Unknown. Manuscript not found.]

There is a river in the ocean — *i.e.* the gulf stream.

Notes

Some further notes on the text are offered to complement the "Note on the Text" at the start. Here only a passing glimpse at the poet's restless process of revision and publication is presented, along with a few random annotations. I've drawn generously from *Leaves of Grass: A Textual Variorum of the Printed Poem*, ed. by Sculley Bradley, Harold W. Blodgett, Arthur Golden, and William White (NYU Press, 2008; 3 vols.), Joel Myerson's *Walt Whitman: A Descriptive Bibliography* (University of Pittsburgh Press, 1993), and the articles online at the Walt Whitman Archive, particularly Ed Folsom's "Whitman Making Books/Books Making Whitman," which readers are directed to for much more detailed information.

"The Ocean": From *Walt Whitman of the New York Aurora*, ed. Joseph Jay Rubin and Charles H. Brown (Bald Eagle Press, 1950).

"The Mississippi at Midnight": from *The Collected Writings of Walt Whitman: The Early Poems and the Fiction*, edited by Thomas L. Brasher (New York University Press, 1963). Later appears in a much altered form in the "Pieces in Early Youth" section of *Collect*.

Leaves of Grass (1855)

First edition; self-published in a quarto-size edition of 795 copies. No table of contents; no name printed on title page or cover, though "Walter Whitman" appears on the copyright page, and an engraved portrait of the bearded, young author appears in the frontispiece. Contains twelve untitled poems (or each poem with the same title, "Leaves of Grass"), plus what has become known as the "1855 Preface." Bound in dark-green, ribbed morocco cloth with blind-stamped foliage; title gold-stamped on front with letters sprouting roots and leaves.

A reminder that the many two-to-four dot ellipses throughout are Whitman's except for the editor's ellipses in brackets that denote excised text. Each of the seven poems represented here were eventually titled, in sequential order, as follows: "Song of Myself," "A Song for

Occupations," "To Think of Time," "The Sleepers," "I Sing the Body Electric," "There Was a Child Went Forth," and "Great Are the Myths."

Leaves of Grass (1856)

Second edition; self-published, "neat pocket volume"; printed in a stereotyped edition of 1,000 copies with the help of the phrenologist and bookseller business Fowler & Wells, who assumed distribution. Author's name (now "Walt Whitman") appears only on the copyright page, as well as on the spine with a quote taken from a letter Ralph Waldo Emerson had written to him: "I greet you at the beginning of a great career." Twenty new poems added to the previous twelve, each one titled and numbered sequentially. Also includes a table of contents, the same author portrait as frontispiece, and a selection of correspondence (including Emerson's letter) and reviews in the back called "Leaves-Droppings."

"Poem of Salutation": Becomes "Salut Au Monde" in 1881.

"Sun-Down Poem": Title changes to "Crossing Brooklyn Ferry" in
   1860. In this version, first line becomes "FLOOD-TIDE below
   me! I see you face to face!"; the whole poem is divided into
   twelve sections; the phrase "solitary committer" excised.
   Other differences between the two versions mostly involve
   the punctuation.

"Poem of Perfect Miracles": Becomes the eight poems in the
   "Leaves of Grass" sequence in 1860 and "Miracles" in the
   "Autumn Rivulets" sequence in 1881.

"Bunch Poem": Becomes the fifth "Enfans d'Adam" poem in 1860
   and "Spontaneous Me" in the poem cluster "Children of Adam"
   in 1867. See below.

"Poem of the Sayers of the Words of the Earth": Becomes "To the
   Sayers of the Words" in 1860, then "Carol of Words" in 1871, then
   "A Song of the Rolling Earth" in 1881.

Leaves of Grass (1860–61)

Third edition; one hundred and forty-six new poems added; sequential numbering of poems abandoned for other organizing principles, such as the clustering of poems into different sequences. Publisher's name, Thayers and Eldridge, appears for the first time on the title page, along with spermatic typography, illustrations of a finger with a butterfly, a cloud-encircled globe, and an ocean with a rising or setting sun scattered throughout. A new engraving of the poet inserted in the frontispiece. Whitman's envisioned "New Bible" with an estimated two printings of 2,000 to 5,000 copies total (at least four more unauthorized printings followed).

"Proto-Leaf": Becomes "Starting from Paumanok" in 1867. See below.

"Chants Democratic and Native American": This grouping of poems doesn't appear in later editions.

"Apostroph": "In rhetoric, a *diversion* of speech; a *digressive* address, a *changing* the course of a speech, and addressing a person who is dead or absent, as if present" (from John Oswald's *An Etymological Dictionary of the English Language* [1840]). Subsequently cut from *Leaves*, though lines from it appear in "O Sun of Real Peace" in 1871.

"Something startles me": First version appears in 1856 edition as "Poem of Wonder at the Resurrection of the Wheat." Becomes "This Compost" in 1881.

"Poem of Joys": Becomes "Poems of Joy" in 1867 and "A Song of Joys" in 1881.

"A Word Out of the Sea": Becomes "Out of the Cradle Endlessly Rocking" in 1881. See below.

"Enfans d'Adam": A group of fifteen poems retitled "Children of Adam" in 1867, later expanded to sixteen poems.

"You and I — what the earth is, we are": This first line is later deleted.

"Inquiring, tireless, seeking that yet unfound": A new first line is later added: "Facing west from California's shores."

"Calamus": A cluster of forty-five poems cut and revised to thirty-nine by 1881. Earlier, never-published incarnation titled "Live Oak, with Moss." Whitman: "Calamus is a Latin word — much used in Old English writing, however. I like it much — it is to me, for my intentions, indispensable — the sun revolves about it, it is a timber of the ship — not there alone in that one series of poems, but in all, belonging to all" (from Horace Traubel's *With Walt Whitman in Camden*, vol. 6 [1982]). Whitman: "Calamus is a common word here. It is the very large & aromatic grass, or rush, growing about water-ponds in the valleys — spears about three feet high — often called 'sweet flag' — grows all over the Northern and Middle States" (from a letter to W. M. Rossetti). Whitman: "sweet-green bulb and melons with bulbs grateful to the hand" (from a notebook).

"Longings for Home": Becomes "O Magnet-South" in 1881.

"Mannahatta": Heavily revised until 1881, and certain lines cut, including: "The free city! no slaves! no owners of slaves!"

Drum-Taps (1865) and *Sequel to Drum-Taps: When Lilacs Last in the Door-yard Bloom'd and Other Poems* (1865–66)

Lincoln was assassinated during the initial printing of *Drum-Taps*, which Whitman then limited to only one-hundred copies in order to deal more fully with the president's death. To the original fifty-three poems, eighteen more were added as a *Sequel to Drum-Taps*; forty-three of the poems from this collection were eventually rearranged into later editions of *Leaves*.

"The Ship": Becomes "The Ship Starting" in 1881.

"Out of the Rolling Ocean, the Crowd": Comma deleted from title in 1881.

"World, Take Good Notice": Comma deleted from title in 1881.

"When Lilacs Last in the Door-yard Bloom'd": Hyphen deleted from title and made one word "Dooryard" in 1881. The editor Edward Grier says, "'When Lilacs Last in the Dooryard Bloom'd' can be traced from some notes on mourning displays in New York, through some notes on the habits of the hermit thrush that Whitman got from John Burroughs, through a list of appropriate words, and finally through a few scattered lines."

Leaves of Grass (1867)

Fourth edition; cheaply printed in three or four different versions of separately paginated books stitched together, including *Drum Taps* and *Sequel to Drum-Taps.* The new opening poem "Inscriptions" added, plus five other new poems, as well as the new grouping of poems as coda, "Songs Before Parting."

"Starting from Paumanok": See "Proto-Leaf" above. "Paumanok" is the Algonquin name for Long Island that possibly means "place of tribute." Whitman traced its meaning to be "the island with its breast long drawn out, and laid against the sea." Cf. "Out of the Cradle Endlessly Rocking" in "Sea Drift," and "Paumanok, and My Life on It as Child and Young Man" in *Specimen Days.*

"Children of Adam": See "Enfans d'Adam" above.

"From Pent-Up Aching Rivers": First appears as poem number two in "Enfans d'Adam" without the first line. An obvious typo in the 1867 edition was corrected in line 42: "as to is" changed to "as it is."

"Facing West from California's Shores": First appears as poem number ten in "Enfans d'Adam" without the first line.

"Song of the Open Road": First appears in 1856 as "Poem of the Road."

"Respondez!": Originally appears as "Poem of the Proposition of Nakedness" in 1856, then as untitled poem number five in "Chants Democratic and Native American" in 1860. Eventually whittled down to two small poems in 1881: "Reversals" (six lines) and "Transpositions" (three lines).

"As If a Phantom Carress'd Me": First appears untitled in the poem sequence "Debris" in 1860, with the first line dropped.

"Songs Before Parting": Becomes "Songs of Parting" in 1871.

"As I Sat Alone by Blue Ontario's Shores": One of the most heavily revised of Whitman's poems. Lines first appear in "Poem of Many in One" (a quarter of it lifted from the 1855 Preface) in 1856, then further expands untitled in "Chants Democratic and Native American" in 1860, and later becomes "By Blue Ontario's Shores" in 1881. Between 1860 and 1867, the poem expanded from fifteen sections to twenty, including a new opening section (that introduces the "Phantom"), making section six presented here formerly section five. Before the Civil War, the last two lines read: "Slavery, the tremulous spreading of hands to shelter it—the stern opposition to it, which ceases only when it ceases."

Song At Sunset: First appears as untitled poem number eight in "Chants Democratic and Native American" in 1860.

Leaves of Grass (1871–1872), *Passage to India* (1871), and *As a Strong Bird on Pinions Free* (1872)

Fifth edition, with at least two printings and three different arrangements; some count a pirated printing distributed in England as a sixth edition. *Passage to India*—consisting of seventy-four poems (twenty-four new)—was published as a separate book, and then annexed as a supplement to the fifth edition. *As a Strong Bird on Pinions Free* was also published as a separate little book and contained seven new poems plus a significant preface. A third individual book published in 1871, *After All Not to Create Only*, formed a second annex to the fifth edition before becoming "Song of the Exposition."

"Inscriptions": Nine poems in this new grouping now open *Leaves*; later expands to twenty-six poems.

"Songs of Insurrection": Cluster of six poems; title discarded after 1876.

"France, the 18th Year of These States": Becomes part of the "Birds of Passage" cluster of poems in 1881.

"Gliding o'er all . . .": First published as an epigraph on the title page of *Passage to India*. Becomes its own poem as part of "By the Roadside" in 1881.

"Passage to India": Title poem becomes a separate poem in 1881, and then part of "Autumn Rivulets."

"Warble for Lilac-Time": Becomes part of "Autumn Rivulets" in 1881.

"Now Finale to the Shore": Becomes part of "Songs of Parting" in 1881.

"The Untold Want": Becomes part of "Songs of Parting" in 1881.

"Joy, Shipmate, Joy!": Becomes part of "Songs of Parting" in 1881.

"As a Strong Bird with Pinions Free": Commencement poem recited at Dartmouth College in June 1872. Becomes "Thou Mother with Thy Equal Brood" in 1881 with a new first section.

"O Star of France!": Becomes part of "Autumn Rivulets" in 1881.

"By Broad Potomac's Shore": Becomes part of "From Noon to Starry Night" in 1881.

Leaves of Grass (1876) and *Two Rivulets* (1876)

A two-volume set published in celebration of the United States centennial and known as the "Centennial Edition," or "Author's Edition." The first volume was a reissue of the fifth edition of *Leaves of Grass* "with Portraits and Intercalations" — two portraits of Whitman and four new short poems pasted onto blank spaces. The second volume Whitman titled *Two Rivulets*, which referred to the "two flowing chains of prose and verse, emanating the real and ideal" that made up the first section of the book after an introductory preface, followed by "Democratic Vistas," "Centennial Songs," "As a Strong Bird on Pinions Free," "Memoranda During the War," and "Passage to India."

"The Beauty of the Ship": Only appears in the first volume of the Centennial Edition.

"Two Rivulets": The title poem for a cluster of fourteen poems. Lines four and five of the title poem appear as an epigraph on the title page of the edition. Unfortunately the typesetting of this section could only approximate Whitman's original design, in which poetry and prose flow together on every page — poetry above, prose below, divided by a bold wavy line.

"Or from that Sea of Time": Only appears in the second volume of the Centennial Edition, though this poem and the previous one are later dismantled and heavily revised into "As Consequent, Etc." See below.

"Eidólons": From the Greek meaning "ideal," "concept," "phantom," "image of the ideal." From Whitman's "Notebook on Words": "Ei-do-lon (Gr) phantom—the *image* of a Helen at Troy instead of real flesh and blood woman." Becomes part of "Inscriptions" in 1881.

"Spain, 1873–74": Becomes part of "From Noon to Starry Night" in 1881.

"Prayer of Columbus": After 1976, the prefatory prose section is deleted and it becomes its own poem without the running prose on the bottom. Note part of the last sentence of the prose half from "vices" to "enslaved" has been run in from the next page of the original edition in order to complete the sentence. On another note, both Dickinson and Whitman had read Washington Irving's 1828, four-volume Christian romance of Columbus disguised as biography, and each wrote poems inspired by its depicted messianic figure. Whitman also thought highly of historian George Ticknor's portrayal of Columbus as a religious aspirant.

Leaves of Grass (1881–82)

Sixth (or seventh) edition, reprinted fifteen times, plus multiple issues of certain printings. Whitman rearranged and regrouped many poems, cut thirty-nine poems and added seventeen new ones, and continued to revise hundreds of lines. Author name still left off of title page; 1855 engraving inserted opposite "Song of Myself." First *Leaves* to be published by a commercial publisher, James R. Osgood and Co., "markedly plain & simple even to Quakerness" as Whitman wanted it. Subsequent volumes of *Leaves of Grass* used the printing plates of this edition. Threats of official obscenity charges caused Whitman to find a new publisher, twenty-one-year-old David McKay at Rees Welsh; between 1882 and 1891, approximately 6,414 copies were sold.

"Sea-Drift": First appearance of this grouping, which is included here in its entirety. Expanded from the 1871 "Sea-Shore Memories" cluster in *Passage to India*.

"Out of the Cradle Endlessly Rocking": First appears in an early version as "A Child's Reminiscence" in the New York *Saturday Press* on December 24, 1859, and then, much revised, becomes "A Word Out of the Sea" in 1860, with the heading "Reminiscence" at the start of the second section. Note the added repetitions in the mockingbird's song in this version.

"As I Ebb'd with the Ocean of Life": First appears as the untitled first poem in the "Leaves of Grass" cluster in 1860 with the first two lines: "Elemental drifts! / O I wish I could impress others as you and the waves have just been impressing me." Then appears as "Elemental Drifts," with numbered sections, in the "Sea-Shore Memories" cluster in *Passage to India* (1871).

"Tears": First appears as the second untitled poem in the "Leaves of Grass" cluster in 1867.

"To the Man-of-War Bird": First appears in the London *Athenaeum* on April 1, 1876.

"Aboard at a Ship's Helm": First appears as the third untitled poem in the "Leaves of Grass" cluster in 1867.

"On the Beach at Night": First appears in the "Sea-Shore Memories" cluster in *Passage to India* (1871).

"The World Below the Brine": First appears as the untitled sixteenth poem in the "Leaves of Grass" cluster in 1860 with the first line replaced with "Sea-water, and all living below it."

"On the Beach at Night Alone": First appears in a much longer version as "Clef Poem" in 1856.

"Song for All Seas, All Ships": First appears in the group of "Centennial Songs" in *Two Rivulets* in 1876.

"Patroling Barnegat": Title refers to Barnegat Bay, New Jersey.

"After the Sea-Ship": First appears in *Two Rivulets* in 1876.

"Autumn Rivulets": New grouping of poems.

"As Consequent, Etc.": A heavily revised combination of the two earlier poems "Two Rivulets" and "Or from the Sea of Time." See above.

Specimen Days & Collect (1882–83)

Specimen Days, the first half of the book, is an expansion of *Memoranda During the War* (1875), with other prose vignettes compiled from a long letter to a friend, as well from notebook scraps and diary entries, that make up a "wayward, spontaneous" autobiography from early life, through the Civil War, and after. The second half, *Collect*, contains the prose stream from *Two Rivulets*, *Democratic Vistas*, various prefaces, letters, plus other essays and notes, as well as some early fiction and pre-*Leaves* poetry. Also includes the infamous "Butterfly Portrait," a photograph of Whitman with a cardboard butterfly on his finger he publicly claimed was real. The image of the butterfly perched on finger was also gold-stamped on the spine. Note Whitman thought of this book as a companion volume to the 1881 *Leaves*, though in this case he allowed his name to be printed on the title page.

Leaves of Grass (1891–92)

Last published volume of *Leaves*; often called the "Deathbed Edition" (some number it the seventh, or eighth, or ninth, or tenth edition) as Whitman's impending death compelled him to make a last, "definitive" compilation. It remains the most widely circulated volume of *Leaves of Grass*, with 389 poems. To the 1881 edition Whitman added two new annexes of poetry—*Sands at Seventy*, first published in *November Boughs* (1888), consisting of sixty-four poems plus a selection of prose, and *Good-Bye My Fancy*, first published separately in early 1891 as an appendix to *November Boughs*. The volume ends with Whitman's essay, "A Backward Glance O'er Travel'd Roads." A posthumous edition published in 1897 added another annex, *Old Age Echoes*, edited by his Executor Horace Traubel.

> *"Come, said my Soul"*: Originally published as an epigraphic poem to the 1891 edition.
> "A Backward Glance O'er Travel'd Roads": First published in *November Boughs*; pieced together from four previously published essays.

"There is a river . . .": From *Notes and Fragments: Left by Walt Whitman*, edited by Richard Maurice Bucke (1899). Reprinted in *The Collected Writings of Walt Whitman: Notebooks and Unpublished Prose Manuscripts*, vol. 5, edited by Edward F. Grier (New York University Press, [1984]).

Index of Titles

Titles in parentheses refer to poems originally untitled in the 1855 edition.